A History of
Music in Canada 1534-1914

A History of
Music in Canada 1534-1914

Helmut Kallmann

University of Toronto Press

Foreword

Most people, I imagine, do not think of Canada as having a musical history; certainly few could give anything more than the most meagre account of it. One must admit that the story, measured against that of older countries, is not impressive. The life of the pioneer is not conducive to high artistic achievement, although even here music of a simple kind plays a valuable part in mitigating arduous toil, lending colour to leisure hours and often adorning religious observances. Much music of this type was brought to Canada by the early settlers and from then on our "new Canadians" of many races have continued to enrich its store.

Creative musical activity in Canada—especially French Canada—however goes back further than most people suppose. Much of our earliest music is lost and we know of it only through references —often casual—in contemporary documents. It has remained for Helmut Kallmann to focus his very observant eye on this and later phases of our musical history. Knowing his enthusiasm, thoroughness and methodical industry, I fancy that little has escaped him.

Music has of late years come to play an important role in Canadian life and it was high time that someone undertook to trace its history. It was Mr. Kallmann's own idea to do so and with him it has been a labour of love. I for one have had occasion to watch the progress of his book from stage to stage and can assure the reader in advance that he has a most interesting story to tell. In addition to its intrinsic interest this book represents a valuable contribution to the growing store of Canadiana. No one has up to now dealt with its subject on such a scale, and as Canadians all of us owe a debt of gratitude to the author.

ERNEST MACMILLAN

Acknowledgments

The collection of musical data in Canadian history, begun in 1948, had grown by 1950 to the size which seemed to warrant its assembly into the form of a book. Encouragement for this project was given by Professor George W. Brown of the University of Toronto Press, Mr. A. E. H. Petrie, and Sir Ernest MacMillan. In the following years Professor Brown, Miss Francess Halpenny and Miss Ruth Charlesworth of the University Press have given editorial advice, and Sir Ernest contributed generously from his fund of knowledge of music in Canada.

I am grateful to the Humanities Research Council of Canada for the grant in aid of research in 1955 which enabled me to travel and collect additional source material, and again for the grant given in 1959 in aid of publication of the book itself, from funds supplied by the Canada Council. I should also like to acknowledge assistance from the Publications Fund of the University of Toronto Press.

My thanks go to the dozens of people who replied to inquiries with valuable information. The contributions of some are acknowledged in the text and footnotes. In addition the following have been especially helpful: in Toronto—Mr. F. Renwick Brown, Mr. Peter Cheetham, Mr. John Cozens, Dr. Richard Johnston, Mr. David McFall, Mrs. Ogreta McNeill, Mr. Erland Misener, Miss Molna O'Connor, Mr. Geoffrey Payzant and Mr. Godfrey Ridout; in Ottawa—Dr. William Amtmann, Mr. Jack Cavill, Dr. W. Kaye Lamb and Mr. Jaroslav Mracek; in Quebec—M. Lucien Brochu,

M. Gérard Morisset and Abbé Honorius Provost; in Montreal—
Mr. Rudolf M. Kestler, M. Jean Papineau-Couture and Mlle
Térèse Rochette; Mrs. H. A. Beckwith (Victoria), Mrs. Jean Coult-
hard Adams and Miss Melva J. Dwyer (Vancouver), Mr. E. C.
Kinsman (St. Mary's, Ontario), Mr. Nicolas Slonimsky (Boston),
Mr. Perry W. Teale (Halifax), and Mr. L. E. Thompson
(Winnipeg).

My sincere appreciation goes to the following for their critical
reading of portions of the manuscript: Mr. John Beckwith, Mr. Ray
de Boer, Mrs. Jocelyn Classey, Mr. Thomas C. Fairley and my wife
Ruth.

Painstaking comparison of printed source material revealed dis-
crepancies which belied the accuracy of some of it. As this book
owes part of its data to the co-operation of many helpful and
interested persons, a deeper knowledge of early Canadian musical
history may well come from further information supplied by its
readers. It will be welcomed.

H. K.

Contents

Illustrations

TEXT FIGURES

A History of
Music in Canada 1534-1914

1 / Introduction

The aim of this book is the description of music at various stages of Canadian history and of the meaning it held in the life of the Canadian people. To entitle this description a "history of music" requires an unorthodox approach, for customarily musical history relates the sequence of great composers and changing styles of composition and endeavours to demonstrate the continuity and cohesion of musical effort throughout a defined period and locale whereby mature nations assume a distinct musical character and unity. In Canada, these conditions do not yet prevail. To appreciate the fascination of the subject, one has to define musical history in different terms: such a history must deal with the planting of seeds rather than the harvesting of the fruits of a thousand years of civilization. The record of music in Canada's first three centuries takes as its subject not creative giants who determine the course of world music history but humble musicians who instil a taste for their art among pioneers preoccupied with establishing the physical and economic foundations of a new nation; instead of mirroring the entertainment of the *élite* in the world's musical capitals, it reflects the musical pastimes and aspirations of the many; and instead of noting the changing styles which express the spirit of the age and nation, it deals with the collecting and assimilating of traditional forms from outside sources. In short, the record is concerned more with social than with artistic aspects of music.

The social aspects of music are complex from the beginning: we find that even in its relatively short history music has held a great variety of meanings in the life of Canadians. To some it has been a means to implant, express and strengthen religious beliefs; to others an amusement contrary to the teachings of the church. Under varying circumstances and needs it has been regarded as a companion to daily labour and play; a pastime for idlers and dreamers; a career to be discouraged for moral and economic reasons; a social asset for daughters of the well-to-do; the expression of patriotic feeling; or a comfort in a life full of physical hardship and monotonous drudgery. Many examples for these sometimes contradictory values will be cited throughout the book.

In his search for elements of continuity and cohesion, the student of music in early Canada again finds it difficult to satisfy traditional criteria. The growth of music has been uneven in time and space, just as immigration and exploration have been spread over three centuries. Beginning at a time before Bach, Couperin, Handel and Purcell were born, music has been introduced to various regions of Canada from various mature countries, each with its own social and religious traditions, and it has been nourished with the help of vastly different mechanical means. Folk song, transmitted orally from generation to generation, and Roman Catholic liturgical music were brought to the wilderness of New France by French peasants and missionaries in the seventeenth century; folk music also found a home in the fishing and farming communities of the Anglo-Saxon settlers on the Atlantic coast. Secular concert music and Protestant choral singing were introduced with the help of the printed page about the end of the eighteenth century to the small towns in the eastern part of Canada by the Loyalist immigrants from the United States, the British and the German bandmasters in their regimental bands. A hundred years later immigrants from many different countries entered Canadian cities and the western frontier districts carrying with them a variety of musical skills in the folk, popular and sophisticated idioms; at the same time the dissemination of music was aided by the introduction of railways and steamships which enabled star artists and opera troupes to travel on an extensive scale, and by such devices as the phonograph, the player-piano and, a little later, radio.

These technological aids to the spread of music were of special importance as they helped to balance geographical factors which retarded the formation of a unified cultural life. A vast but thinly populated territory is not an encouragement to the exchange of artists and the sharing of musical resources and experiences. On the contrary, very often closer cultural links were established with nearby American cities than with Canadian cities a few thousand miles away, as likely as not speaking a different language, and separated by mountains, rivers and primeval forests.

It follows from the preceding observations that it is impossible to speak of music in Canada as an autonomous organism growing from primitive origins (after all, the origins were more highly developed than the offshoots!) through infancy and adolescence to adulthood. What convenient chapter headings these stages of development would make (although after reading W. D. Allen's *Philosophies of Music History*, American Book Company, 1939, one hesitates applying such biological terms to the music of any country or civilization!). It would be absurd to try to trace a chain of influence from the liturgical chants of the French Récollet and Jesuit missionaries to the choral societies of Upper Canada; or from the compositions of Dessane and Couture to those of a generation or so later. When Quebec and Halifax could look back over a century of organized musical activity, Vancouver and Winnipeg were struggling new outposts.

This isolation and interruption of musical effort is revealed not only in the comparison of different regions of Canada but often within one and the same city. Many cities have an old and distinguished record in the cultivation of music and have produced brilliant musicians, but too often the impact of each new wave of immigrants, of each new generation of Canadian-born music students returning with the latest techniques and aesthetic gospels from Paris or Leipzig, swept aside the teaching and views of the older Canadian generation. The impact from outside as well as the insufficiency of patronage and shifting population made it difficult to establish permanent institutions or home-grown "schools" of composition.

Unity in Canada's musical history, therefore, is found less in chronology, locale and musical repertoire than in the ever present themes of transplantation, assimilation and search for identity which will be traced throughout this book. The following chapters will describe what music was received in Canada, how it was accepted, and how Canadians began to make their own creative contribution to music.

The selecting of material and apportioning of space reflect to some degree the success with which material was obtained from or about various cities, provinces or historical periods, by means of printed literature, investigation in archives, correspondence or interviews. A more important criterion for selection was the need to record names of musicians and musical organizations and document events (assembled for the first time in form of a book) without degenerating into a mere catalogue of the countless available data. Fortunately the example of a few cities or careers usually serves to illustrate the essential features in many others; conversely those sections of the book which are preoccupied with the necessary registration of facts contain observations of general pertinence. The choice of examples and the thoroughness of treatment had to be determined according to both intrinsic musical value and historical interest. Description of a colourful pioneer like Frederic Henri Glackemeyer, Bishop John Medley, or David Willson helps to characterize a whole musical era; on the other hand, the careers of many erudite European-trained musicians of the late nineteenth century, more distinguished but also more routine, can be sketched adequately in summary form.

The most problematic task in selecting from the raw material is the search for a clear view of basic developments, uncluttered by an abundance of discursive asides and facts for facts' sake. But desirable though it is, clarity of structure must not be made an end in itself, if it is not inherent in the subject-matter. Space must be given to a variety of themes and topics. Altogether the first book on Canada's musical history should emphasize description rather than evaluation according to a preconceived point of view. The foremost aim must be to make the facts available, to tell "what actually happened" and to let events speak for themselves. For this reason the application of extraneous critical standards is kept to a minimum: the historian would miss the point of his task if he examined early Canadian concert life simply to show how primitive it was in comparison with music in London or Paris, or how wonderful it was because it took place in a frontier setting.

Although it is hoped that the many factors involved in selecting and proportioning material have been evenly balanced, a definitive judgment of composition and other individual achievements can be gained only under far more advanced conditions of archival collections and when the subject becomes one of wider discussion and research. Only then will it be possible in many cases to penetrate beyond the statistical and biographical facts of a musician's career and bring to life his personality, his aesthetic views, his human qualities, his working methods, his hopes and disappointments. Some musicians, little known now, may gain in stature, others may have received undue emphasis here, because their life happens to be particularly well publicized and documented.

A word about the scope of this book. Being concerned mainly with the European heritage in Canada, it does not attempt to deal with Indian and Eskimo music. The social role of folk song is described and the names of many songs are mentioned in passing, but for the survey of Canadian folk music literature and its musical analysis readers are referred to the articles written as introductions to the song collections of Marius Barbeau, Ernest Gagnon, Helen Creighton, Elisabeth Bristol Greenleaf, Grace Yarrow Mansfield, Richard Johnston, Edith Fowke and others.

For a thorough discussion of developments in the mid-twentieth century readers may turn to the book *Music in Canada*, edited by Sir Ernest MacMillan (Toronto, 1955) and to other sources listed in the Bibliography. While this literature will help in an understanding of the contemporary scene, the specific aim of this book will be fulfilled if it helps to enlarge consciousness of a part of Canadian history which is not as well known as it deserves; if it revives and preserves the memory of many a worthy, though forgotten musician; and if it contributes to the understanding of the preparations, problems and processes involved in establishing music in colonial surroundings.

2 / Music in New France

THE EARLIEST RECORDS: Music has been with the European
settlers in Canada from the days of their arrival on the newly
discovered shores. Indeed, even before any settlement took place the
hardy mariners who sailed with Jacques Cartier greeted the new-
found land by singing a mass. The first of several references to
the celebration of the mass in Cartier's report is that for June 14,
1534, when, he says, "we had mass sung" at Brest (Bonne Espé-
rance Harbour on the south coast of Labrador).[1] It was on his
second voyage to the new continent that Cartier for the first time
ascended the St. Lawrence River. He visited the Indian village of
Hochelaga, a palisade settlement of some three thousand Iroquois
on the site of present-day Montreal. The welcome was a most
friendly one. The visitors with their strange apparel and manner
must have impressed the Indians as supernatural beings, for the
Indians presented their sick to the French for healing. Thereupon
Cartier recited some verses from the Gospel according to St. John,
and the Indians were given hatchets, knives, rings and other
presents. "The Captain [Cartier] next ordered the trumpets and

[1]H. P. Biggar, ed., *The Voyages of Cartier* ("Publications of the Public
Archives of Canada," no. 11) (Ottawa, 1924), p. 24. Nazaire LeVasseur, in his
series of articles "Musique et Musiciens à Québec," *La Musique* (1919–22),
claims that when Cartier's ship entered Gaspé Bay in August 1534 and the
land was claimed for King Francis I, the *Ave Maris Stella* and *Te Deum* were
sung. This is quite possible to imagine, but there is no proof for it in Cartier's
writings. Besides, his ship entered Gaspé Bay in July, not August, 1534. We
shall have occasion again later to doubt the accuracy of LeVasseur's writing.

other musical instruments to be sounded, whereat the Indians were much delighted. We [the French] then took leave of them and proceeded to set out upon our return."² Thus music formed the climax of the first ceremonial meeting between European and Indian in Canada. The day was October 3, 1535.

Cartier's visits to Canada did not result in permanent settlement. It was not until about 1600 that French interest was renewed in the search for a northwest passage leading to the fabulous riches of the Orient, and in the fur trade with the land that Cartier had discovered. In 1605 the first French settlement in Canada was founded. This was Port Royal, now the town of Annapolis Royal, Nova Scotia.

Again musical records date from the earliest days. At Port Royal, Marc Lescarbot (ca. 1570– ca. 1630), a young lawyer from Paris, wrote a masque to celebrate the return of Baron de Poutrincourt, the leader of the colony, who had been away on an expedition. *The Theatre of Neptune* was performed on barques "upon the waves of the harbour" on November 14, 1606. This "gay piece of courtly fun," as it has been called, is of musical interest because it contains not only a trumpet cue but a short piece of verse to be sung in four parts. Marius Barbeau, the eminent authority on Canadian folklore, has assumed that the tune used for this song was that of *La Petite Galiotte de France*, a popular French song of the fifteenth or sixteenth century.³

Lescarbot was also the first to write down Indian songs. He recorded the words and music of four Micmac songs to which he listened outside the wigwam of the chief Membertou. Unfortunately, he gives only the scale-steps and does not indicate the rhythm. An example follows:

haloet	ho ho hé hé ha ha	haloet	ho ho hé
re fa sol	*sol re sol sol fa fa*	*re re sol*	*sol fa fa*⁴

²*Ibid.*, p. 166.
³Port Royal is the scene of Healey Willan's ballad opera *The Order of Good Cheer* (1928).
⁴Marc Lescarbot, *Histoire de la Nouvelle France* (Paris, 1609), ed. W. L. Grant and H. P. Biggar (Toronto, 1914, based on 3rd ed. of 1617), III, 106 (English), 360–1 (French). Father Gabriel Sagard-Théodat in his *Le Grand Voyage du pays des Hurons* (Paris, 1632) reprinted them in four-part arrangements. They are reproduced in the Champlain Society edition (Toronto, 1939), opp. p. 120.

MUSIC AS A HANDMAID OF MISSIONARY WORK: Most of the early immigrants were not farmers but explorers or priests. The music they brought with them was that of the Catholic church and rural western France. In the new country there was none of the pomp and splendour of aristocratic life in Paris or Versailles, and one would never hear graceful suites and ballets such as were performed at the court of the *roi soleil*.

The two main groups of immigrants differed widely in their reasons for coming to the New World. The explorers and adventurers, the *coureurs de bois*, were eager to discover the country's riches, to obtain furs, and to adapt themselves to the new environment by studying the Indians' way of life. The priests, on the other hand, had come to convert the Indians to Christianity. With unselfish devotion the hard-working missionaries attempted to convert the Indians to the Catholic faith and to introduce to them the ways of occidental civilization. Their efforts are of great interest to us because of the important place given to music. To appreciate this we must compare the attitude of the French in their cultural relations with the Indians with that of the English and Spaniards. It has been pointed out that the English made little attempt to civilize the Indians, whereas the settlers from Catholic countries were deeply interested in the Indians' conversion.[5] The Spaniards attempted to force their own way of life upon the rich Indian civilization of Mexico, while the French attempted a more gradual approach; "Sa Majesté désire qu'on francise ainsi peu à peu tous les sauvages, afin d'en faire un peuple poli. L'on commence par les enfants. Monseigneur notre Prélat en a pris un grand nombre; les Révérends Pères en ont pris aussi en leur collége de Québec. Tous sont vêtus a la Française, & on leur apprend à lire & à écrire comme en France. . . ."[6]

While language and reasoning presented difficulties, the missionaries soon discovered one key to their ambitions and employed it to great advantage: the Indians' strong inclination and receptiveness towards music. For instance Father Gabriel Sagard-

[5]Mrs. L. Spell, "Music in New France in the Seventeenth Century," *Canadian Historical Review* VIII (June 1927), 119–131.

[6]Lettres de Marie de l'Incarnation, # 85, September 27, 1650, quoted in E. M. Faillon, *Histoire de la colonie française en Canada* (Montreal, 1866), III, 271.

Théodat, who in 1623–4 travelled along the Ottawa River by canoe to the country of the Hurons, reported:

Il se faut aussi estudier à la douceur & monstrer une face ioyeuse & modestement contante, & chanter par fois des Hymnes, & Cantiques spirituels, tant pour sa propre consolation, le soulagement de ses peines, que pour le contentement & edification de ces Sauuages, qui prennent un singulier plaisir d'ouyr chanter les loüanges de nostre Dieu plustost que des chansons profanes, contre lesquelles ie leur ay veu quelquesfois monstrer de la repugnance. O bon Jesus, qui condamne les mauvais Chrestiens chanteurs de chansons dissuluës & mondaines.[7]

Nothing could summarize more briefly the experience of these pioneers than the remark, made two hundred years later by the wife of a missionary: "All the Indians are passionately fond of music and . . . it is a very effective means of interesting and fixing their attention."[8]

Exploiting this musical inclination, the Jesuit Fathers taught the Indians around them the simpler parts of the services. They translated hymns into native dialects, and accompanied the singing with instruments where these were available. The Fathers were well equipped for these tasks, for in this period every educated person possessed at least rudimentary training in music. Furthermore it is very likely that in the selection of the Fathers for service in Canada consideration was given to musical qualifications, once it was known how well the Indians responded to sacred song. Records prove the success of this musical diplomacy. Even before the arrival of the Jesuits, when Jesse Fléché, a lay priest, came to Port Royal in 1610, he began to teach the simpler parts of the church service to the Micmacs. When he baptized the chief

[7]Sagard-Théodat, *Histoire du Canada et Voyages que les frères mineurs Recollects y ont faicts pour la conversion des infidèles*, I (new ed.; Paris, 1866), 173–4. One must also train oneself to good-humour and present a cheerful appearance of modest satisfaction, and sing hymns sometimes and spiritual songs, both for one's own comfort and relief from toil and for the edification of the savages, who take peculiar delight in hearing sung the praises of God rather than profane ditties, to which I have sometimes seen them show impugnance. O Jesus, who condemnest evil Christians, singers of dissolute and worldly songs!" Tr. by H. H. Langston, unpublished manuscript (in University of Toronto Library), pp. 146–7.

[8]Anna Jameson, *Winter Studies and Summer Rambles in Canada* (1st ed., New York, 1839; reprinted, Toronto, 1923), p. 372 (1923 ed.). Told to Mrs. Jameson by Mrs. MacMurray, wife of a missionary to the Chippewas.

Membertou and his tribe in the same year, the converts joined in the singing of the *Te Deum*.[9]

As years went on, the missionaries' musical pioneer work was richly rewarded. In 1676 Father Jean Enjalran reported on the singing of the Indians from the Huron seminary at what is now Sillery, near Quebec: "One is charmed to hear the various choirs, which the men and women form in order to sing during mass and at vespers. The nuns of France do not sing more agreeably than some savage women here; and as a class, all the savages have much aptitude and inclination for singing the hymns of the church, which have been rendered into their language."[10] Antiphonal singing between men and women, referred to in this passage, was a frequent mode of performance.

No doubt the Indian children took more readily to sacred songs than did their elders who were steeped in ancient traditions. An account from the mission of Notre Dame de Foye, near Quebec from 1672–3 stated:

The example of the French pupils—who every night, on leaving school, go to sing at benediction in the chapel of Notre-Dame de Foye—has had the good effect that the little savages, in order to imitate them, have learned to sing beautiful hymns in their own language; and they sing them even in their houses, in the streets, in the fields, and wherever they happen to be. Thus these little creatures, ignoring all the profane songs of their ancestors, have on their lips only the spiritual motets that the Father teaches them. The result is, that in a short time they learn with pleasure the mysteries of our faith, and all their prayers, which they are made to sing to various airs, changing the words and the music as is done in the church, on the return of the yearly festivals.[11]

The Fathers who translated the *Magnificat*, the *Ave Maria*, the *Te Deum* and other sacred songs into native dialects usually preserved the original melody or altered it slightly to fit the Indian words. At times, however, it must have been difficult to find a translation that could be sung to the original melody. In these

[9]*The Jesuit Relations and Allied Documents*, ed. Reuben Gold Thwaites (Cleveland, 1896–1901), II, 137. This edition is referred to throughout. Page numbers refer to the English text.
[10]*Ibid.*, LX, 145.
[11]*Ibid.*, LVII, 61–3.

cases, or when an entirely new text was written, French folk songs and Indian melodies were made use of or new tunes were invented.

One of these songs which has survived is the carol "Jesous Ahatonhia" ("Jesus is Born"), also known as "Noël huron." It is generally assumed that Father Jean de Brébeuf was the author of the Indian words of "America's first Christmas carol." This famous missionary spent many years among the Huron Indians near Georgian Bay and acquired an intimate knowledge of the Indians' language and mentality.[12] The purpose of his song was to tell the Christmas story to the Indians in a way they would easily comprehend. Thus the imagery of the story was changed to fit the Indians' environment. The tune (Fig. 1) is that of a French song of the six-

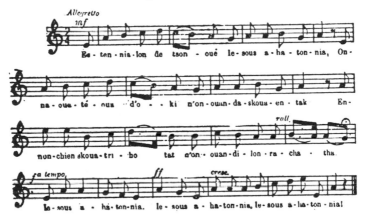

FIGURE 1. "Jesous Ahatonhia," the *Noël huron*, as printed in Myrand's *Noëls anciens de la Nouvelle-France.*

teenth century, "Une Jeune Pucelle," with minor changes. Its beginning resembles the melody of "God Rest Ye Merry, Gentlemen." The exact date of "Jesous Ahatonhia" is not known; it was written sometime between 1634 and 1648, and 1641 has been cited as its approximate date. Huron Indians who fled to Lorette (near Quebec) from the Iroquois in 1649, after the series of raids in which Brébeuf met a martyr's death, preserved the carol, which was then translated into French. In recent years it has been harmonized

[12]Brébeuf is the subject of a choral-orchestral pageant with words by E. J. Pratt and music by Healey Willan.

and translated into English several times. It should be pointed out that the widely used translation by J. E. Middleton (1926) does not adhere very closely to the Indian words.

From several reports we know also that the missionaries invented new tunes for the songs they wished to teach the Indians. For instance, a letter written by Sister Anne de Ste-Claire from Quebec on September 2, 1640, states that Father René Menard (1605–61) "avait composé quelques motets que nous chantions après l'éléva-tion."[13] The earliest example of composition in America north of Mexico, however, comes not from a missionary, but from Poutrin-court, the leader of Port Royal settlement. It dates from the years 1610–12. These are the words of Marc Lescarbot: "Let us return to Port Royal. When the Sieur [Poutrincourt] arrived there he found Martin[14] and his friends, baptized, and all strongly imbued with zeal for the Christian Religion, listening very devoutly to divine service, which was usually sung to Music composed by the Sieur."[15]

The whole range of the missionaries' musical work—attracting the Indians with instruments, teaching them to sing religious chants and inventing new tunes—is epitomized in the account of Father Louys André (1631–1715), who in 1670 set out from Sault Ste Marie on a missionary assignment to an island on Láke Huron. After his arrival on the island he conceived the plan of composing some spiritual canticles. "No sooner," he writes, "had I begun to have these sung in the Chapel, accompanied by a sweet-toned flute . . . than they all came in crowds, both adults and children; so that, to avoid confusion, I let only the girls enter the Chapel, while the others remained without, and thus we sang in two choruses, those without, responding to those within."[16]

In spite of the many favourable reports about the Indians' love for the chants of the church, a note of scepticism should be sounded. Is it possible that a people, no matter how "primitive" its civiliza-tion, would give up its musical traditions without resistance? Indeed, since many tribes opposed conversion, they must also have

[13]Les Ursulines de Québec (Quebec, 1863), I, 39.
[14]Martin was a Souriquois chief who, with his tribe, had been baptized by Jesse Fléché.
[15]Marc Lescarbot, Relation Dernière (Paris, 1612), reprinted and translated in Jesuit Relations, II, 147.
[16]Jesuit Relations, LV, 147.

defended their traditional songs and dances against the music of a foreign faith. We may assume that the Fathers were so proud of their musical successes that in their reports they did not record failures with the same thoroughness. Further, as the report from the mission of Notre Dame de Foye indicates, it was chiefly the younger generation, raised under the missionaries' guidance, that accepted and excelled in the new music.

Although the work of the missionaries resulted in no music which was part aboriginal and part European, it has left a permanent mark on the music of certain Indian tribes in eastern Canada[17] in the sense that these Indians accepted elements of Gregorian chant and French folk music. Even today some Indian tribes, such as the Micmacs of New Brunswick or the Hurons of Lorette, sing the chants taught them three hundred years ago by the French missionaries. The permanence of this influence is indicated in the following impressions of two nineteenth-century observers. The first quotation tells of Peter Jones, a missionary to the Mohawks in 1830:

At the conclusion of his discourse, he gave out a hymn in the Chippewa tongue, in which he was joined by the Indians present, who all have excellent ears for music; indeed it would be difficult to find one who has not. The squaws sang very sweetly, and much more naturally than the over-strained voices of many of our fair cantatrices in Old England and the colonies.[18]

The writer's sister observed:

We had so often listened with pleasure to the Indians singing their hymns of a Sunday night that I requested some of them to sing to us; the old hunter nodded assent; and, without removing his pipe, with the gravity and phlegm of a Dutchman, issued his commands, which were as instantly obeyed by the younger part of the community, and a chorus of rich voices filled the little hut with a melody that thrilled to our very hearts.

The hymn was sung in the Indian tongue, a language that is peculiarly sweet and soft in its cadences, and seems to be composed

[17]French-Canadian song, on the other hand, has hardly been influenced by Indian music. For a good summary see A. G. Bailey, *The Conflict of European and Eastern Algonkian Cultures, 1504–1700* (Saint John, N.B., New Brunswick Museum, 1937).

[18]Samuel Strickland, *Twenty-Seven Years in Canada West* (London, 1853), II, 59.

with many vowels. . . . I was pleased with the air of deep reverence that sat on the faces of the elders of the Indian family, as they listened to the voice of their children singing praise and glory to the God and Saviour they had learned to fear and love.[19]

QUEBEC, EARLIEST CENTRE OF MUSIC: Although Port Royal was the first French colony in Canada, its everyday existence was much too unstable to permit any real musical development. Many times the village was abandoned and resettled, attacked and resettled. To find settlements with a more continuous history we must follow the priests and explorers inland to the outpost of Quebec, founded in 1608, and to the country stretching west to Lake Huron. In Quebec, the largest French settlement and centre of missionary activity, Europeans and Indians lived side by side. Since the Jesuit Fathers wrote to their superiors in France detailed reports about day-to-day happenings —the famous Jesuit *Relations* —we possess a wealth of information about musical as well as other activities. The references to music concern two closely related spheres: education and performance.

The first to promote music in the colony was Father Le Jeune (1591–1664), who arrived in 1632 as superior of the mission. In striving to adorn religious services with music, he realized the importance of training the young people who would be the future leaders of the colony. In the winter after his arrival, Le Jeune started a school for native children. Every day classes ended with the singing of the *Pater Noster*. A proper schoolhouse was erected in 1635 and thereafter systematic instruction in the elements of Gregorian chant and musical notation was given to the Indian and French boys.[20] Boys who showed musical aptitude were given such instruments as were available and received individual instruction. Of the Indian boys it is said that their lack of enthusiasm for academic studies was compensated for by their great attraction to music.

A few years later Mother de St.-Joseph, one of the first Ursulines to come to Canada, began to teach native and French girls. After giving a lesson on the Catechism she would teach her pupils to sing religious songs and to play the viol, and sometimes she would

[19]Catharine Parr Traill, *The Backwoods of Canada* (London, 1836; Toronto, 1929), pp. 221–2 (1929 ed.).
[20]In 1635 there were about 85 French people in all of New France.

let the Indian girls perform their traditional dances.[21] As the "merry-hearted" Mother de St.-Joseph "had a beautiful voice and understood Music well, not only did she sing and chant the psalms, but she also led the Choir, for which office she doubtless had aptitude; for she succeeded in it marvellously, notwithstanding her lung troubles."[22]

A fire put a temporary stop to education in 1640, when both the boys' school and church were destroyed. But a new church was soon built and henceforth music assumed a larger role in divine worship.

Father Le Jeune's efforts now began to bear fruit. So often do the *Relations* refer to music at Quebec in the 1640's that we can trace its course almost year by year. It appears that every musical boy or man was called upon to assist in church service. The musicians were drawn from the school boys and from the clergymen and "gentlemen" who sang or played instruments. At Christmas 1645 we read that Martin Boutet "played the violin; there was also a German [transverse] flute, which proved to be out of tune when they came to the Church."[23] The beginning of musical criticism in North America! The carols sung at midnight mass included "Chantons noe" and "Venez mon Dieu."[24] On November 27 there was a wedding at which "there were two violins for the first time."[25] We should note that in the seventeenth century the violin—if indeed a violin is referred to—and the transverse flute were new instruments and that in France, lutes and recorders still surpassed them in popularity.

In 1646 the choir was enlarged by a musically gifted soldier who took the treble part and on St. Thomas Day, in December, four-part singing was begun.[26] According to Myrand, the carol "Mortels, préparez-vous" was sung that Christmas.[27] Two years later, we read, psalms were sung in "fauxbourdon," meaning at that period the

21Letter written by Sister Anne de Ste-Claire, Quebec, September 2, 1640. Printed in *Les Ursulines de Québec*, p. 41.
22*Jesuit Relations*, XXXVIII, 149; written after her death, which occurred in 1652.
23*Ibid.*, XXVII, 113.
24*Ibid.*
25*Ibid.*, 101 (November 27, 1645).
26*Ibid.*, XXVIII, 249.
27For a detailed study of French-Canadian carols consult Ernest Myrand, *Noëls anciens de la Nouvelle-France* (Quebec, 1899, 1907).

practice of adding ornamental, usually improvised, counterpoint to the plain-chant. One day there was "music with viols for the elevation" during communion and mass. The report for 1650 describes a Christmas celebration "with an order and pomp that increase devotion. There are eight choir-boys, besides Chanters and Officials."[28]

In the same year a boarding school was opened where children of the colonists were taught "reading, writing, plain chant and the fear of God." The teacher was the same Martin Boutet, a French immigrant, who had played the violin at Christmas 1645. He is mentioned both as cantor and as leader of the children's choir. Not only children were trained in music; the Church expected its priests as well to be competent church musicians. Bishop Laval's order (dated Paris, March 26, 1663) establishing the Quebec Seminary listed "le plain-chant grégorien" among the subjects in which the clerics were to be trained. The missionaries at Quebec also sustained and encouraged talented musicians. In 1662 François d'Augé (or Daugé), a musician, was taken on as a boarder at the mission and three years later a nineteen-year-old drummer, "an excellent musician" who arrived with the Carignan regiment, was given a subsidy to pursue his musical studies.

MUSICAL INSTRUMENTS: There are many instances of the use of musical instruments in addition to the few already noted. Claude Dablon, one of the Jesuit missionaries who had established an outpost at Onondaga (near Syracuse, N.Y.) in 1655, is known to have taken several instruments with him. He was an excellent player who used music in teaching the native girls.[29] These must have been the same instruments which are the "heroes" of a story told by Mother Marie de l'Incarnation in her letter of October 4, 1658. The French at Onondaga had discovered that the Iroquois were plotting to kill them. There was nothing for the French to do but escape. They conceived a counterplan according to which they let the Indians enjoy a noisy festivity, so noisy indeed that the French could secretly prepare their departure. After the Indians had feasted, eaten, danced and shouted to the sound of flutes, trumpets and

[28]*Jesuit Relations*, XXXVI, 173–5.
[29]*La Vie du R.P. Pierre Joseph Marie Chaumonot* (1688; reprinted New York, 1858).

drums, a French boy who had been adopted by an Iroquois lulled the tired men to sound sleep with his guitar playing. At this point the French made a safe escape.

In his notes on the musical history of Quebec, LeVasseur says that the records mention an organ as early as 1657. Unfortunately my search has not yielded any such document.[30] We do know, however, that an organ was played in the parish church at Carnival time in 1661. The Jesuit *Relations* refer to the instrument for the first time in these words: "The organ played while the Blessed Sacrament was being taken down, and during benediction." Pierre Duquet and Michel Feuillon assisted with the music during these festivities.[31] The date is significant not only in Canadian, but in all North American musical history: there is no record of an organ in the United States until about 1700. What type of organ was played in Quebec in 1661 and where it was built is not known. It cannot have been a very satisfactory instrument, for on his journey to France two years later, Mgr Laval, anxious to foster the spirit of religious devotion among the eight hundred settlers, purchased a better instrument. He brought it with him on his return to Quebec in September 1663. At least, so we are told by Bertrand de la Tour, who published Laval's biography in 1761 and who had lived in Quebec as a parish priest: "On commença à se servir des orgues que M. l'Evêque avait apportées de Paris." However, the only contemporary evidence is an entry in the churchwarden's accountbook in November 1663, recording the purchase of 300 nails for putting up a staircase to the organ (*l'escalier des orgues*) and for the preacher's chair.[32] This indicates that the work of installing the new organ was begun soon after its arrival. Yet the records for the following year show that the organ was not used regularly, perhaps because of mechanical problems or because a skilled player was not always available. The Jesuit *Relations* tells us that there was organ music on Shrove Tuesday (February), while the candles were being lighted, but at Easter "there was benediction at the parish church, with instrumental music—then for the first time—in the Jube near the organ. All went well, except that the voice and instruments are weak for

[30]LeVasseur, in *La Musique* (1919), I, 26.
[31]*Jesuit Relations*, XLVI, 163–5.
[32]Archives du Séminaire de Québec, carton Polygraphie 22, #51.

so vast a structure.[33] Obviously there was a reason for not using the organ at Easter. In a letter which an expert has dated August 1664, Bishop Laval reported to the Pope:

There is here a cathedral made of stone; it is large and splendid. The divine service is celebrated in it according to the ceremony of bishops; our priests, our seminarists, as well as ten or twelve choir-boys, are regularly present there. On the more important festivals, the mass, the vespers, and the eventide Salve are sung with an instrumental accompaniment in counterpoint with viols, and are each arranged according to its own style; blending sweetly with the singers' voices, the organ [or all the instruments] wondrously embellishes this harmony of musical sound.[34]

De la Tour states that the organ was first used near the end of 1664, at the time of the blessing of the first three bells poured in Canada. The "officiers de musique" at the Christmas services in 1664 were Louis Jolliet and Germain Morin, the first Canadian to be ordained priest. As a reward for their work they were invited by the Jesuits to a New Year's Day supper. Of these two men, Louis Jolliet (1645–1700) has been suggested as the more likely one to have played the organ. He was one of the first Canadians to further his studies in Europe (1667–8), where he became an accomplished harpsichord player. On his return to Canada, however, he did not enter the career of a professional organist, but "worked his way through college" as a musician, as a recent biographer has phrased it.[35] This was the Jolliet who achieved fame as the discoverer of the source of the Mississippi River.

Further information about the instruments in use at this time is supplied by LeVasseur. He relates that during reconstruction work in the nineteenth century, about ten viols and viol basses with six strings each were discovered in a vault at the Hôpital-Général.

33Jesuit Relations, XLVIII, 233.
34A. Leblond de Brumath, Bishop Laval (Toronto, 1906), pp. 84–5. The crucial last sentence reads in Latin: "In maioribus festis missa, vesperae, ac serotinum salve musica cantatur, hexacordo diversum et suo numero absolutum, et organa vocibus suaviter commixta musicum mirifice hunc concentum adornant." It is given here in a translation specially made for the author by Mr. Edward J. Barnes of Toronto, as De Brumath's rendition is not very accurate. The date of Laval's letter was suggested by Abbé Honorius Provost of the Quebec Seminary archives.
35Jean Delanglez, Life and Voyages of Louis Jolliet (1645–1700) (Chicago, 1948), p. 2.

Possibly they had been stored there for safety during an attack on Quebec and were later forgotten. The instruments were built by Nicolas Bertrand in Paris. All had similar dimensions and structure and varied in size only. According to this source, one of the bass viols, dated 1672, won a first prize at the Philadelphia World Exhibition (1876) as the "oldest instrument on the North American continent."[36] One of the other instruments was dated as early as 1646. This last was sold to a Toronto music house in the early twentieth century, but its present location is not known. If we knew at what period these instruments had been brought to Canada we would have a valuable clue to the history of secular art music in New France—a field as yet unexplored.[37] Instruments were also associated with military life and various reports describe how trumpets, fifes and drums accompanied expeditions and ceremonies.

From the existence of an organ in Quebec, the desire grew to have such an instrument in other outposts. A priest of a mechanical bent took the organ brought by Laval as a model and built copies.[38] Unfortunately, we know neither his name nor the place where these instruments were installed. To continue with the early history of organs in Canada we turn to Montreal, founded in 1642 as Ville-Marie. In a well-documented study O. Lapalice has recorded the names of the organists and music directors at the Church of Notre Dame.[39] The purchase of an organ for Montreal was considered in 1698 but records do not mention an organist until 1705. The first known organist was Jean-Baptiste Poitiers du Buisson (1645–1727), a native of France, who took over the post at the age of sixty. While the documents do not describe his musical work, they do reveal something about his economic status. Du Buisson received no salary, but from time to time got an arbitrary sum of money or goods, depending on the momentary wealth of the parish

[36]LeVasseur's articles were written in his old age and although they abound in facts and figures, these are not always correct. For instance, he gives 1878 as the date for the Philadelphia World Exhibition.

[37]I have not detected any positive evidence of the cultivation of secular art music among the educated governors and *seigneurs* of New France. Professor Graham George in the issue of *Culture* for December 1955 cites reasons to postulate the probability of secular *soirées*.

[38]E. C. B. de Bourbourg, *Esquisse biographique sur Mgr de Laval* (Quebec, 1845), p. 24.

[39]O. Lapalice, "Les Organistes et maîtres de musique à Notre-Dame de Montréal," *Le Bulletin des recherches historiques*, XXV (August 1919), 243.

and the good grace of his superiors. Thus in 1715 he was given what was thought a generous sum of 100 *livres* and he received the same amount in 1718 "for having played the organ for several years." He must have been a patient man indeed. Charles François Coron, who assumed the position in the early 1720's received the sum of 83 *livres*, 15 *sous* for twenty months' work. In 1725 and 1726 he obtained as annual salary an overcoat and a jacket valued at 45 *livres*. In the following year, his income was fixed at 45 *livres* in money or 50 in merchandise. This brings to mind the kind of salary received by Bach, which included coal and cords of firewood.

THE OLDEST PRESERVED COMPOSITION: One cannot help being impressed by the number of famous pioneers of New France who were also musicians or lent a hand to musical enterprises. Baron de Poutrincourt, the leader of the settlement at Port Royal, Martin Boutet, the first teacher at the boarding school in Quebec, Bishop Laval, Louis Jolliet, Germain Morin and others were remarkable for their political, religious or educational achievements. Yet each made a significant contribution to the beginning of musical life in Canada. Clearly this is more than coincidence. The leaders of New France considered music as an essential part of the pioneer's equipment and way of living, in contrast to the leaders of later centuries who too often regarded art as a mere frill unworthy of their attention.

It is hardly surprising then that the second Canadian to be ordained priest, Charles-Amador Martin (1648–1711), was also an accomplished musician.[40] He received his general education at the Jesuit college in Quebec and studied theology at the seminary there. A priest in several parishes near Quebec, and later canon of Quebec cathedral, Martin was a fine singer, and has also been credited with writing the first composition in Canada which has been preserved. This piece of plain-chant was written in celebration of the Holy Family at the behest of Mgr Laval. This celebration had been instituted by Laval in 1665 for the second Sunday after Epiphany but from 1685 it was held on the third Sunday after Pentecost.

Martin has been credited with the music for the mass and the

---

[40]He was the son of Abraham Martin *dit* l'Ecossais whose name was later immortalized in the Plains of Abraham.

office,[41] but it is doubtful that he wrote anything apart from the "prose" section of the office (Fig. 2). The manuscript of the office is preserved at the ancient Hôtel-Dieu in Quebec City, bound together with a *Messe du St. Nom de Jésus*. Neither work is signed or dated. Both are written in square-note notation on red lines, covering 24 pages in all. The Hôtel-Dieu also has the manuscript of the *Messe de la Sainte-Famille*.

In his biography of Louis Jolliet, Ernest Gagnon has written of Martin's composition:

La prose de l'office de la sainte Famille (pour ne parler que de cette partie de l'office entièrement composé par lui) indique du talent et une excellente formation. Cette prose n'est plus chantée, croyons-nous, que dans la cathédrale de Québec, et seulement le jeudi dans l'octave de la sainte Famille. C'est une pièce de plain-chant d'une incontestable beauté, écrite dans le premier mode authentique de la tonalité ancienne. Le style de cette composition est d'une correction remarquable, tant au point de vue du rhythme qu'au point de vue des affinités des notes modales.[42]

FOLK SONG: Nothing has been said so far about secular French folk music. Are we to conclude that the only music in New France was that of the church? Certainly, the Jesuit *Relations* foster such an impression. Let us realize, however, that the missionaries were interested chiefly in recording those musical events which con-

[41]Auguste Gosselin, *Vie de Mgr de Laval* (Quebec, 1890), I, 598; also Sœur Duplessis de Ste-Hélène, "Notice sur la Fête de la Ste-Famille" (unpublished manuscript), p. 11. (The latter was a historian of the Hotêl-Dieu.)

[42]Ernest Gagnon, *Louis Jolliet* (3rd ed.; Quebec, 1926), p. 136. The dating of Martin's music presents several problems. The year 1670 is given in Eugène Lapierre's article on music in Canada under "Canada, musique" in the *Encyclopédie Grolier* (Montreal, 1947) and has been taken over in the *Catalogue of Canadian Composers*. However, further investigations have made this date appear highly improbable. Not only was Martin very young and inexperienced in 1670 (he was ordained in 1671), but of four Canadians who are said to have sketched the Latin words for the prose, the last did not arrive in Canada until 1673 (the first death among the four occurred in 1697). The sketch was sent to Abbé de Santeuil, canon at Saint-Victor Abbey in Paris, who rendered it into more elegant language. It is unlikely that all this work was accomplished in one year; hence 1674 may be assumed as the earliest possible year.

Another aspect remains to be considered. When Laval moved the feast date in 1684 he proposed that a new office be written. This was supplied by Father Gourdan of Saint-Victor Abbey in Paris before 1700. (E. M. Faillon, *Histoire de la colonie française en Canada*, Montreal, 1866, III, 547.) The possibility that this was the text composed by Martin should be kept in mind.

FIGURE 2. Part of the Prose for "La Fête de la Ste. Famille" as printed in the *Graduel romain* (1854 edition).

cerned their own field of activity. Many of them looked with apprehension and hostility upon "impious songs" and worldly pleasures. For instance, when Louis-Théandre Chartier de Lotbinière held the first ball in Canada, in February 1667, a Jesuit's pen exclaimed "Dieu veuille que cela ne tire pas à conséquence."[43] In a field related to music, the theatre, there were performances of works by Corneille and others, but clerical opposition put a stop to "impious comedy" towards the end of the seventeenth century and the theatre suffered an eclipse until the latter part of the eighteenth century.

Clerical unconcern, however, is not the only reason why we know so little about secular folk song. Transmitted by voice alone, folk song by its very nature left few written traces of its history throughout the centuries.[44] Despite this, it can be said that the singing of the peasants, explorers, and adventurers was by far the most common form of music in New France.

It has been estimated that of the seven to ten thousand songs that have been collected in the province of Quebec in recent years, fully nine-tenths are derived from songs brought to Canada before 1673. This has been established through their texts, and through comparison of Canadian with French versions, and of variants within different regions of Canada. The study of the history of French migration to Canada allows us to place the introduction of these songs still more accurately—in the years between 1665 and 1673. In this period, large-scale immigration was initiated by Jean Talon, an energetic Intendant of New France. His various inducements to immigrants helped to double the population in a short time. The number of French-Canadians rose from 2,500 in 1663 to 6,700 in 1675. After Talon's time the population increased by natural growth rather than immigration. The great wave of immigrants under Talon's administration consisted mainly of people from the Normandy, Brittany, and other districts of northwestern France. Many of them had been farmers and fishermen before emigrating and with their arrival agriculture became an important activity in Canada. The settlers brought with them a great love of song, dance and fiddle playing. Often a group from

[43]Faillon, *Histoire de la colonie française en Canada*, III, 397.

[44]Ernest Gagnon, in his article "La Musique à Québec au temps de Monseigneur de Laval," *La Nouvelle-France* (May 1908), mentions a note from the year 1638 which apparently refers to the song "Pauvre Bonhomme."

the same village would settle together, and this homogeneity of traditions and customs was as much responsible for the preservation of their songs through the generations, as was the vitality of their musicianship, their relative isolation in the new country, and their loyal memory of "la douce France." Song was ever present at work and at leisure, at home or on a journey. It sped the paddle of the *voyageur*, it helped to pass hours of loneliness, it preserved the memory of the homeland, it mirrored the exploits, sufferings and adventures of the pioneers. In short, song played an infinitely more vital part in everyday life than it does in our present-day urban society.

3 / Diversification of Folk and Church Music

CANADA IN THE EIGHTEENTH CENTURY: The eighteenth century, except for its final decades, is a rather dark age in the recorded musical history of Canada. There is a dearth of source-material, such as the Jesuit *Relations* of earlier days, describing the details of everyday life. Most accounts of the period, whether contemporary or more recent, are lengthy discussions of military and political affairs. Look for the word *music* in the index of almost any book of Canadian history and you will find that the M's stop at "Murray, James, governor of Quebec"! It is a sad fact that almost all histories of Canada, even those dealing with social and cultural life, dismiss music in a scant paragraph or two, or simply ignore it altogether. Unless new discoveries of documents enlarge our knowledge, it may be assumed that during the first sixty or seventy years of the eighteenth century music continued much along the lines established in the seventeenth century: as faithful companion of religion, work, travel and leisure hours. There was some expansion of musical activities as new settlements arose and more churches were equipped with organs, the most notable addition being the organ in Montreal. The Church employed the services of many amateurs and perhaps a few musicians of professional accomplishment. Few of these are known to us by name.

Unfortunately for Canada this period was one of frequent warfare with resulting unrest, destruction of property, and uprooting of entire settlements. The rivalry between France and England in North America, dating from the early seventeenth century, came to a climax of clashing arms. To complicate the picture, Indians were often drawn into the fight, enlisting now on one side, now on the other. Quebec had been under British rule between 1629 and 1632; Acadia—the eastern part of New France—from 1654 to 1667 and permanently after 1713. The struggle raged most violently in the Maritimes. As the result of war, about 6,000 French settlers were expelled from Acadia in 1775. In their place new settlers arrived from New England, Yorkshire, Ulster, and Scotland. Hardly had British rule over all of Canada been confirmed in 1763 when the country became involved in war once more. In 1775 revolutionary American forces captured Montreal and made an unsuccessful attack on Quebec, but had to withdraw in the following year. Soon a steady stream of United Empire Loyalists—in all about 40,000—began to flow from New England, New York, and other American colonies to the Maritimes and the still unsettled regions of Upper Canada. Among the Loyalists there were many whose former situation in life had afforded them broad opportunities for education and culture.

The fortunes of war found a reflection in music. During the decisive battle for Quebec in 1759, a two-manual organ built in Paris and installed only six years before, was destroyed in the bombardments—a heavy loss to musical life. On the British side victory was celebrated in song. "A Thanksgiving Anthem, for the taking Montreal [sic] and making us Masters of all Canada" is preserved in the British Museum. It was written by James Nares, composer in the service of the Chapel Royal. Although hardly as numerous as his portraits, there are several songs about General Wolfe, the most famous being "The Death of the Brave General Wolfe" or "Brave Wolfe." This beautiful ballad, of which several versions are known, has long been popular in eastern Canada and New England. An instrumental tone-picture of the battle of Quebec was begun by Franz Kotzwara, who had achieved fame with his "Battle of Prague" and obviously wanted to duplicate his success. After Kotzwara's death in 1791, a London publisher prevailed upon W. B. de Krifft to complete the composition. The "Siege of Quebec," a sonata for the harpsichord or piano with accompaniments for a violin, violoncello, and tympano ad libitum, has nine parts describing in turn such events as the signal for the attack, the "ascending of the heavy artillery up the rocks," fighting with swords, a heavy cannonade, the capitulation, and the lamenting for the death of General Wolfe and the officers and soldiers killed. It ends with a march of victory and a finale entitled "General Rejoicing."

In discussing Canadian history from the late eighteenth century on, one must bear in mind that Canada's population consists of two major groups: the French, centred in the province of Quebec; and the Anglo-Saxons who form the majority in all other provinces. Europeans from other countries also came at an early date, but only in recent years has a great variety of people from many parts of the world settled in Canada. They live as minorities among the English-speaking population whose language and customs they gradually assimilate. Among the minority groups the Germans, Ukrainians, Scandinavians, and Dutch are strongest numerically. Despite the common environment, the contrast between the French- and the English-speaking population is a striking one. It is so striking, indeed, that throughout Canada's musical history few generalizations can be made that apply equally to both sections of the Canadian people.

The first French settlers left a feudal and agricultural France behind them. Many came from the same district, and in Canada they founded villages and towns in which communal life was closely knit. Since the eighteenth century the population of Quebec has grown less by immigration than by natural increase. The Roman Catholic faith is shared by all and the French language forms a linguistic island in North America. Only of late has industrialization become a serious force. These factors have combined to make French Canada a very homogeneous and conservative society. No wonder ancient traditions in song and handicrafts, as in other fields, have been preserved in a purer state than in France.

In contrast, many of the Anglo-Saxon immigrants came from the cities of a dawning industrial age. They arrived from New England, Scotland, England and Ireland. More often than not, neighbours in the new settlements spoke different dialects, belonged to different religious sects, and sang different songs. Settlements were often miles apart and old neighbours might leave for the west, making room for new immigrants. The English-speaking Canadians were also much more open to influence from the large American cities a short distance across the border which had developed into strongholds of a modern commercial and technological outlook. Under such conditions folk traditions were easily forgotten. These statements do not apply equally to all provinces, however, for within English-speaking Canada one must distinguish between a region such as Nova Scotia, with its two centuries of history and wealth of traditional folk song, and the Prairies, which grew up with the railway and the automobile and possess no distinct song of their own.

These brief observations indicate a variety of social environment in Canada. They do not imply that there are two antagonistic peoples with irreconcilable conflicts. On the contrary, the cultural and social forces uniting all Canadians are becoming stronger every year. But as our description of musical history passes from one region of the country to another, it will be useful to keep in mind the above essential social characteristics of French- and English-speaking Canadians.

THE SETTING: At the end of the eighteenth century only the eastern part of present-day Canada was settled; the west and north were begun to be charted by explorers such as Alexander Mackenzie and George Vancouver. There were four separate political units, each with its own Governor and Council: the colonies of Upper and Lower Canada, Prince Edward Island, New Brunswick and Nova Scotia. The total population was about 300,000 of whom the majority lived in Lower Canada, now the province of Quebec. Material conditions of everyday life were still very primitive and extreme distances made transportation difficult. As roads were impassable in winter and spring, rivers and lakes served as the main avenues of traffic. Constantly in the presence of physical danger, the hardy pioneers had to fight such odds as famine, disease, wild animals and bush fires. There were attacks from Indians and armed clashes with the Americans. Medical and educational facilities were of the most elementary kind. Nevertheless, although people's thoughts were preoccupied with material and political problems, cultural activities were pursued in such towns as Quebec, Montreal, Kingston, Halifax and Saint John, all with populations below 15,000 (at this time Toronto had about 300 inhabitants; Ottawa and Hamilton did not exist; Edmonton was a trading post).

Musical documents became more plentiful towards the end of the eighteenth century, making it possible to draw a detailed picture of musical life. Our chief sources of information are the books in which visitors and immigrants laid down their impressions of the new country. Such reports were published in great numbers, some superficial and prejudiced, but many throwing interesting and even amusing sidelights on music. From these I shall quote liberally. A few newspapers made their appearance as well, starting with the Halifax *Gazette* in 1752. Newspaper advertisements and announcements reveal many details of musical interest.

In the early days of British rule in Canada, music had three main manifestations: the spontaneous and untutored music-making by the people in song, dance and instrumental playing; church services with their chants, psalms and hymns; and regimental bands in the garrison towns. In comparison with earlier times, folk music and religious music increased in variety as they now represented different nations and denominations. Band music, on the other hand, can be regarded as an entirely new musical element in Canada and one of great importance. Military instruments had been used in New France, but the British regimental bands stationed in Canada exercised an influence far beyond the military sphere. They gave impetus to the cultivation of secular art music and made orchestral concerts possible.

FOLK MUSIC: By far the strongest musical impression travellers took back with them to Europe was that of folk-singing. Indeed, folk music remained a vital and integral part of everyday life. From generation to generation the *habitants*, trappers and *voyageurs* of Quebec and the fishermen and farmers of Newfoundland and Nova Scotia handed down the songs of their ancestors. Even though transmitted orally, these songs were carefully preserved, with but few changes in words or tunes. To the old songs many new ones were added, taking their themes from current events and serving much the same role as a newspaper does today.

Tourists were amazed at the extent to which song pervaded all the activities of French Canadians in particular. In the words of a twentieth-century writer, people in the French settlements along the Detroit River "were mostly a carefree, jovial lot. The streets of the town were noisy day and night with the folksongs of the old homes across the ocean. The sound of violins could be heard from many houses and dancing was the popular amusement. . . ."[1] This description holds true equally for other parts of the country. Whether we turn to the St. Lawrence valley, the Gaspé, or Acadia, we find that the people were great lovers of the dancing, singing and fiddling which whiled away long winter evenings and made the hours of work go faster. As one writer puts it: "If a Frenchman has a fiddle, sleep ceases to be a necessary of life with him."[2] A few decades later another observer of *habitant* life stated, "Of dancing, fiddling, and singing, they are also fond, after vespers on Sunday; considering it no sin, but a harmless recreation, never attended with dissipation or vice."[3]

One group of singers is always singled out in the travellers' reports: the *voyageurs* or boatmen whose canoes plied the rivers and lakes between the wild bush area of northern Ontario and Manitoba and the trading centres such as Bytown (Ottawa) and Montreal. This emphasis can be explained in part by the obvious fact that the travellers associated for a longer period of time with the canoemen than with the rural farming and fishing population. The deeper reasons were the uniquely romantic setting and the high degree to which song had become a part of the canoemen's work.

The boatmen were of French, Indian, or mixed descent. Their language, according to Washington Irving, was a French patois intermingled with English and Indian words and phrases. To one accustomed to Parisian French much of this dialect sounded unintelligible. A fine picture of the singing is drawn by John Mactaggart:

As *voyageu:s*, or ramblers of any kind, they find much delight, so that a number of them be together. They will endure privations with great patience; will live on peas and Indian corn for years together. . . . They are good at composing easy, extemporaneous songs, somewhat smutty,

---

[1]G. B. Catlin, *The Story of Detroit* (Detroit, 1923), p. 25.
[2]William Dunlop, *Statistical Sketches of Upper Canada* (London, 1832), p. 54.
[3]John M'Gregor, *British America* (2nd ed.; London, 1833), II, 337. Some traditional fiddle music survives in French Canada. It is also preserved in a very pure form among the Métis, people of mixed Indian and French origin in the Prairie provinces.

but never intolerant. Many of their *canoe-songs* are exquisite; more particularly the *air* they give them. . . . We must be in a canoe with a dozen hearty paddlers, the lake pure, the weather fine, and the rapids past, before their influence can be powerfully felt. Music and song I have revelled in all my days, and must own, that the *chanson de voyageur* has delighted me above all others, excepting those of Scotland.[4]

Mrs. Jameson gives some details about the manner of performance: "The men sang their gay French songs, the other canoe joining in the chorus. . . . They all sing in unison, raising their voices and marking the time with their paddles. One always led, but in these there was a diversity of taste and skill."[5] The songs she heard included "En roulant ma boule," "La Belle Rose blanche," "Trois Canards" and "Si mon moine voulait danser."

Singing went on from early morning, when the canoemen picked up their paddles, until sundown: "Songs follow the paddle, beginning as soon as it is picked up and ending when it is dropped."[6] "Fifty songs a day were nothing to me. I could carry, paddle, walk, and sing with any man I ever saw. . . . No water, no weather, ever stopped the paddle or the song."[7] A note of appreciation is struck by John M. Duncan who listened

. . . to the boat songs of the Canadian voyageurs, which in the stillness of the night had a peculiarly pleasing effect. They kept time to these songs as they rowed; and the plashing of the oars in the water, combined with the wildness of their cadences, gave a romantic character to our darksome voyage. In most of the songs two of the boatmen began the air, the other two sang a response, and then all united in the chorus. Their music might not have been esteemed fine, by those whose skill in concords and chromatics, forbids them to be gratified but on scientific principles; my convenient ignorance of these rules allowed me to reap undisturbed enjoyment from the voyageurs' melodies, which like many of our Scotish airs were singularly plaintive and pleasing.[8]

[4]John Mactaggart, *Three Years in Canada* (London, 1829), I, 254–5.
[5]Anna Jameson, *Winter Studies and Summer Rambles in Canada* (New York, 1839; Toronto, 1923), p. 425 (1923 ed.).
[6]La Rochefoucault, quoted in Marius Barbeau, *Quebec: Where Ancient France Lingers* (Toronto, 1936), p. 95.
[7]Alexander Ross, *The Fur Hunters of the Far West* (London, 1855), II, 236. Told to Ross by an old *voyageur*.
[8]John M. Duncan, *Travels through Part of the United States and Canada in 1818 and 1819* (Glasgow, 1823), II, 121–2. This passage refers to the St. Lawrence River between Kingston and Brockville.

In another writer this music awakened old European memories: "The song of the *voyageur* floating over the smooth and silent water, and mellowed by distance, has, in my imagination, equalled the long-lost strains of the Venetian gondolier; . . ."[9]

But singing was not stopped by bad weather: " . . . As we were approaching Fort Alexander in the afternoon it began to rain pretty hard. The sight of their destination set the men a-singing, and we had all sorts of boat-songs, and rowed our four canoes up to the quay to the triumphant tune of 'En roulant ma boule.' "[10]

That the songs were not always equal to drawingroom standards need hardly be mentioned. La Rochefoucault warned that they are "gay, often a trifle more than gay," but perhaps Sir Richard Bonnycastle was too severe in declaring that "in fact very few of them, excepting in their burdens or chorusses, will bear to be printed or translated, on account of their excessive coarseness. In the north-west, these songs either begin or end with the startling and inspiring war-whoop."[11]

This typically Victorian attitude helps to explain why so few of the songs were published during the nineteenth century. The earthiness could prove an embarrassment when sensitive ladies were among the passengers. So shocked were the four Grey Nuns who travelled by canoe from Montreal to the Red River Settlement in 1844 that one of them, Sister Lagrave, made up new words for some of the spicier songs—with how much success we can imagine—and also taught hymns to the boatmen, "much to the amusement of Sir George Simpson" who happened to be in Fort William on their arrival.[12]

The song of the *voyageurs* also inspired the pen of true poets. In the minds of many British people two poems signified for many years the closest link between Canada and the muses. Both poems bear the same title: "Canadian Boat Song." The first was written in 1804 by Thomas Moore, who was paddled down the St. Lawrence River in a canoe from Kingston to Montreal. The impact of

[9]Pierre de Sales Laterrière, *A Political and Historical Account of Lower Canada* (London, 1830), p. 135.

[10]Marchioness of Dufferin and Ava, *My Canadian Journal* (London, 1891), p. 350, entry of September 7, 1877, written in Manitoba.

[11]Sir Richard Bonnycastle, *The Canadas in 1841* (London, 1842), II, 16–17. See also quotation on p. 179.

[12]J. M. Gibbon, *The Romance of the Canadian Canoe* (Toronto, 1951), pp. 115–16.

the magnificent scenery along the river and the ring of a song his boatmen repeated again and again—"Dans mon chemin j'ai rencontré Deux chevaliers très bien montés"—stirred the poet to write words of his own to go with the melody.

> Faintly as tolls the evening chime,
> Our voices keep tune and our oars keep time.
> Soon as the woods on the shores look dim,
> We'll sing at St. Anne's our parting hymn.
> Row, brothers, row, the stream runs fast,
> The Rapids are near, and the daylight's past.

One must agree with the opinion of Professor Needler that this is a true boat song and in a real sense Canadian.[13]

The other Canadian Boat Song, "The Lone Shieling," has caused much speculation because it was published anonymously. The poem appeared in *Blackwood's Edinburgh Magazine* in 1829, and purported to be a translation from the Gaelic. More than a hundred years later, Needler proved that the author was David Macbeth Moir, a practising physician in Scotland who had received many letters describing Canadian life from his friend John Galt. Needler states that the poem is not "in any real sense a boat-song, but the Lament of Highlanders from the Hebrides exiled in Upper Canada . . . the only thing Canadian about this otherwise remarkable poem." Of this poem we quote the well-known second stanza:

> From the lone shieling of the misty island
> Mountains divide us, and the waste of seas—
> Yet still the blood is strong, the heart is highland,
> And we in dreams behold the Hebrides.

The glorious period of *voyageur* song was the first half of the nineteenth century. Later, when transportation was mechanized, the number of boatmen began to dwindle and the romance of their adventures became a melancholy memory:

I have seen four canoes sweep round a promontory suddenly, and burst upon my view; while at the same moment, the wild, romantic song of the voyageurs, as they plied their brisk paddles, struck upon my ear, and I have felt the thrilling enthusiasm caused by such a scene: what, then, must have been the feelings of those who had spent a long,

---

[13]G. H. Needler, *The Lone Shieling* (Toronto, 1941). Moore's arrangement for three voices was published in London in 1805.

dreary winter in the wild North-West, far removed from the bustle and excitement of the civilised world, when thirty or forty of these picturesque canoes burst unexpectedly upon them, half shrouded in the spray that flew from the bright vermilion paddles, while the men, who had overcome difficulties and dangers innumerable during a long voyage through the wilderness, urged their light craft over the troubled water with the speed of the rein-deer, and with hearts joyful at the happy termination of their trials and privations, sang with all the force of three hundred manly voices, one of their lively airs, which, rising and falling faintly in the distance as it was borne, first lightly on the breeze, and then more steadily as they approached, swelled out in the rich tones of many a mellow voice, and burst into a long enthusiastic shout of joy! Alas! the forests no longer echo to such sounds.[14]

This excerpt dates from 1848. At about the same time a travelling clergyman stated that "the occupation of the gay voyageurs who were wont to make the 'Ottawa tide' resound with their choral ditties, is almost now amongst the things that have been. . . . All the traffic on the Ottawa is now done by the steamers."[15]

Even though the *voyageurs* disappeared from the main rivers, their song was kept alive for many more years in those regions where the steamer cannot penetrate, and a faint echo rings in the lumber camps of today. Ernest Gagnon's collection of Canadian songs, published in 1865, contains many *voyageur* songs, and even in the twentieth century, when the collecting of folk songs began in earnest, it was not too late to record many more. Nevertheless it is certain that dozens of beautiful songs have been lost forever.

As communication with Europe became more rapid and as immigrants arrived in larger numbers, Canadian taste was more easily influenced by European fashions. In the early days songs had travelled to Canada with individual folksingers. Now they were imported on printed paper, on so-called broadsheets and calendar pages, or in song books. Thus the French ballad gained a tremendous popularity in French Canada in the early nineteenth century. A typical example, cited by Marius Barbeau, was the poem of "Pyrame et Thisbe," a long "complainte" based on the old story made famous by Ovid. The Canadians adapted some of the ballads to old melodies, but others already had tunes of their own. In Upper

---

[14]R. M. Ballantyne, *Hudson's Bay* (Edinburgh, 1848), pp. 245–6.
[15][A. W. H. Rose] *The Emigrant Churchman in Canada*, ed. H. Christmas (London, 1849), II, 132–3.

Canada, as in the United States, ballads with psalm-tunes enjoyed great popularity. In his book *Early Life in Upper Canada* (1933), Edwin C. Guillet names some of the favourite songs: "The Soldier's Joy," "Money Musk," "Old Dan Tucker," and "Pop Goes the Weasel."

DANCING: Among the popular amusements and pastimes, such as sleighing, skating, horse-racing, and card-playing, dancing ranked second to none. The winter season in particular was one of dance and festivity. People would travel for miles on their sleighs to attend rural balls and informal gatherings of merriment. Dancing was the ruling passion of the Canadians, according to a letter written in the 1790's by an Englishman.[16] The dance tunes were played by the village fiddler or piper, and when no instrumental performer could be found, clapping, whistling, or singing would mark the rhythm. In French Canada the *giumbarde* (Jew's-harp) was also a popular instrument, and during the nineteenth century the clarinet and guitar became common. Even when several musicians were available, they played in unison rather than in harmony. The rustic musicians performed entirely by ear and developed an amazing facility for memorizing new tunes.

French and English Canadians each had their favourite dances. But as dances usually have no text, they are not restricted by language barriers and migrate from one nation to another more easily than do songs. What were the popular dances in Canada? In the second half of the eighteenth century De Sales wrote enthusiastically, "Jamais je n'ai connu nation aimant plus à danser que les Canadiens; ils ont encore les contre-danses françoises et les menuets, qu'ils entre-mêlent de danses angloises." To dance forty menuets at a wedding was considered nothing unusual in French Canada.[17] Around 1800, cotillons, quadrilles and, to a lesser extent, polkas and mazurkas were in vogue, while in Upper Canada and the Maritimes square dances, reels, jigs, and hornpipes were danced. In the towns, waltzes, menuets, schottisches and quadrilles gained special favour. No Scottish settlement was complete without bagpipe music. But, as one traveller explains, "At their dances within

[16]"Canadian Letters . . . 1792 and '93," *Canadian Antiquarian and Numismatic Journal*, ser. 3, IX (1912), 96.
[17]J. A. Hadfield, Diary, published as *An Englishman in America, 1785*, ed. D. S. Robertson (Toronto, 1933), p. 127.

doors, they, however, generally prefer the old Highland fiddler, or the young one who has learnt the same music, which is at all times played with the spirit and rapidity of which the Scotch reels and strathspeys are so eminently susceptible."[18]

In both parts of the country religious opposition to dancing flared up now and then. For example, LeVasseur tells us that in the convents waltzes and other dances in triple time were repressed as being lascivious. However, such victories were never lasting.

Thus all the evidence indicates a light-hearted and universal love of music among the people of early Canada (with the exception of a few religious sects soon to be noted). We should once and for all discard the unfortunate habit of regarding Canadians as a people without a tradition in the enjoyment and cultivation of music. That prejudice refers particularly to English-speaking Canadians and finds some justification in the prevailing attitude of the all too commercially minded middle classes of a much later time. Their utilitarian and practical outlook on life did indeed frown upon art, regarding music as either an eccentric pastime, a luxury, or, at best, a business; an artistic career indicated, to them, a doubtful moral character. It is therefore important to know that there was an earlier age, an age in which untutored music-making prevailed, and in which music was one of the essentials of living. A Merry Canada it must have been!

CHURCH MUSIC—A CONTRAST OF ATTITUDES: The only powerful opposition towards "ungodly" songs and dancing came from certain religious denominations, especially fundamentalist sects such as the Quakers and Methodists. These put popular music on a par with drinking, cursing and card-playing. The fiddle was condemned outright as a sinful instrument because it was the frequent associate of dance music. Only psalms, hymns (such as those of Isaac Watts and the Wesley brothers), and religious folk songs were recognized as legitimate music by these sects. This attitude was common in the early Protestant settlements in Canada and the United States and continued through the nineteenth century, when the use of instruments in church or the proposed purchase of an organ was often bitterly opposed by the older members of the congregation. In a Baptist church in Saint John, N.B., the deacons

[18]M'Gregor, British America, II, 451.

objected to what they called dance music in the church, but at long last the pastor was prevailed upon to let the choir sing a "copper tune" during the collection. At St. Andrew's Presbyterian Kirk in the same city, no organ was permitted until 1867, and then only a weak-sounding instrument was tolerated. Voluntaries and solo sing ing were also restricted.[19] The epitome of this attitude is the comment of a Presbyterian minister from Nova Scotia when he was told that the gallery in the Temple at Sharon, Ontario, was employed for no other purpose than as a place to hold a monthly musical concert: "*Vanity* is inscribed on human affairs and here truly is an exemplification of human extravagance and folly not often to be surpassed."[20]

It is hardly surprising that music in early Protestant congregations remained in a state of "rustic simplicity," as a Toronto writer reminiscing in 1878 termed it. The accompaniment to psalm and hymn singing, when it was available at all, was often provided by instruments other than the organ. In St. Mather's (or St. Matthew's) Church in eighteenth-century Halifax, a bass fiddle led the singing of the Presbyterians and Congregationalists.

One must be careful to point out that this puritan—not indeed Puritan—attitude which stands in such marked contrast to that of the missionaries of New France was limited to a few sects only. The very opposition testifies to the widespread popular indulgence in worldly song and dance. As a matter of fact the churches themselves made a large contribution to music by forming choirs and sponsoring oratorio performances and even concerts of both sacred and secular music. Organs can be found very early in the history of many Anglican and Roman Catholic Cathedrals. Quebec's Holy Trinity Cathedral (Anglican) had an organ about a decade after its consecration in 1804 and Toronto's St. James Cathedral (also Anglican), opened in 1807, had an organ in 1834 or before. In Saint John, N.B., a prosperous merchant contributed £ 200 towards an organ for Trinity (Anglican) Church, imported from London in 1802. Another London-built instrument was installed in the Quebec Basilica at the beginning of the nineteenth century. This centre of Roman Catholic worship had been left without an organ

19J. Russell Harper of Ottawa in "Spring Tide" (manuscript).
20Wm. Fraser, Diary, 1834–5, entry of March 24, 1835, in *Transactions of the London and Middlesex Historical Society*, XIV (1930), 121. See also p. 73 of this book.

in the bombardments of 1759. Many of the clergy were fond of music, and a few were accomplished musicians. At least one priest, the Abbé Charles Ecuyer (1758-1820) even engaged in composition. He wrote a Sanctus for three voices, a Magnificat, psalms, motets and vespers, all for the Yamachiche parish church, to which Ecuyer was appointed in 1802 and where he formed a fine choir.[21]

A good example of both positive and negative attitudes towards music is provided by St. Paul's (Anglican) Church of Halifax, which was opened for service in 1750, the year after the city was founded. It is the oldest non-Roman Catholic church building on the Canadian mainland and its choir has had a continuous history since the 1760's. In 1762 the Legislature of Nova Scotia joined in a subscription for an organ. Tradition has it that this organ, installed in 1765, was built in Spain for a South American convent and was brought to Halifax as a prize of war and purchased by the wardens of St. Paul's. Its sweet sound and beautiful mahogany case were long the pride of Haligonians. Earlier writers assumed that the Spanish organ was the second one used in St. Paul's and that it was used until the early nineteenth century. In a more recent history of the church[22] it is pointed out, however, that a new organ was purchased in 1784 for £ 86. 1 s. 7 d. In any case the richly ornamented Spanish organ-frame was used to house succeeding instruments.

The first organist was a Mr. Evans who apparently had installed the instrument himself. He left Canada in 1766 and was succeeded by several short-term organists. Among these was the young Irish officer Richard Bulkeley, provincial secretary since 1757 and aide-de-camp to Governor Edward Cornwallis, the founder of Halifax. Bulkeley was a man of wide culture and must have wielded considerable influence in musical circles, for Archdeacon Armitage praised him as "the father of music in English-speaking Canada."[28]

Bulkeley was in turn succeeded in 1768 by Mr. Viere Warner, who received a salary of £ 50 and held the position for at least three years. Warner must have been an accomplished musician,

[21]N. Caron, *Histoire de la paroisse d'Yamachiche.* (Trois Rivières, 1892), pp. 65-6.
[22]R. V. Harris, *The Church of St. Paul in Halifax, Nova Scotia, 1749-1949* (Toronto, 1949), p. 37.
[28]Ven. Archdeacon Armitage, "Music in By-gone Days," *Acadian Recorder*, Jan. 16, 1913, p. 7.

because it was during his term of office that an oratorio was performed at St. Paul's (see p. 56) and because he was heavily censured by the church authorities for his elaborate performance. This document, which is reminiscent of similar censure directed against Johann Sebastian Bach, deserves to be quoted in full. Let a historian of St. Paul's Church introduce it:

It may be that the organist and his choir indulged their taste for artistic music too freely on the state occasion just referred to [church attendance by His Majesty's Council, clergy, and House of Assembly in June 1770], and that those in authority could no longer stand the assumed power of the organist and his assistants.[24]

The resolution reads as follows:

At Vestry held at Halifax the 24th of July 1770.

Voted, that whereas, the Anthems Sung by the Clerk and others in the Gallery, during Divine Service have not Answered the intention of raising the Devotion of the Congregation to the Honour and Glory of (God) in as much as the Major part of the Congregation do not understand either the Words or the Musick & cannot join therein,

Therefore, for the future the clerk have express Orders, not to Sing any such Anthems, or leave his usual Seat without directions & leave first Obtained from the Reverend Mr. Breynton.

Voted, That whereas: also the Organist discovers a light mind in the Several tunes he plays, called Voluntaries, to the great Offence of the Congregation, and tending to disturb, rather than promote true Devotion.

Therefore he be directed for the Future, to make a choice of such Tunes as are Solemn, & Fitting Divine Worship, in such his Voluntaries, and that he also for the future be directed to play the Psalm Tunes in a plain Familiar Manner without unnecessary Graces.———

Voted, That a copy of the foregoing Votes be sent by the Clerk of the Vestry, to the Clerk & Organist.

A true Copy

Edwd. Godfrey Clerk to the Vestry

PUBLICATIONS OF RELIGIOUS MUSIC:

The turn of the century marked one of the most important "firsts" in all Canadian music, the publication of printed music. Le Graduel

[24]G. W. Hill, "History of St. Paul's Church, Halifax, Nova Scotia," in Report and Collections of the Nova Scotia Historical Society, I, (1879), 35–38.

romain, Le *Processional romain,* and Le *Vespéral romain* appeared in 1800, 1801 and 1802 respectively, printed in Quebec by John Neilson and destined for the use of the Roman Catholic diocese of Quebec. These publications were planned in 1797, when Neilson, a printer, journalist and politician, announced in the Quebec *Gazette* that he was willing to satisfy widespread demand for portable editions of the *Graduel* and *Vespéral,* provided 400 copies would be subscribed for. He proposed to base his edition on that published at Vannes in France, with addition of certain chants used in Quebec.[25]

The preface to the first volume deplores the lack of music books in the parish and emphasizes that it is the first Canadian book of its kind: "C'est le premier essai de ce genre qui ait été fait en Canada et l'on éspère qu'il ne sera pas sans mérite."

The books are small but bulky—the *Vespéral* alone numbering over six hundred pages—and music is printed on almost every page. The notation is in square notes on a four-line staff. The text is Latin. Often additional verses are printed below the music. A short method of plain-chant is appended to the *Processional,* dealing with the elements of notation and intonation and giving examples of the eight tones of the church modes.

A significant publication of a later date was the *Nouveau Recueil de cantiques à l'usage du diocèse de Québec,* published anonymously in 1819.[26] Today we know that its author was Father Jean-Denis Daulé (1765-1852), who had come to Quebec in 1794 as a refugee from the French Revolution. From 1806 to 1832 he was chaplain in the Ursuline convent. He was also an amateur violinist. Following the practice of the time, Daulé's hymn book contained the words only and a separate book included almost two hundred melodies. Some of the melodies have no accompaniment, whereas others sound like keyboard arrangements or duets for wind instruments. The tunes were partly traditional, partly new. What is significant about this collection is its attitude towards secular song,

[25]M. Tremaine, *A Bibliography of Canadian Imprints, 1751-1800* (Toronto, 1952). It is a curious oddity that, were all Canadian music publications sorted out according to number of pages, these earliest publications would stand at the very front.

[26]"Nouveau" appears to distinguish this work from the *Recueil de cantiques des missions, des retraites et des catechismes,* by Jean-Baptiste Boucher-Belleville, a collection of devotional songs without printed music which first appeared in Quebec in 1795 and went through many editions.

so completely different from that of the Protestant sects. Far from condemning secular songs—some of the melodies in the *Nouveau Recueil* are actually drinking songs—the Roman Catholic Church made these tunes serve its own purpose by fitting new words to them. LeVasseur thought that the new words added a graceful naïveté to the tunes and upheld the practice: "Les paroles lui servirent de passe-port dans le temple."

The first music book with English text was the work of Stephen Humbert (1767–1849), a New Jersey Loyalist who settled in Saint John, N.B., in 1783. Versatile as only a pioneer could be, Humbert was at various times a baker, a bookseller, a captain in the militia, a singing teacher, and a politician who would engage in heated discussion with the City Council over the weight of loaves of bread and the allocation of fishing rights.[27] He was an ardent champion of Wesleyan Methodism at a time when the Church of England was the only officially recognized church. In this religious pioneer work, his musical talent stood Humbert in good stead. Thus in October 1796 he opened a Sacred Vocal Music School in "Mr. Harper's large and commodious Upper Room in King Street."[28] Always enterprising, Humbert did not let the lack of suitable choral music worry him for long. He published his own collection of sacred music, which he called *Union Harmony, or British America's Sacred Vocal Musick*. No copy of the first edition, published in Saint John but printed in New England, is known to have survived, but it is known that its price was $1 per copy. It appeared in October 1801, only one year after *Le Graduel romain*, the first Canadian book of music. Humbert's collection enjoyed wide popularity, going through three more editions (1816, 1831, 1840). The second edition, "much improved and enlarged," contains over three hundred pages of music from the "most approved English and American Composers, with some original Musick on special occasions." In the introductory Advertisement the author defends the practice, very popular in North America, of "Fugueing Tunes,"

[27]Letter written to the author by J. Russell Harper, then librarian-archivist at the New Brunswick Museum, Saint John, now Curator of Canadian Art at the National Gallery, Ottawa. Mr. Harper's manuscript "Spring Tide," an inquiry into the lives, labours, loves and manners of early New Brunswickers, is an excellent source of information about music in Saint John. Through Mr. Harper's kindness, I was able to make copious notes from "Spring Tide," to which frequent references will be made.

[28]Harper, "Spring Tide," p. 168.

namely, letting one or two of the voices in a hymn drop out momentarily and then enter in a sort of contrapuntal imitation:

. . . fugueing musick, when judiciously performed, will produce the most happy effect, without the least disorder of jargon, especially when it is considered we do not sing to please men, but the Lord. If those who are hearers, while others are performing that part of divine worship, were as assiduous to learn Sacred Musick, as they too generally are the giddy amusements of the day, we should have less hearers and more performers of this animating part of divine worship.

Most pieces in the *Union Harmony* are set in four parts, some in three. The fourth edition, further enlarged, contains many new hymns of Humbert's own composition, some named after New Brunswick localities. At the time he published the fourth edition, Humbert also founded a Sacred Music Society, which made its first public appearance at the Baptist Church in November 1840.

4 / The Appearance of Secular Art Music

THE BACKBONE: BANDS AND THEIR VARIED FUNC-
TIONS: People in the garrison towns enjoyed a great advantage
over the country dwellers in being able to listen to the bands
stationed with the British regiments. Canada had no regular army
of her own before Confederation but was manned by British regiments who took turns in Canadian service. Thus there was a great
variety of British regimental bands, including some of great fame,
which could be heard in such cities as Halifax, Quebec, Montreal,
and Toronto over a period of about one hundred years. Many of
the bandmasters and players were of non-British origin, coming
very often from Germany, which then stood in the front rank as an
exporter of musicians. Upon retiring from service some of these
men settled permanently in Canada, where they wielded wide
influence as music teachers and performers. Unfortunately little
information is available about the size and instrumentation of the
bands.

The bands achieved great popularity because of their many
activities apart from military functions proper. They might assist at
theatrical performances or provide the nucleus of an orchestra—
augmented by civilian amateurs—in the rare event of a concert.
They would be called upon to entertain officers and their guests at
social affairs, or to play during church service. Their participation
in religious and national festivals, such as the St. Jean-Baptiste
celebrations in French Canada, and their concerts on public squares
gained the bands an even wider, and warmly appreciative,

audience.[1] They also provided the occasion for the writing of the earliest Canadian marches. Without doubt the regimental band was the first great musical contribution of Britain to Canada. If it had not been for the bands, the formation of orchestral societies in nineteenth-century Canada would have been delayed by decades or, in many towns, altogether.

The variety of the bands' functions is illustrated by one of the earliest and most notable ones, that of the Royal Fusiliers or 7th Regiment, which came to Quebec in August 1791 under Prince Edward Augustus (later Duke of Kent, father of Queen Victoria). The regiment was greeted by a march specially written in honour of its arrival by Charles Voyer de Poligny D'Argenson, a notary of Quebec, and named *Royal Fusiliers Arrival at Quebec, 1791.* Before speaking about the band itself, it is worth relating the story of this march and a sister composition, the *March de Normandie,* written by the same composer about the same time. After being neglected for more than a century and a quarter, this music received a new lease on life in 1928. On Dominion Day of that year a memorial tablet commemorating the service of the Fusiliers in Canada was unveiled in Quebec. On this occasion the Royal Fusiliers were presented with the original manuscript of the two marches, which was then framed and hung in the officers' mess of one of the battalions. In 1930 the Fusiliers provided a historical display at the Royal Tournament. Ever since, the *March de Normandie* has been regarded as the slow march of the regiment and is still played regularly. After the revival, a trio was added which does not blend well with the march itself. The march is the oldest secular Canadian composition still performed.[2]

Mrs. Simcoe, wife of the first Lieutenant-Governor of Upper Canada has left some interesting notes about the Royal Fusiliers and other bands in her famous diary. Within two weeks after her landing in Quebec, on Monday, November 21, 1791, she "went to a subscription concert. Prince Edward's band of the 7th Fusiliers

[1]See H. J. J. B. Chouinard, *Annales de la Société St. Jean-Baptiste de Québec,* IV (Québec, 1903), 504–27.

[2]J. M. Gibbon, in *Canadian Mosaic* (1938), p. 167, made the very plausible statement that Frederic Henri Glackemeyer composed the *March de Normandie.* The original manuscript (now at the Depot of the Royal Fusiliers in the Tower of London) bears the inscription "Copied by Jouve, bandmaster to the Duke of Kent." However, at the bottom of the frame in which the manuscripts are placed is printed under each of the two marches: "Composed by Charles Voyer de Poligny D'Argenson, Notary of Quebec, who died there 1820."

played, and some of the officers of the Fusiliers. The music was thought excellent. The band costs the Prince eight hundred [pounds] a year."[3] The band also played in church service, which the Prince always attended.

The musical inclination of the regiment was also apparent on less formal occasions. On Friday, March 2, 1792, Mrs. Simcoe reported:

I gave a dance to forty people. The Prince was present. . . The Fusiliers are the best dancers, well dressed, and the best-looking dancers that I ever saw. They are all musical and like dancing, and bestow as much money, as other regiments usually spend in wine, in giving balls and concerts, which makes them very popular in this place where dancing is so favourite an amusement. . . .[4]

In 1794 the regiment moved to Halifax. It is reported that when Prince Edward laid the cornerstone of Masonic Hall on June 5, 1800, "the band of the Prince's own regiment, the 7th Fusiliers, performed under the direction of Mr. Selby, organist of St. Paul's, one of the craft."[5] A bandstand is still preserved in Halifax which the prince had built to serenade a lady friend living in a nearby lodge. The band also gave promenade concerts on Saturday mornings.

A few examples may serve to illustrate band music in other towns. In Montreal about 1792, the band of the first battalion of the 60th, or Royal American, Regiment played, "generally . . . for a couple of hours," on summer evenings on the Parade, the great public promenade.[6]

In Niagara (now Niagara-on-the-Lake) the officers held balls once a fortnight during the winter season. From nearby Queenstown (now Queenston), Mrs. Simcoe wrote in April 1793: ". . . the band plays on parade before the house until six o'clock. The music adds cheerfulness to this retired spot, and we feel much indebted to the Marquis of Buckingham for the number of instruments he presented to the regiment. The bugles sound at five every morning."[7]

Fourteen years later, a ball was given at Niagara by Lieutenant-

[3]*The Diary of Mrs. John Graves Simcoe, 1791–1796*, ed. J. Ross Robertson (Toronto, 1911), p. 55.

[4]*Ibid.*, p. 79.

[5]T. B. Akins, "History of Halifax City," in *Collections of the Nova Scotia Historical Society*, VIII (1895), 129.

[6]"Canadian Letters . . . 1792 and '93," *Canadian Antiquarian and Numismatic Journal*, ser. 3, IX (1912), 106.

[7]*Diary of Mrs. Simcoe*, p. 158.

Governor Gore to celebrate the King's birthday, June 4. The evening before, "the ball commenced at 8 o'clock in the Council House, which was fitted up and lighted in an elegant manner, with an orchestra of the charming band of the 41st Regiment."[8] There were about fifty couples dancing and the festivities lasted until one o'clock in the morning.

THE MUSIC-LOVERS: PATRONS, AMATEURS AND MUSICIANS: The officers' patronage of the bands is the closest parallel to be found in Canada to the aristocratic sponsorship of music in European countries. This patronage was enhanced by the abundance of leisure time available to the officers. Except during the few short periods of war, military duties were not arduous. Music, like reading, hunting, dancing or drinking, was a pleasant antidote to the loneliness of the country and helped monotonous days pass more quickly.

The British officers and their regimental bands provided one important factor for the encouragement of secular art music; the wave of immigrants which caused the population figure of Canada to soar from 70,000 in 1760 to 400,000 in 1814 provided another. The new arrivals, whether from the British Isles, the United States or Germany, included many who possessed musical training. Although music may have been cultivated in the homes of individual *seigneurs* of New France, the impression is that secular art music developed faster in a few decades after the British conquest than it had in a century before. Even in Quebec and Montreal the names of musicians and amateurs are often English and German and the documents relating to concert performances are usually written in English. There also arose two important English-speaking cities: Halifax which enjoyed the advantage of being the port most easily accessible from Europe and Saint John, N.B., which dates back to 1631 as a settlement. Its development as a city dates from 1783 when some 10,000 United Empire Loyalists landed in its harbour. It must be borne in mind that the United States had far surpassed Canada in population and cultural development by this time. There were musical societies and concert halls; hymn collections and sheet music were published; and a few composers, such as Francis Hop-

[8]York *Gazette*, June 13, 1807, quoted in Edwin C. Guillet, *Early Life in Upper Canada* (Toronto, 1933), p. 325.

kinson, arose to earn wide acclaim. Thus many of the Loyalist immigrants to Canada were men of good education and refined tastes. In Saint John, for example, music was first cultivated by a select group of upper-class Tories such as Ward Chipman, Sr., Solicitor-General of New Brunswick in whose house elegant musical evenings were held. The host, who had a fine deep voice, performed the latest songs, which he brought back from London "for the express pleasure of the ladies."[9]

The meeting of a British prince, a Loyalist lawyer, and a German bandmaster in the French city of Quebec and the benefit to music resulting from it provides a striking example for the blending of the factors just discussed. Musical life in Quebec was closely interwoven in this period with the personalities of Prince Edward Augustus, a patron with the means, Jonathan Sewell, an educated amateur with the taste, and Frederic Henri Glackemeyer, a professional musician with the skill, to promote music-making. These men not only represent different social roles in musical life, but also symbolize the variety of national influences on which the musical growth in Canada has always depended. We have already had testimony to Prince Edward's love of music from contemporaries who heard the band which he maintained in Quebec and, later, in Halifax when he was commander of the 7th Fusilier Regiment. "He delighted in musical reunions, and organized a society of amateurs of which the late Chief Justice Sewell, an accomplished violinist, was leader."[10]

Jonathan Sewell (1766–1839), a New Englander by birth, was educated in England and New Brunswick and called to the bar of Lower Canada in 1789. At the time when Jonathan left school, his proud father wrote to a friend: "You seem pleased with Jonathan's drawings, but if you are fond of music, his astonishing proficiency on the violin, the best instrument in my opinion, would raise your admiration greatly. He now plays the overtures of the first masters with great correctness."[11] There is not much exaggeration in these words, for it is a sign of young Sewell's skill and enlightened taste that he took an interest in the most recent quartets and quintets of Haydn and Mozart. Some of this music, which he acquired and

[9]J. Russell Harper, "Spring Tide," p. 166.
[10]W. J. Anderson, *The Life of H. R. H. Edward Duke of Kent* (Toronto, 1870), p. 8.
[11]Quoted in Harper, "Spring Tide," p. 167.

performed as early as 1791 and 1793, is still preserved in Quebec. A biographer has summed up Sewell's talents as follows:

Not only was Mr. Sewell a profound lawyer, but he was a good dramatist, a fair musician, a critical student of poetry, and a very facile writer of verse. Having attained much efficiency as a violinist, he was chosen as the leader of the amateur band of the late Duke of Kent, when His Royal Highness, as commander of the forces in Canada, resided at Quebec.[12]

Sewell maintained his interest in chamber music throughout his life. In the second or third decade of the nineteenth century we find him, now Chief Justice of Lower Canada, as leader of a string quartet. It is curious that the enthusiasts of chamber music were not professional musicians but musical amateurs in legal circles: the notaries Archibald Campbell and Edouard Glackemeyer (son of the musician) took the second violin and flute parts respectively, and J. Harvicker played the cello. One may speculate that the second violinist took the viola part and the flautist one of the violin parts.

The story must now be told of a man whose career was interwoven with all the musical activities of his time. Friedrich Heinrich Glackemeyer (he later changed his given names to Frederic Henri) was, to our knowledge, the first professional musician of excellence in Canada, and one whose pioneer work has had a lasting influence. He was born in the German city of Hanover in 1751 and died in Quebec in 1836. The span of his life embraced those of both Mozart and Beethoven. From his earliest youth he showed a remarkable gift for music. When Glackemeyer was five, his father, a flautist, put a violin in his hand, and a few years later the gifted child had become the darling of aristocratic circles, where he was invited to perform.

When and why Glackemeyer came to Canada is not quite clear. To be sure, we have a very detailed report about him by LeVasseur, who knew one of his sons, but in LeVasseur's writing it is sometimes hard to distinguish anecdote from fact.[13] According to this story, the boy heard about Canada one day and took a fancy to visit the country himself. Warned about the wildness of life there, he retorted that if life was rugged, his violin would soften it! Nothing

12W. Notman, *Portraits of British Americans,* II (Montreal, 1867), 250.
13N. LeVasseur, "Musique et musiciens à Québec," in *La Musique* (1919-22).

could hold him back, and at the age of 15 or 16 he landed in Trois Rivières with a bagful of instruments under his arm. Sieur de Tonnancour gave him a hearty welcome and treated him as a guest. Soon afterward Glackemeyer moved to Quebec where his reputation had already preceded him. In a short time he attained eminence as a musician in the city where he was to reside the rest of his life.

Had not LeVasseur endowed his story with such a wealth of detail, we would be tempted to dismiss it as fiction. However, we do know for sure that Glackemeyer was bandmaster in one of the Brunswick mercenary regiments under Baron von Riedesel, which arrived in 1776 to help the British suppress the American Revolution. We should not altogether discard the possibility that he came to Canada with the regiment. At the end of the war, the bandmaster declined a position as organist in Riedesel's home village. He preferred to stay in Canada, as did some two and a half thousand German soldiers who settled as craftsmen or farmers.

For a time, Glackemeyer taught music to von Riedesel's children, as we know from a note written in English and signed by Glackemeyer:

I was teacher of music to the family Riedesel, in the winter 1783; was lodged and treated with the greatest politeness and civility. My two pupils were misses Augusta and Fredericka,[14] who would have made great progress, had they had a better instrument [than] a miserable old spinet, which they had bought of the Revd. Mons. Noiseux, curé at Beloeil, at present Grand-Vicar at Three-Rivers; there being only one piano in Quebec.[15]

Prince Edward Augustus knew and appreciated Glackemeyer, for he appointed him music master of a regimental band which gave open-air concerts twice a week on the Esplanade.

We know of only one composition by Glackemeyer, a march. It is a musical reminder of the war of 1812–13 when the Americans invaded Canada but were ultimately turned back at the battle of Chateauguay in 1813. This march is dedicated to the hero of the battle, Colonel Charles de Salaberry.

[14]Aged about 12 and 10 years. There is no reference to Glackemeyer in the writings of Baron and Baroness Riedesel.
[15]Quoted by P.-G. Roy, "La Famille Glackemeyer," *Le Bulletin des recherches historiques*, XXII (July 1916), 195.

Glackemeyer remained an important musical figure in Quebec for the remainder of his long life. He taught music and imported printed music and instruments. For a few years during his sixties he was organist at the Basilica. The culminating point of his career was his appointment as the first president and director of the Quebec Harmonic Society (1820).[16]

Two aspects of Glackemeyer's career have now to be discussed in the larger context of the period: music education and the import of instruments.

THE AUXILIARIES: EDUCATION AND TRADE: Patrons, connoisseurs and musicians alone cannot maintain concert life. Equally essential is a circle of intelligent listeners and amateur musicians. Music education has to step in here. The first people to teach music outside the Roman Catholic institutions were the singing masters who appeared in the late eighteenth century, often from New England, and who organized so-called singing schools (or classes, as they would be called today). They taught the rudiments of musical notation and singing, thus enabling their pupils to help with the musical part of church service. Some singing masters might also teach the violin, flute, and piano, instruments very popular at dances and parties.

One of the first singing masters to come to Canada was Amasa Braman, a native of Connecticut. After spending some time in Halifax he lived in Liverpool, N.S., for about 16 months from 1776 to 1778. There he opened a school, taught singing, and practised law. We read in Simeon Perkins' diary that the author spent the evening of Sunday, February 23, 1777, at "Mr. Joseph Tinkham's singing psalm tunes. I have for about six weeks attended all the evenings I could conveniently, on a school for that purpose, taught by Mr. Amasa Braman. . . ."[17] A few weeks later the singers gave a public performance. "In the afternoon, Mr. Braman, ye singing master, has a singing in the new Meeting House, and delivers an oration upon musick. A very genteel performance, and the singing was by good judges thought extraordinary for the time

16Students of United States musical history will note a certain parallel between the careers of Glackemeyer and of Gottlieb Graupner (1767–1836), a Hanoverian.
17The Diary of Simeon Perkins (Toronto, 1948), p. 141.

we have been learning."[18] Whether it was his law practice or his teaching activities which proved a financial failure, certain it is that, pressed by debts, Mr. Braman absconded one morning in a shallop, leaving as suddenly as he had appeared.

The singing schools appear to have flourished most strongly in the Maritimes. In Halifax, Reuben McFarlen offered to teach the rules of psalmody to young gentlemen and ladies in his singing school in 1788. I have already mentioned the Sacred Vocal Music School, which Stephen Humbert set up in Saint John, N.B., in 1796. These are only a few of the many instances of singing schools that can be found in newspaper advertisements of the day.[19]

European opinion as to the state of general education among Canadians, in particular among Canadian men, was however quite severe: "The Canadian women are better educated than the men, who take care of their horses and attend little to anything else. . . ."[20] Even among the ladies, potentialities were higher than accomplishments. In the view of John Lambert, who travelled through North America from 1806 until 1808:

Reading is not altogether so general an amusement as it is in England; and I believe that the Canadian ladies spend the greatest portion of their time in doing nothing, or at least in doing that which amounts to nothing. The polite accomplishments of drawing and music are almost strangers in Canada. I never heard of more than half a dozen who understood either, and they were but moderate proficients. But the Canadian ladies labour under the disadvantage of indifferent teachers, in almost every branch of polite education. . . . Many of them, however, have natural genius and abilities, that only require to be properly cultivated to render them in every respect equal to the European females.[21]

As for the lack of music teachers, Lambert found only two music masters in Quebec, and "one of them is a good violin performer; but for any other instrument, they are both very indifferent teach-

[18]Ibid., p. 146.

[19]"Singing schools" survived far into the nineteenth century, at least in small and pioneer communities. One such example is Professor R. B. George's "convention" held in Regina in 1888. Thirty persons enrolled and in five days learned to read and sing in chorus. At the end of this period the chorus gave a concert together with George's troupe. Then the professor and his troupe moved on to the next town. (Musical Journal, Toronto, 1888, issue of June 15).

[20]Diary of Mrs. Simcoe, p. 91.

[21]John Lambert, Travels through Canada and the United States of North America in the Years 1806, 1807, & 1808. (3rd ed.; London, 1816), I, 328.

ers."[22] Glackemeyer's first instrument was the violin, and he also played the cello, piano, and organ. Probably he was the one "good violin performer." He taught violin and piano to girls and ladies during the day, and violin and bass viol three nights a week to men. The initiating fee was a guinea and each subsequent lesson cost a shilling. The distinction between the sexes is significant. There was a strong prejudice against teaching music to men, so strong indeed that Glackemeyer, who made accomplished musicians out of his daughters, refused to teach music to his sons. One of these, Edouard, who took an irresistible liking to the flute, had to study it in secret for fear of his father. Paradoxically, it was not considered proper for a woman to appear in public concerts.

It is easy to see the tremendous difficulties connected with the teaching of music. Printed music was scarce and as a rule a pupil had to copy the music from her teacher's book. A few beautiful examples of such handwritten compilations of music can be seen at the museum in Jordan, Ontario.

Another severe handicap was the shortage of instruments. We have quoted Glackemeyer's remark that only one piano existed in Quebec in 1783. He himself did much to improve this situation. In an advertisement in the Quebec *Herald* of November 24, 1788 (Fig. 3), he offered for sale: "Two new excellent Piano Forte's, with a neat leather cover warranted to be of the best tone, and to stand tune a long time." In February 1789 "an elegant PIANO FORTE, made upon a new construction in the year 1787," was offered by a gentleman who had got it in payment of a debt. Apparently he was unable to sell it, for only four months later, Glackemeyer advertised "An Excellent Second Hand PIANO FORTE," for sale at ten pounds, or for hire. Three pianofortes were also advertised in June 1789 by another music dealer and teacher, Francis Vogeler. The arrival of five pianos within a year must have been a great impetus to music in Quebec, and it seems hard to believe a report that there were only three pianos in the city in 1812.

Guitars and violins were advertised by John Smith of Halifax as early as 1752. In 1770 a merchant imported from London to Halifax a number of German flutes, violins, and books of duets and Scotch tunes, as well as fiddle strings and ruled music paper. Glackemeyer and Vogeler also sold guitars, flutes, violins, and

[22]*Ibid.*, p. 302.

1-4   QUEBEC *Nov.* 24 1788.

FOR SALE,
By FR: GLACKEMEYER, *oppofite the*
HERALD PRINTING-OFFICE.

TWO new excellent Piano Forte's, with a neat leather cover warranted to be of the beft tone, and to ftand tune a long time, The following Harpficord Mufic, Niccolais Sonatas, Opers 3 and 7. Overture by Jomelly, do. to the Opera Rofina. A choice collection of Songs neatly bound, Operas, the Padlock, Poor Soldier, and Gretten Green. A Collection of Divine Mufic. Two Volumes of Military Mufic fit for bands, compleat by feveral Mafters. 3 Volume do. Flack's Divertimento's Compleat. Baffoon and Hautboy Reeds. Fiddle Pegs & Bridges, The Beft Harpficord, Piano Forte and Guitar ftrings. The beft Roman Fiddle ftrings. A Collection of Country Dances and Minuets for the years 1787 1788. with their proper figures. Tuneing hammers and Pitch Forks.

HARPSICORDS, PIANO FORTIES, GUITARS *repaired and tuned, on the fhorteft notice and moft reafonable terms.*

FIGURE 3. An advertisement in the
Quebec Herald and Universal Miscellany
of November 24, 1788.

accessories, such as reeds for oboes, clarinets and bassoons, harpsichord strings, and fiddle bridges. In December 1791 a fine single-manual harpsichord by Kirkman was auctioned at Quebec.

In Saint John, Colin Campbell advertised in 1801 the latest shipment of music from Edinburgh: violins, with or without cases, military and common fifes, and an Aeolian harp, as well as the most fashionable music from Scotland, Italy, and other countries.

THE RESULT: CONCERT PERFORMANCES: The various factors and circumstances which encouraged art music combined to produce lively, though irregular concert activities. Examples will be quoted here from Halifax and Quebec, where many concerts were held in coffee houses, taverns, churches or private parlours, concert halls being unknown.

It was in Halifax that the first Canadian newspaper, the Halifax *Gazette* (1752), and the oldest Canadian literary periodical, the *Nova Scotia Magazine* (1789), were published. Here too, a theatre was opened in 1789, fifteen years earlier than in Montreal. Another memorable date in Canadian history is the year 1769, when an oratorio was performed at St. Paul's Church. According to Archdeacon Armitage, this performance was given in April by the Philharmonic Society augmented by officers of the Army and Navy.[23] The society had the exclusive privilege of occupying the organ loft of the church. It is the first musical society reported to have existed in Canada. The church records preserved refer to the sale of tickets only; they mention the word oratorio, but not the title of the work performed.

In her research on musical life in Nova Scotia Miss Phyllis Blakeley of the Nova Scotia Public Archives[24] found the earliest reference to a concert of secular music in a letter from Edward Winslow, Sr., to Ward Chipman, Sr., dated September 26, 1783:[25]

. . . have been at two Balls and one concert, at the concert was exceedingly good musick vocal and instrumental there appeared to be nothing wanting to make it compleat but your voice to have been added to the same; altho' there was a Gent that sang extremely well, I can truly say I had much rather hear you than him, there is something so sprightly in your Singing that affords me more pleasure than almost any other person. There was present at the Concert, Gov'r Parr, Gov'r Wentworth and Gov'r Fanning, with a number of Brilliant Ladies & Gent'n of the Navy & Army, had you been there, how you would have danced.

On May 20, 1789, divine service was held at St. Paul's for the recovery of King George III from insanity. The musical portion of

[23]Ven. Archdeacon Armitage, "Music in By-gone Days," *Acadian Recorder*, Jan. 16, 1913, p. 7.

[24]Information about the musical history of Nova Scotia has been enriched vastly by Miss Blakeley's work. This kind of systematic investigation has been followed by provincial archivists in New Brunswick, Quebec and British Columbia, and it is to be hoped that it will inspire archivists and local historians in the other provinces as well. Throughout this book much of the information about Nova Scotia is based on Miss Blakeley's articles. See also the bibliography.

[25]*The Winslow Papers*, ed. W. O. Raymond (Saint John, N.B., 1901), p. 135.

the celebration included the final chorus from Handel's *The Messiah* as well as one of Handel's Coronation Anthems, performed by "several Gentlemen and the Musick Bands of the Regiments" with the support of the organ.

A concert given by Mrs. Mechtler on September 29, 1790, at Mrs. Sutherland's Coffee House was of a different kind. Mrs. Mechtler sang arias from "the much admired Opera of Rosina" and Dibdin's "Was I a Shepherd Maid to Keep." The bandmaster of the 20th Regiment played a concerto on the harpsichord and his band concluded with an overture—in modern terminology probably a symphony—by one of the Bachs. Among the many famous composers of the Bach family, the most popular at this time was Johann Christian, the "London" Bach.

In 1792 fortnightly concerts were planned at the British Tavern, to last two hours in the evening. At a concert given in December 1797 for the benefit of Mr. Scavoye, a symphony by Leopold Anton Kotzeluch and a concertante for violin, oboe, and cello by Ignaz Pleyel were performed. An ambitious programme, requiring skilled performers indeed! Here is evidence that symphonic music, even though possibly in mutilated form, was heard in Canada before the nineteenth century.

Musical performance took an astonishing upward stride during the 1790's, not only in Halifax but in Quebec, and achieved an intensity that unhappily was not maintained during the early decades of the nineteenth century. Prince Edward Augustus did much to encourage musical performance. He was not the first, however, to promote a musical organization. In November 1790, the English-language newspaper the Quebec *Herald and Universal Miscellany* carried a report of the first subscription concert of the season 1790–1, which took place on November 15:

On Monday evening the Winter Concert commenced, at Free-Masons-Hall, it is to continue ever [sic] Monday Evening for twenty four weeks. His Honor Major General Clarke, our Lieutenant Governor, added sanction to the Concert with his presence, and enlivened the female part of the auditory by his affability and attention.

The Concerts are supported by subscription: From the genteel manner in which the first was conducted, the convenience of the Hall, and musical abilities of the gentlemen institutors, we augur a few pleasing hours weekly to the Amateurs of Apollo.

That we have here a musical society in all but name, becomes obvious from the fact that the subscribers were requested to meet in order to elect a treasurer and a committee "agreeable to the Rules." Provided the series continued regularly, as planned, the twenty-fourth concert would have taken place on April 25, 1791. It appears likely that the plans were carried through, for two weeks later, on May 12, the newspaper published the following financial statement:

Herald Miscellany & Advertiser: Thursday May 12, 1791.
Subscription Concert.

Cash received from one hundred and four subscribers	£ 130	0	0
PAID AS FOLLOWS			
To Mr. Franks for his Rooms, for fire and candles	37	10	0
To seven hired Performers	49	0	0
To copying musick, ruled paper and to extra hired Performers	5	3	6
For delivering the Tickets and collecting the money	3	17	6
For the use of a Piano Forte	3	10	0
To Mr. McKutcheon for making an Orchestra, musick stands, sconces, and for putting up and taking down the Orchestra at different times	8	0	0
To Mr. Moore for printing tickets, rules and advertisements, &c.	3	9	0
To a servant for receiving the tickets at the door and attendance at supper	1	11	3
Balance paid by order of the managers to Mr. Taylor to be distributed to the poor	17	18	9
	130	0	0

John Rotton, Treasurer.

The most curious item in this balance sheet is the £ 8 spent for Mr. McKutcheon's services. "Putting up and taking down the Orchestra" obviously does not refer to a librarian's job but to the installation of a special podium. Mr. McKutcheon then was a carpenter, and that his pay was higher than that of the musicians can be explained only by the expenses he incurred for tools and materials. One other notable fact is the absence of a conductor in the list of expenses.

That the subscription concerts continued the following season is confirmed by a notice, in the Quebec *Gazette*, of the postponement of a Monday concert in February 1792, as well as by Mrs. Simcoe's mention of the subscription concert she attended on a Monday in November 1791. According to her account (see p. 46), the performers during the second season were "Prince Edward's band of the 7th Fusiliers . . . and some of the officers of the Fusiliers." Perhaps in the first season, too, there were more than "seven hired performers," for it is unlikely that the officers would have played for a fee, and thus they would not be listed on the balance sheet.

The use of musicians from the regimental bands for orchestral concerts became an established custom in following years. About 15 years later John Lambert stated:

The tedious evenings of the winter are sometimes relieved by a private concert. The performers are some gentlemen of Quebec, assisted by a part of the regimental bands in the garrison. But entertainments of this description very seldom take place, either from the expense which accrues to them, or the want of performers on particular instruments.[26]

Unfortunately the newspapers remain silent about the musical contents of the subscription concerts. However, at least one printed programme for a concert held outside the series has been preserved. This concert was given on Tuesday, February 21, 1792, for the benefit of Sieur Jouve, musician to His Royal Highness. Jouve had arrived in Quebec in 1791 with the Duke of Kent and set about to teach vocal music, harp, cello, and French guitar and to sell imported music. We reprint the entire program of his concert, tickets for which sold at 3s. and 1s. 6d.

CONCERT[27]

vocal et instrumental

Au Bénefice du Sieur JOUVE, Musicien de Son Altesse Royale,
Demain (Mardi 21 fevrier) dans la Nouvelle Salle des Spectacles

---

PREMIER ACTE

1. Ouverture d'Iphigenie, Musique de Gluck.
2. Second Quatuor, de Jouve.
3. Ariettes Boufonnes d'Opéras Comiques, avec accompagnement de Guitare Française.
4. Pièce d'Harmonie, pour Clarinet et Basson obligé.

[26]Lambert, *Travels through Canada*, I, 302.
[27]Quebec *Gazette*, February 23, 1792; separate sheet attached to the newspaper.

5. Duo de Blaise et Babet, par Glackmeyer et Jouve [by Dézède, 1783].
6. Carillon des Cloches de France, à grande orchestra, Musique de Jouve.

SECOND ACTE

1. Ouverture de Panurge, Musique de Grétry [1785].
2. Ariette du Soldat lassé des alarmes de la Guerre, qui a été redemandée, chantée par Madame Allen.
3. Ariette, de la Melouranie, avec tous les instrumens et le canon obligé, redemandée au concert, et chanté par Jouve.
4. Concerto de Cor de Chasse par Rhen.
5. Une Scène et Ariette d'Atis [Atys by Piccini, 1780?], avec accompagnement de Harpe.
6. Le Sommeil d'Atis avec Harpe, chanté par Messieurs Bentley, Glackmeyer et Jouve.
7. Le Concert sera terminé par la Grande Chacoune de Cephale et Procris, musique de Grétry [1775].

Le Concert commencera à sept heures. On trouvera des Billets à la porte; depuis Quatre Heures à trois Chelins les premiers et un chelin et demi les seconds.

: : : : : : : : : : :

Even though concert programmes are rare, there are, fortunately, several other types of sources which give information about the music performed in this period. Not only did a pupil often copy music by hand from his teacher's book but an amateur fiddler or flautist would compile his own anthology of dances, national songs, marches, and other popular pieces. Some of these "tune books" are still preserved in museums and archives.

A far more important source is the advertisements of imported music in newspapers. Glackemeyer and Francis Vogeler advertised the following (and many other) titles in Quebec newspapers between 1788 and 1790. These sample titles may indicate the variety of styles cultivated and the level of technical achievement.

Harpsichord sonatas by Niccolai, Bach, and Butler; six pieces by Haydn; vocal scores of the operas *Poor Soldier* and "*Grettna* [sic] *Green*"; Two Volumes of Military Music fit for bands, compleat by several Masters; a collection of country dances and menuets for the years 1787 and 1788; six overtures by Haydn and six symphonies in four parts by Stamitz; five symphonies by Pleyel for violin or flute, op. 12 and op. 14; a selection of Scottish songs, adapted for harpsichord and violin accompaniment, including some 80 songs, published by William Napier in London.

Even if only a small part of this music was sold and performed, musical activities must have been lively indeed.

The best evidence as to the music performed, however, can be gathered from a collection of music still preserved in Quebec. It is reasonable to assume that most of it was brought to Canada through Glackemeyer's efforts. LeVasseur states that Glackemeyer imported instruments and music not for commercial gain but solely for the cause of good music. From the earliest owners, who included Jonathan Sewell, Edouard Glackemeyer and the Quebec Harmonic Society, the music passed through the ownership of the Septuor Haydn, a chamber music ensemble, into the hands of Laval University. Together with other early nineteenth-century collections (notably that of Miss Desbarats), this oldest body of printed music in Canada was left in storage for many years. Through the efforts of an indefatigable music librarian, M. Lucien Brochu, it was finally catalogued and given an honoured place on the shelves of Laval University Library in 1958. Altogether there are about two hundred volumes. Some of these form sets of parts for chamber ensemble or small orchestra, each volume containing the parts for one instrument of compositions by several composers.

The earliest part of the collection dates from the time of the advertisements cited. A volume of Haydn quartets bears an ink note "Sewell, August 1791"; the last three Mozart quartets are inscribed "Sewell, 1793." Second-violin parts of Mozart's string quintets in C major and G minor are bound together with the quartets; on both quintets is the handwritten inscription "Quebec Subscription Concert 1793." Two of the most complex and majestic works by Mozart were played, in part or in their entirety, in Canada only six years after their composition! How this music must have astounded the audience by its difficulties and modernism!

The string quartets also include such well-known eighteenth-century composers as Abel, Gossec, Gyrowetz and Viotti. The symphonies (sometimes labelled overtures) include works by Abel, Johann Christian Bach, Gyrowetz, Pleyel, Andreas and Bernard Romberg, Karl Stamitz, Vanhal and Woelfl. Many of the editions bear a London imprint.

LeVasseur's claim that many of the works cannot be found anywhere else in the world must have been prompted by enthusiasm and ignorance of Eitner's *Quellen-Lexikon*. Nevertheless the collection is of great value as a library of eighteenth- and early nineteenth-century music in contemporary editions. By importing much of this music to Canada Glackemeyer has earned for himself a monument in the annals of Canadian music.

THE THEATRE AND JOSEPH QUESNEL: Theatrical perfomances were rare and of low artistic quality in eighteenth-century Canada. Theatre, like music, was encouraged by the officers of the British regiments and a select group of educated people. In French Canada clerical opposition stifled the development of drama for a long time. In consequence even Molière was introduced to Canada by the British, who organized stage performances in Halifax from about 1775 on. Whenever possible, music was added to the spectacle. Advertisements for English-language plays in Quebec newspapers *ca.* 1790 refer to hornpipes (dances) and singing between the acts of a play, or between the play and the farce following it. For a theatrical performance at the Coffee House in Saint John, N.B. in 1799 "several gentlemen gathered together to form a band of music." Light and comic songs were popular between the acts of plays.[28]

There was at least one performance of an opera in the Theatre Royal of Halifax. Grétry's *Richard Coeur de Lion* was performed on February 14, 1798, under the patronage of Prince Edward and Lieutenant-Governor Sir John Wentworth. In the fashion characteristic of the time the advertisement does not mention names of composer, conductor or singers, but it assures the public that the opera will be performed with "new dresses, scenery, decorations, &c." This opera, very famous in its day, had been introduced to the United States only the previous year. It may have been presented in Halifax by the same troupe that gave it in Boston and, later, in Philadelphia.

The first French-speaking promoter of theatre in Canada was not only a poet and playwright but also a talented musician and composer. Unlike Glackemeyer, Joseph Quesnel (1749-1809) came to Canada not by free choice but by sheer accident. Whereas

[28]Harper, "Spring Tide."

the German had enlisted on the British side against the American rebels, the Frenchman came to Canada as captain of a ship carrying munitions to the Americans. Quesnel was born in the seaport of St. Malo, the ancestral home of many French Canadians, but, unlike the bulk of French emigrants, he did not set foot in Canada until he had travelled around half the globe. Having finished school at the age of 19, Quesnel became a sailor. His first voyage lasted three years and led to Pondicherry, Madagascar, and the West African coast. Another journey took him to the Antilles and Brazil. In his thirtieth year Quesnel took command of a ship carrying munitions and supplies to the American revolutionaries. However, before the ship reached port, it was captured by an English frigate off the coast of Nova Scotia, and Quesnel was taken to Halifax. His enthusiasm for the cause he served was not deep enough to prevent him from deciding quickly to settle in Canada. Friends introduced him to General Haldimand, the governor of Quebec, and although technically an "enemy alien," Quesnel soon received his naturalization papers. The spirit of adventure led him to one more excursion, this time on land, during which he explored the Mississippi valley. The rest of his life was spent quietly in Montreal and nearby Boucherville, where he managed the village store. In Montreal, Quesnel helped to foster theatrical performances. It is said that he envisaged the foundation of a school of declamation and singing.

Quesnel had three faithful companions on all his travels: the writings of Molière and Boileau and a violin. Once settled in Canada, he had plenty of leisure to try his own hand at writing and composing. He "has been described as gentleman of cheerful temperament and nice tastes, who was happy in promoting the happiness of other people. He is still remembered as the author of some dramas and drawing-room operas, which at the time were very popular with the French Canadian population."[29] Quesnel wrote at least four plays and a number of epistles, epigrams, and other poems.[30] All the plays are said to have contained music, but there is no

[29]Notman, *Portraits*, III (Montreal, 1868), p. 43.

[30]Quesnel's dramas and other literary works have been discussed by several critics, including J. Huston in *Le Répertoire national* (Montreal, 1848), A. B. Routhier in his introduction to a new edition of this work, written in 1893, and J. Charbonneau in *Des Influences françaises au Canada*, II (Montreal, 1918), 167–71.

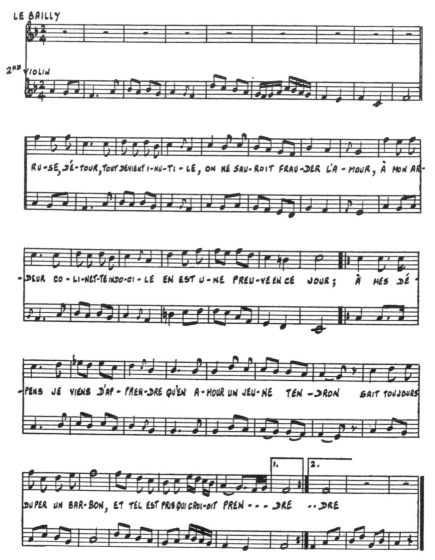

FIGURE 4. Vocal and second violin parts of the beginning of the Vaudeville-Finale of Quesnel's *Colas et Colinette*. Copied with permission of the Archives, Séminaire de Québec, Université Laval.

evidence of any overtures. *Lucas et Cécile* is called an opera. It contains 17 musical numbers of which the vocal parts, but not the accompaniments, are preserved in the Quebec Seminary. Five singers appear in twelve solo numbers, two duets (called "dialogue en chant"), two trios and a finale. The manuscript contains a number of corrections made at a later date. *L'Anglomanie*, subtitled *Le Dîner à l'anglaise*, is a one-act comedy which satirizes the aping of British manners among the upper ranks of French-Canadian society. We should not infer from this play, however, that the author's attitude was anti-British. True, he had come to this continent in the cause of republicanism, but he became an admirer of British monarchy and detested the "hideous anarchy" to which republican France had fallen victim. In the prose comedy *Les Républicains françaises* (or *La Soirée du cabaret*) he made fun of the new order. The only play still available in print is *Colas et Colinette* (or *Le Bailli dupé*), a prose comedy in three acts. This is a pleasant and expertly written piece in the manner of Molière and built around a stereotype plot. The characters are the stock figures of French, not Canadian, village society. The vocal parts and a second-violin part of this work have been preserved (Fig. 4). As in *Lucas et Cécile*, there are numerous arias and duets, and in the end everyone on stage joins in the vaudeville finale. Many of the melodies are pleasing. The second violin frequently underlines the vocal part in thirds or sixths. We may assume then that the first violin played in unison or octaves with singer. It would not be very difficult to restore the remaining instrumental parts so that the work could be revived. The music belongs to the style of "Comédie mêlée d'ariettes" cultivated by Grétry, Philidor, and Monsigny.

A contemporary of Mozart's last operas, *Colas et Colinette* was written in 1788 and first performed in Montreal in 1790. It was revived in Quebec in 1805.

Literary critics have labelled Quesnel's writing "classicism in decline" and have described his style as elegant, ironic, and graceful. Quesnel was entirely a product of French education; Canada had little if any influence on his art. None of his plays, except *L'Anglomanie*, have any connection with Canadian life. Perhaps the absence of Canadian inspiration and the resulting lack of vital interest to his audience more than any inherent weaknesses caused the eclipse of Quesnel's muse.

In an autobiographical poem, *Epitre à M. Généreux Labadie* (1804) the artist admits how little appreciated his works are in Canada. His reaction is one of bitterness against the Canadians, mingled with a good-humoured acceptance of his fate.

> Parcours tout l'univers, de l'Inde en Laponie,
> Tu verras que partout on fête le génie,
> Hormis en ce pays; car l'ingrat Canadien
> Aux talents de l'esprit n'accorde jamais rien.

When the poet arrived in Canada, he was treated with great hospitality. But alas! there was no good music!

> A table, ils vous chantaient vieille chanson bachique;
> A l'église c'étaient deux ou trois vieux motets
> D'orgues accompagnés qui manquaient de soufflets.

To terminate this state of affairs Quesnel wrote a piece of music which was performed at Christmas. A colourful piece it must have been, for it contained music "fast and slow, gay and sweet and mournful, flats, naturals and sharps." Unfortunately the audience had no appreciation for this masterpiece. They thought the music fit for the stage and for dancing rather than the church and thrust insult upon the unsuspecting composer.

> Pour l'oreille, il est vrai, tant soit peu délicate,
> Ma musique, entre nous, était bien un peu plate;
> Mais leur faillait-il donc des Handels, des Grétrys?
> Ma foi! qu'on aille à Londres ou qu'on aille à Paris.

Recognized by only a few faithful friends, he abondoned the sterile field of music and sought his luck in drama.[31] Near the end of the poem we find these lines:

> Pour nous, cher Labadie, dans ce pays ingrat,
> Où l'esprit est plus froid encore que le climat,
> Nos talents sont perdus pour le siècle où nous sommes;
> Mais la postérité fournira d'autres hommes,
> Qui goûtant les beautés de nos écrits divers,
> Célébront ma prose aussi bien que tes vers.

It is regrettable that the *Epistle* does not confirm Huston's assertion that Quesnel also wrote symphonies for grand orchestra, quartets, duets, and sacred music for the Montreal Parish Church.

[31]Poetic Licence! Of course Quesnel went on writing music.

TWO TYPES OF CANADIAN MUSICIANS: A brief comparison between Quesnel and Glackemeyer indicates two characteristic types among Canadian musicians of later times. Quesnel, the cultured amateur, was a more outstanding individual. He was doomed to disappointment and obscurity because his activities were on too high a plane to be appreciated by his contemporaries. While his literary influence was considerable, as a creative musician he was isolated from his environment and had no successor for several decades. Glackemeyer, on the other hand, aimed less high, but, precisely because his versatility on various instruments and his spadework as a teacher and importer of instruments and printed music supplied the needs of the time, his contribution was both immediate and lasting. Both men deserve to be remembered not for their creative achievements, but for their artistic courage and their pioneer spirit.[32]

[32]Both had distinguished sons. Frédéric Auguste Quesnel, Q.C., was a lawyer and deputy for two counties. A town in British Columbia is named after another son, Jules Maurice Quesnel, who was a fur trader and a companion of Fraser on his famous journey. Louis-Edouard Glackemeyer, the flautist, was several times president of the Quebec Notary Chamber as well as city councillor.

5 / The Dawn of Urban Musical Life

A PREVIEW OF THE NINETEENTH CENTURY: The pioneer settlers of a new country must direct all their energies to the struggle for elementary physical comfort and security. Exploring new territory, clearing the bush, searching for mineral wealth and supplies of raw materials, building roads and railways, and establishing democratic self-government: these were foremost problems in nineteenth-century Canada. Under such conditions there was little time for contemplation and artistic pursuits; cultural refinement was a secondary concern.

Nevertheless this century of national formation and consolidation, of social and industrial change, could not but upset the old cultural pattern and create new musical needs. The growth of the towns and the emergence of a strong middle class are reflected in the appearance of a characteristically urban type of musical life. In earlier days a person who wanted to hear music went to church, watched the marching soldiers, joined the dancers, sang, or played an instrument in the circle of his friends or family. "Learned" music, as we have seen, was the property of very few people. But as the population grew in the towns, enough people became interested in music to organize a choir or an instrumental group or to fill a concert hall. As in the field of fine arts and literature, societies were formed to practise and propagate music. Halifax was the first town from which a musical society has been reported (1769); the Quebec subscription series of the 1790's had much the character of a musical society. Then followed Saint John, N.B. (1824), Mon-

treal (1837?, 1848), and Toronto (1845), and even Victoria in
the far west had a Philharmonic Society by 1859. Now there were
opportunities to listen to music made simply for contemplation, as
an end in itself, not as an adjunct to other activities. Instead of
being chiefly a spontaneous amateur activity, music moved into
the hands of professionals, people who made music in order to
earn a living. Music became a business.

The first half of the nineteenth century was a period of transition
between these two patterns of musical life. Only in the fifties and
sixties did musical societies and concerts become a regular institution (rather than occasional extensions of regimental bands and
churches) in all cities. The societies took the lead in musical
colonization, but spice was added by the guest recitals of world-
famous artists or ensembles who set a standard of performance
which local musicians strove to emulate.

As the need for skilled musicians increased, many immigrants
were drawn to Canada. The number of native musicians was
small, but after the middle of the century, a number of excellent
French-Canadian musicians achieved distinction not only at home
but also abroad.

Secondary features of urban musical life appeared as the century
went on. Music found its way into schools and higher educational
institutions; conservatories were opened. Periodicals were published,
although few could be sustained for any length of time. The music
trade at first depended largely on import, as it still does with regard
to printed music. On the other hand, instrument-building rapidly
developed into a lively industry.

There arose a modest demand for Canadian compositions.
Patriotic and national songs seem to be historically a product of
middle-class society; by the middle of the century French Canada
had produced a number of them, and after Confederation they
were written in all parts of the country. Composition also encompassed church, band, and dance music, but there was little
stimulus for the creation of large-scale works.

Such, in brief, was the path of music in a century which saw
Canada's rise from a backward colony to a rich and powerful
nation. The present chapter examines in detail the period of transition which resulted in the establishment of a distinctly urban
pattern of musical customs and institutions. In the early nineteenth

century conditions differed from those sketched in the previous chapter in degree rather than character: continuing on the foundations of secular music-making laid previously, musical societies and concerts increased in number. Musical organizations were still rare and irregular, but showed signs of emancipation from the regimental band and the church, on which they largely depended.

It would be a mistake to conclude that the change from the spontaneous and untutored music-making of rural and small-town communities to the sophistication of concert halls and conservatories was one of gradual merging. The farmers, fishermen and *voyageurs* did not begin to cultivate art music. Their music continued to flourish as folk song and folk dance transmitted orally from one generation to another, remaining alive with especial freshness and vigour in French Canada and the Atlantic provinces. However, folk music found no shelter in the cities with their predominantly middle-class population, and it grew only shallow roots in many of the newly settled regions of Upper Canada and the West, largely because of geographical and social conditions in these regions: the isolation of farms from one another and the different national origins of new neighbours.

In the cities musical taste became distinct from that prevailing in the countryside. Oral tradition faded and taste was determined by sheet music imported from abroad. Music teachers, far from fostering folk traditions, were often ignorant of them. What one writer remarked a century later was true in the early 1800's: "The vocal and instrumental teaching is said to be driving out the old custom of united family singing of the old folk songs."[1]

There was only one force which may be said to have "grown" from simple rustic to complex urban conditions: church music. When an organist assembled one or two dozen people to rehearse for a Christmas or Easter service, the resulting performance was considered quite a rare musical treat. If the leader was capable, the singers might volunteer to spend some time each week trying out new music, sacred or even secular. Outsiders might be invited to these sessions, or the choirs of several churches might combine for a concert. Singing schools (see p. 52) were held and glee clubs

[1]E. Hesselberg, "A Review of Music in Canada" from *Modern Music and Musicians* (New York and Toronto, ca. 1913), p. xx. Hesselberg is speaking about Nova Scotia.

formed. As Hesselberg observed with reference to Nova Scotia, "On the Sabbath they sang the old chants and Psalms, thus keeping alive a love for the music of their church. As the settlements grew the custom of meeting together to sing became prevalent, and singing schools for the old and young were established."[2]

BAND MUSIC IN THE CITIES: One of the important new features of the early nineteenth century was the formation of the first purely Canadian bands, often in the service of a patriotic cause. Just as choirs stemmed from the music required for church services, so instrumental music owed much to the British regimental bands. In addition, regimental musicians often acted as teachers and leaders after they had retired from military service.

One of these was Jean Chrysostome Brauneis (1785–1832), who came to Canada from his native Germany as a young man and for some years was active in the band of the 70th Regiment. He left the band to devote himself to teaching and in 1823 obtained a shop licence in Quebec, presumably to sell musical instruments. Business must have been slow, for in 1827 Brauneis applied for a permit to open a billiard room to supplement his income. There had been a long-standing desire to form a native musical band in Quebec and in 1831 Brauneis was chosen as the person best suited to organize it. For about half a year the band was very busy, and it presented a concert on February 20, 1832. Unfortunately the bandmaster fell a victim to the cholera epidemic then sweeping Canada. A successor could not be found, and owing to this and to political unrest the band ceased to function.

All musical life stopped for a number of years. When the band was finally revived in 1836 it bore the proud name Musique Canadienne. It did much to stir the patriotic sentiments of the French Canadians, then engaged in the struggle to gain a greater share in Canadian government. The instruments included two clarinets, a piccolo, serpent, and bassoon, three horns, a trombone, and percussion. The leader was a native of Quebec, Charles Sauvageau (1809–46). Like many other Quebec musicians, including cathedral organists, Sauvageau—as its "premier chef de musique"—and his band participated in the St. Jean-Baptiste celebrations. His "Compagnie de Musique" led the patriots with tunes such as "Par

[2] *Ibid.*

derrière chez mon père" ("Vive la Canadienne"), the quasi-national song of the time.

Brass bands appeared also in various parts of Upper Canada during the thirties and forties. A York [Toronto] Band existed at least as early as 1824. The Police Board of Hamilton gave permission to a band in 1837 to rehearse one evening each week. In the same year, during the rebellion which sought to overthrow the "Family Compact" (the unpopular governing class of Upper Canada), the strains of band music stirred the fighting spirit of the rebels marching on parade in Toronto.

Bands were also founded in many settlements, particularly the German ones of western Ontario. They ranged in type from informal and nameless groups formed to amuse a family or neighbourhood circle on summer evenings or idle winter nights to uniformed town bands parading on official ceremonies and "name" bands hired for dances, weddings, and other entertainment. People in Europe would not have travelled farther to hear a famous star in an opera performance than did the villagers and townspeople of Canada to enjoy the sounds of a band.

BAND MUSIC AT SHARON, ONTARIO: It would appear logical that in early nineteenth-century Canada anyone wishing to hear a band play had to visit one of the garrison towns. He would have heard some fine music, but he would have missed one band, which, though belonging to a small village, had few equals anywhere in the country. Nor was this a regimental band made up of European musicians. Its members were Canadian settlers and they provide the exception to the rule that urban music was superior to that of the country. The village, which for half a century maintained a reputation for its music-making, was originally called Hope and was later renamed Sharon. It lies half-way between Newmarket and Lake Simcoe in southern Ontario. The story of music at Sharon cannot be separated from the personality of the founder of the settlement, David Willson (1778–1866). Born in New York State, of Irish parentage, Willson had but little formal education and successively became a joiner and a sailor. In order to please his young wife, he quit the sea and in 1801 settled in Upper Canada. Here he secured a Crown deed to a 200-acre farm and, being strongly interested in religion, joined the Society of Friends. His was an independent mind, and some years later he broke with the Friends, taking some seceders with him. In 1814 he started meetings in his own home and five years later the new sect, the Children of Peace, opened their first church. In reaction to the simplicity and severity of the Quakers, this sect evolved an original and colourful type of worship. The symbolism expressed in their rites and the architecture of their buildings was naïve and literal—the Temple being of square design to emphasize square-dealing with everyone—and their Christianity emphasized above all the practical virtues of fellowship.

Under Willson's leadership the Davidites, as they were sometimes called, erected a number of buildings of strangely symbolic design; one of which, the Temple, is still preserved and is now a museum. Whereas leaders of other religious sects bitterly fought attempts at giving music a prominent place in worship, Willson was passionately fond of music and promoted it inside and outside church as a pillar of good community life. About 1819 the first singing classes are said to have been held. Sleighloads of young people drove to the Meeting House. Two young women led the choir with their flutes and from this nucleus in 1820 a band was organized and led by Patrick Hughes, and an organ was purchased. At present we can neither substantiate nor disprove the claim that this was the first native band in Canada, and the same might be said for the claim that the first organ built in Canada was for the Children of Peace, were it not for the story, previously mentioned, that a clergyman of New France made copies after the organ imported by Mgr Laval.

The man who succeeded Hughes as leader of the band, who trained the members of the band on their individual instruments, and who built three organs for the sect was Richard Coates, a veteran bandmaster of the Battle of Waterloo and the Peninsular War. Two of the organs are preserved and have been returned to the museum at Sharon. The oldest, dating from *ca.* 1820, has no keyboard but two barrels of ten sacred tunes each. Its case is 8½ feet high, 2½ feet deep, and 4½ feet wide, and it has 133 pipes. Museum visitors are still charmed by its sounds. The second organ no longer exists. According to Ethel Willson Trewhella's series of articles, which traces the history of Sharon in great detail,[3] it had three barrels with ten tunes each. The tunes included old-

[3]E. W. Trewhella, "The Story of Sharon," *Newmarket Era and Express* (1951–2), written in 42 instalments.

time ballads such as "Blue Bells of Scotland," "Henry's Cottage Maid," and "Lochaber No More." The third Coates organ was placed in the town meeting house in 1848 and is now in the museum.

Construction of the Temple, the only building which has survived, started in 1825, and the first service was held there in 1831. While the Temple was being built, William Lyon Mackenzie, who was to become the first mayor of Toronto, described the music room to be built:

Here will be placed, as in a gallery, the musicians and organist, at least thirty feet above the congregation. And when the full-toned and soft-set organ, built by Mr. Coates, of York, shall be set up in this room, together with the players on the flutes, violins, bass-viols, bassoons, clarionets, and flageolets, used by the society in their worship, the effect will remind a visiter [sic] "the music of the spheres" about which bards of old have sung, and poets, in "lofty lays," recorded fancy's fictions.[4]

At the opening of the Temple, a youth, clad entirely in white, was lifted high above the people and his sweet tenor voice rang out in a hymn of praise which he himself had composed. At the end of the very impressive ceremony the band led in a hymn of praise.

Some writers refer to the band as a brass band. It is strange then that the above quotation mentions many instruments but no brass. Mackenzie may not have been a competent music critic, but he must have been able to identify the various instruments when, in July 1831, he reported as follows:

The meeting in East Gwillimbury, to petition the king for a redress of grievances, was followed in the evening by many demonstrations of joy; and the spirited young men of the volunteer amateur musicians, composing the powerful band of the militia regiment, marched up and down the streets of Hope, playing cheerful and enlivening airs. I had the curiosity to count their instruments and there were three or four clarionets, two French horns, two bassoons, besides German and octave flutes, flageolets, &. They have also violins and violoncellos, and are masters of their delightful art.[5]

A possible solution to the puzzle of the brass band lies in the probability that there were players on all types of instruments—

4W. L. Mackenzie, Sketches of Canada and the United States (London, 1833), p. 121. Actually the organ was set up in the Meeting House, not the Temple.
5Ibid., p. 243.

brass, woodwind, string and keyboard—and that they played in various combinations as demanded by the occasion; now as a band, now as an orchestra.

A third quotation from Mackenzie, dating from 1828, testifies to the quality of performance:

Early in the morning after I arrived, I found some of the singers in the chapel practising their hymns and tunes. A number of young females sang a hymn, composed, as is all their poetry, by members of the society. Two young men had bass-viols, and the full-toned organ aided the music which, I will venture to say, is unequalled in any part of the Upper, and scarcely surpassed even by the Catholics in the Lower province.[6]

An ophicleide, a now obsolete brass instrument, was added to the orchestra in 1846. That year marked a new stage in music at Hope, because a professional music teacher, Daniel Cory of Boston, was hired to give systematic instruction in singing. During the two years of his presence, two grand concerts were given, in February and in the summer of 1847. People from the villages and towns around Hope came, either to participate, or to listen to the concerts.

Perhaps Mackenzie's opinions will be considered prejudiced in favour of the Children of Peace because the sect was in sympathy with his anti-Tory policy, and for a time the township of East Gwillimbury was considered a hotbed of radicalism. However, praise for the musical achievements of the sect came from objective and hostile quarters as well. Patrick Swift's *Almanac* for 1834 states that "Their music, vocal and instrumental, is excellent" and a British clergyman of the Anglican church, who judged Willson "a religious enthusiast devoid of all learning and regular training whatsoever," yet had to admit that he was pleased with the music: ". . . the service, if so it may be called, commenced with a very tolerable performance of something intended to be a sacred voluntary on brazen instruments, violins, &c. It really struck me as remarkable that these country farmers could have got it up so well."[7] The writer singles out horns and trombones among the brass instruments.

[6]*Ibid.*, pp. 122–3.
[7]*The Emigrant Churchman in Canada*, ed. H. Christmas (London, 1849), I, 129. The anonymous writer was A. W. H. Rose, who came to North America in 1846.

With the 1860's the Sharon band entered its final period of glory. It appears that there was now more emphasis on secular and less on sacred music. Willson was in his eighties and no longer took any active interest in music, as his lines express:

> Farewell to melody and strains
> That once did fill my listening ear,
> Ye joyful band that peace proclaims,
> I leave you with a glistening tear.

For many years the band was led by Jesse Doan, a skilled clarinetist. He belonged to one of the oldest Sharon families, and one which contributed a number of musicians. Upon Doan's resignation in 1866 his nephew John D. Graham succeeded as bandmaster. By this time the players had reached a stage of accomplishment where they "would transpose the music as they played, thereby saving the trouble of rewriting the original score in a different key, if so required. It has been said by competent judges to be the most perfect in tone, time and execution of any amateur band in Canada."[8]

In the 1860's a set of silver instruments was purchased in the United States for about $1,500 and henceforth the band was known as the Sharon Silver Band. The visual attraction was enhanced when the players received blue uniforms. The band also played in nearby villages and towns, such as Uxbridge and Newmarket, and on St. Patrick's Day in 1871 performed in Toronto. Frequently during the summer months it entertained passengers on Lake Simcoe steamers. On one occasion it ventured even further south than Toronto. According to Mrs. Trewhella, "It is on printed record that the Silver Band of Sharon competed at the great Philadelphia Centennial in 1876, and that there they won the First Prize as the best band in North America."[9]

According to one of the players, Tom Robinson, most of the pieces played by the Sharon Temperance Band (as it was also called) were medleys of American tunes: "Yankee Doodle," "Dixie," "Marching through Georgia," and others.[10] Several Sharon men fought on the Northern side in the American Civil War and

[8]Emily McArthur, History of the Children of Peace (Newmarket, 1898).
[9]Trewhella, "The Story of Sharon," instalment 11.
[10]"Band of Sixty Years Ago: Sweet Strains at Sharon," Toronto Evening Telegram, May 17, 1916.

they took the songs they heard in the United States home to Canada. In Mrs. Trewhella's words, the band in this period had the "American martial swing, and the songs were filled with sentimental appeal." As examples she quotes "Tenting Tonight," "Just before the Battle, Mother," "Old Folks at Home," and others.[11] It has been said that "Popular music was . . . whistled in Sharon a year before first heard in Old Toronto.[12]

Printed music was generally procured from Boston or New York "by single selection, and each bandsman's part was copied by their leader into books of blank forms. . . . Overtures, serenades, and selections from standard operas are among their repertoires."[13]

About 1866, the year of Willson's death, the Fenian Raids, and the rush to California, the sect of the Children of Peace began to decline. People would still gather around parlour organs and pianos to sing the old songs they had learned in Daniel Cory's and Amos Doan's singing classes, and in September 1883 the choir was heard once more at the September Feast; but in August 1886 the last meeting of the Children of Peace took place, and a colourful chapter of musical history came to an end. Looking back, one feels that its distinction was based not on its rather negligible influence on other communities but on the intensity and originality of its musical life, unique in a setting of three hundred villagers.

QUEBEC: Music during the nineteenth century developed on closely parallel lines in different cities and regions of Canada— and, one might add, in the mid-western United States and in Australia. Yet, because of geographical distances and isolation, each centre of population was independent of the others, and there was little exchange of talent or musical news between cities. Musical history was essentially the sum total of innumerable local histories. For this reason our description of musical activities in nineteenth-century Canada has to proceed largely along geographical divisions. The first city to be considered is Quebec, because there were found some of Canada's oldest musical institutions and a number of interesting musical figures. The period under discussion is roughly that from 1820 to 1850.

[11]Trewhella, "The Story of Sharon," instalment 28.
[12]A. Helen Pearson, "The Passing of the Children of Peace," *Saturday Night*, November 30, 1912.
[13]*Ibid.*

It is doubtful whether the tradition of the Quebec subscription concerts of the amazing 1790's was kept up with sustained vigour: evidence is insufficient, but it is probable that concert life depended on occasional visiting troupes and sporadic local efforts. Towards the end of the second decade of the century a German political refugee, supposedly named Barro, a violinist, gave several concerts at the Sewell theatre, for which a Mr. Rod, a dance teacher, conducted the orchestra. Barro stayed in Canada for only about five years, leaving many creditors behind him on his departure in 1823.

The Quebec Harmonic Society held its first rehearsal on January 15, 1820. It was organized to serve both artistic and practical ends: to further the progress of music and to raise money for charitable purposes.[14] It seems to have been a purely instrumental group. In fact, Glackemeyer, its first president, imported instruments to make the ensemble more complete. The society rehearsed and presented its concerts at the Hôtel Union. Many music lovers subscribed to the society, and they and their families were given free admission to the concerts.

Charles Sauvageau, whom we have already met as leader of the Musique Canadienne, was one of the first native Canadians to be remembered as a conductor. His musicians were as adept at dance music as at patriotic band music. In 1833 the Quebec *Mercury* advertised Sauvageau's dance band of six players:

Mr. Sauvageau begs to inform the nobility and gentry of Quebec and its vicinity, that he has at hand a Quadrille Band, and also a fine collection of Quadrilles, Waltzes, Galopades, etc, etc, in which he will make it his whole study to please those who may have the kindness to honour him with their employment, in applying at his residence, no 36, Oliver street, St. John's suburbs, or to Mr. B. Hunt, no 7, Ste. Genevieve, Cape.[15]

Sauvageau also ventured into the field of concert music. On October 25, 1840, he organized a concert at the Salle des Glacis ("weather permitting"). The programme has been preserved.

First Part
String Quartet on motives from Bellini's Somnambula
Group of six singers in a piece by Brugière

[14]*Le Canadien* (Quebec), Jan. 19, 1820.
[15]Quebec *Mercury*, Nov. 19, 1833.

Violin solo with variations by Sauvageau
Trio from a Rossini opera for two concertante violins and clarinet
Theme by Mozart with six variations, played by one of Sauvageau's
pupils

Second Part

Overture "Italian in Algiers" by Rossini, played by string quartet
Air varié for violin, played on one string, by Sauvageau
Piece by Sauvageau, imitating the sound of a horn or trumpet
Trio played by instruments, from the choir sung by six singers in the
first part [sic]

Said to have been a less forceful musician but a better organizer
than Brauneis, Sr., Sauvageau founded his own orchestra in 1840.
It is reported that the orchestra gave several outdoor concerts. After
Sauvageau's untimely death in a theatre fire in 1846, the orchestra
was led by his brother Benjamin, a clarinetist, and later by François
Vézina, father of the Joseph Vézina whose contribution to Canadian music will be discussed later.

Charles Sauvageau was also the author of a little textbook of
musical rudiments, which appeared in 1844 under the title *Notions
élémentaires*. He was one of the first Canadian musicians to have
instrumental compositions published in print. Some of his pieces
of *salon* music and a "chant national" for the St. Jean-Baptiste
Society were printed in the Quebec literary and musical journal
Le Ménestrel in 1844.

There is a special fascination for a historian in a Canadian
musician whose name has not found its way into Canadian reference books[16] but who came into closer contact with one of the
world's great composers than any other Canadian we know of. This
man was Theodore Frederic Molt (*ca.* 1796–1856), like Glackemeyer and Brauneis, Sr., a German who came to Canada as a
young man. The earliest known record about Molt dates from
Spring 1825 when the young music teacher in Quebec City
auctioned off his furniture and "an excellent forte-piano, violins,
flutes, clarinettes etc." in order to return to Europe for study purposes. He must already have established firm roots in Quebec,
for he left with "the sweet hope to return to Canada to take up
again teaching of the liberal art for which the natives show so
much taste."

[16]Except in my *Catalogue of Canadian Composers*.

On his journey, which lasted about a year, Molt met three of Europe's great musicians: Moscheles, then living in England, and Czerny and Beethoven in Vienna. Molt gained the privilege of visiting Beethoven, who seems to have shown much interest in the musician from far-away Canada. Molt introduced himself by writing into Beethoven's conversation book:

Ich bin Musiklehrer in Quebec in Nordamerika. Ihre Werke haben mich so oft ergötzt, dass ich es für meine Pflicht halte, Ihnen auf einer Durchreise durch Wien meinen persönlichen Dank abzustatten, um so mehr als ich so grosses. . . .[17]

The following page, unfortunately, was torn from the conversation book. According to Molt's son, the conversation did not dwell long on music, for Beethoven had just written some verses—rather poor in Molt's opinion—to a young lady and began to talk about her with great enthusiasm.[18]

Soon after Molt wrote the following letter to Beethoven:

Hochzuverehrender Herr!

Als ich letzthin so frey war Sie zu besuchen, sparte ich mir einen Wunsch an Sie auf, welchen ich Ihnen hiermit in diesem Briefe gehorsamst vorzulegen wage: Ich werde nach meiner Abreise von hier nie mehr das Glück haben in Ihre Nähe zu kommen. Verzeihen Sie mir daher wenn ich Ihnen aus meinem Stammbuch ein Blättchen zur Ausfüllung darlege, welches mir in einer Entfernung von beinahe 3000 Stunden (wohin ich von hier aus wieder reise) ein ewig theueres Dokument bleiben soll. Ich preise mich glücklich, mehrere jener berühmten Tonkünstler Europas gesehen zu haben, welche ich in Amerika aus ihren Werken kannte und werde stolz darauf sein, meinen dortigen Freunden, welche zugleich ihre Mitverehrer sind, sagen zu können,

'Seht, diess hat Beethoven aus seiner grossen Seele für mich geschrieben!'

Erlauben Sie mir bis morgen mich um gütige Antwort melden zu dürfen.

Mit ausgezeichneter Hochachtung

Ihr

[17]"I am a music teacher in Quebec in North America. Your works have delighted me so often that I consider it my duty to pay you my personal gratitude on a journey through Vienna, all the more as I had such great . . ." (my translation).

[18]Told by Molt's son to Beethoven's biographer, Alexander Wheelock Thayer, *The Life of Ludwig van Beethoven*, H. E. Krehbiel ed., (New York, 1921), III, 211.

gehorsamst ergebener Diener
Theodor Molt
Musiklehrer
in Quebec in Nord Amerika.[19]

Beethoven complied with Molt's wish and wrote him the canon "Freu Dich des Lebens" (which in an earlier version appears among the sketches for the B flat major quartet). The manuscript bore the date of December 16, 1825, Beethoven's fifty-fifth birthday.[20] Having returned to Quebec in the summer of 1826, Molt took up teaching again and two years later produced his first book, *Elementary Treaty on Music, More Particularly Adapted to the Pianoforte: Traité élémentaire de musique, particulièrement adapté au piano forte*, with text in English and French.

Like Glackemeyer a convert to Catholicism, Molt was the organist of the Quebec Basilica from 1840 to 1849. During these years he published a treatise on vocal music and attempted to compile a collection of Canadian songs, for which he sought the help of local poets.[21] The outcome of this attempt was different from the original plan, for *La Lyre sainte*, published in 1844 and

[19]A. W. Thayer, *Ludwig van Beethovens Leben* (H. Riemann ed.; Leipzig, 1923), V, 273.
Highly honorable Sir!
When I recently took the liberty to visit you I saved (up) one wish to you which I obediently dare to lay before you in this letter: After my departure I shall never again have the luck to come near you. Pardon me therefore if I lay before you a little leaf from my album which shall remain for me in a distance of nearly 3000 hours (whither I am travelling again from here) an eternally precious document. I consider myself lucky to have seen several of those famous musicians of Europe whom I knew in America from their works and I shall be proud to be able to tell to my friends over there, who are likewise fellow-worshippers of you
"Behold, this Beethoven has written for me from his great soul"! Permit me till tomorrow that I may call for a kind answer.
With extraordinary respect
your
obediently devoted servant
Theodore Molt
Music teacher
in Quebec in North America
(My translation.)
[20]The manuscript, once in the possession of Molt's son, passed into the hands of the Berlin antiquarian dealer J. A. Stargardt in 1933. Its present whereabouts are not known.
[21]See "Le Recueil de cantiques de M. Molt," *Le Bulletin des recherches historiques*, XLVI (June 1940), 168.

1845, was a collection of sacred hymns of the most varied origin. A patriot, Molt set to music the poem "Sol canadien, terre chérie," written in 1829 and intended by its author, Isidore Bédard, as national hymn.

Molt was the first organist of the Basilica to participate in the St. Jean-Baptiste celebrations. He did so with great success, and one year,[22] when he organized a choir for the occasion, he was rewarded with a silver snuff box, while the bandmaster, Charles Sauvageau, received a golden pencil.

His wife and two of his sons having perished in the theatre fire of 1846, which also took the life of Charles Sauvageau, Molt left Quebec. Speaking English, as well as French, fluently he accepted a position as music teacher at the Female Seminary in Burlington, Vermont. He wrote another pianoforte manual at this time and died in 1856, at the age of sixty.

A number of compositions, published by Brainard (Cleveland), and bearing the name of T. F. Molt may be assumed to have come from the pen of the Canadian musician.

With the consecration of the Anglican Cathedral of the Holy Trinity in 1804, another important centre of church music was added to Quebec. The first archbishop of the Cathedral, Jacob Mountain, was a music-loving man who was very proud of the organ and the choir. On his initiative the services were obtained in 1816 of a fine musician, Stephen Codman (1792?–1852?). A native of Norwich, Dr. Codman had studied with such well-known English musicians as Beckwith and Crotch. A highlight of his 36 years of service in Quebec was the Grand Performance of Sacred Music, held in the Cathedral on June 26, 1834, for the benefit of the Quebec Emigrant Society. "This new and brilliant public exhibition of music, for which preparations upon an extensive scale had been made"[23] was probably the largest one in the country up to that time. A chorus of 111 singers was supported by an orchestra of over 60 players, composed of 10 first violins, 12 second violins, 4 violas, 6 cellos, 1 bass, 8 flutes, 4 each of clarinets, bassoons, horns, and trumpets, 1 each of trombone, serpent, and bass horn, and 2

[22]The source, H. J. J. B. Chouinard, *Annales de la Société St. Jean-Baptiste de Québec*, IV (Québec, 1903), 521–2, gives 1847 as the date. However, Sauvageau died on June 12, 1846. As St. Jean-Baptiste Day is celebrated on June 24, the year must have been 1845 or earlier.

[23]Quebec *Gazette*, June 25, 1834.

drums. Codman was chairman of the Musical Committee of Management and conductor; J. Brewer acted as his assistant. The two men "alternately presided at the organ and pianoforte."

The concert lasted about three hours and included vocal solos, trios, and quartets and choral selections from the sacred works of Haydn, Mozart, Handel, Cherubini, Rossini, and Beckwith, as well as Codman's own *Invocation* and an organ concerto by Crotch. The Quebec *Gazette* of June 27 contained an extensive review of the concert, from which we quote one paragraph:

> No performance, we believe, more agreeably surpassed even the high expectations that had been formed; and the signal success of the exertions of the whole corps of amateurs and professional gentlemen, was the subject of universal praise. Not only the pieces in which the grand and imposing strength of the whole orchestra was displayed, but the different concertos, and particularly that of Mr. Codman on the organ, who exhibited his distinguished professional talents to the best advantage, gained the warmest approbation of all present. The effect of the different solos, too, and particularly those by the young ladies, excited general surprise.

Not only was this musical effort remarkable for its time, but it may also be regarded as the beginning of the second great musical contribution made by Britain to Canada: the love for choral music and the cultivation of oratorio.

MONTREAL: Next to Quebec, Montreal, founded in 1642, is the oldest Canadian city. It was founded as a French settlement, but unlike Quebec it has had a sizable population of English-speaking people ever since the British conquest. The majority of the population is French-speaking, but about a third is of Anglo-Saxon or other non-French ancestry. Montreal owes its musical importance to its rapid growth of population, the variety and vitality of traditions embodied in its people, and, to some degree, its proximity— compared with other Canadian cities—to New York and Boston.

As early as 1819 a Montreal city directory listed the surprising number of nine musicians (one of them also a grocer), among them Messrs. Champagne and William Andrews, Jr., organists, and Peter Smith, professor and teacher of music. It would be most interesting to know why Mr. Smith made a distinction between *teacher* and *professor*, for it is highly doubtful that he held a university position. Oddly enough the list contains no mention of Guillaume-Joseph Mechtler (1763–1833), Brussels-born organist of Notre Dame Church from 1792 to 1833, who may be considered the city's leading musician of that time.

Concerts were as rare in Montreal as in other towns in the first half of the century. The directory of 1819 admits that "Montreal is not at present over-burthened with amusements," but adds that "By the indulgence of the Colonel of the regiment stationed here, the company assembled are in summer time frequently amused in the evening by the music of an excellent band." The locale of indoor concerts was the Theatre Royal and they were usually undertaken by amateurs or by the garrison bands, which also played during theatrical performances. For instance, in 1829 amateurs performed Molière's L'Avare, and during the intermission the band of the 79th Regiment played. When Charles Dickens visited Montreal in 1842, he saw a play with music provided by the band of the 23rd Regiment, then considered one of the finest bands in the country. At rare intervals a foreign artist would appear. One such instance is the concert given in May 1830 by Signor Jean Muscarelli, advertised as a member of the "Milan Opera."

When Guillaume Mechtler died in 1833, a new organist was appointed at Notre Dame Church at an annual salary of £ 50. This was Jean-Chrysostome Brauneis, Jr. (1814–71), the son of the bandmaster (see p. 71). A native of Quebec, Brauneis, Jr., had just returned from three years' study in Germany. He was the first Canadian musician to complete his studies overseas. Thanks to his thorough training he soon acquired an excellent reputation as a teacher of many instruments, of theory, and, in particular, of singing. He wrote a mass for Notre Dame Church which was performed in the summer of 1835 with the accompaniment of organ, violin, flute, bass viol and bassoon. This was the first occasion on which a Canadian newspaper reviewed a composition by a local musician at length. An article in La Minerve[24] declared that the counterpoint was exact and flawless and that the harmonies satisfied the most exacting ear, and concluded that the performance, especially on the part of the sopranos, did not do justice to the composition. Only one other Brauneis composition is known, a published march dedicated to the St. Jean-Baptiste Society in 1848.

[24]La Minerve, July 16, 1835.

Brauneis also imported instruments and tuned pianos, a job which was not yet done by specialists. We also know that in 1837 he was planning to found a *société de musique*, but evidence is lacking as to whether or not this project was realized.

In his later years Brauneis exchanged his position as organist at Notre Dame Church for that at St. James Cathedral. An excellent musician, he participated in many musical enterprises in Montreal and enjoyed a fine reputation.

HALIFAX AND OTHER CENTRES IN NOVA SCOTIA: Musical life in Halifax in the early decades of the nineteenth century went on in much the same way as has already been described. About 1800 the city had a population of 9,000 and it continued to expand so that by the middle of the century the figure had risen to 20,000. Band music was ever present in this military town, and from time to time a concert was given by regimental musicians or by amateurs among the officers or other prominent citizens. On the whole, concerts were rare. As we read in W. Moorsom's *Letters from Nova Scotia*, published in 1830, "the exquisite powers of musical concert . . . are here almost unknown, and, except in two or three solitary instances, hardly attempted." Again we are indebted to Phyllis Blakeley for our knowledge of some of these "solitary instances." A visiting troupe such as that of Herrmann and Co. of the Royal Conservatory of Munich was such a rare treat that the Mason's Hall on Barrington Street, the customary place for entertainment, was filled to overflowing. Among local organizations were the New Union Singing Society of 1809 and the St. Paul's Singing Society of 1819. That music was cultivated also by the working classes is demonstrated by the Amateur Glee Club which was organized in 1836 by young tradesmen and mechanics of Halifax and which, according to a contemporary newspaper, afforded pleasure to their friends and innocent amusement to themselves. On a May evening in 1837 two hundred persons assembled at the Lecture Room of the Mechanics' Institute and for nearly three hours were entertained by glees, catches, duets, and songs.

Perhaps some may be disposed to smile at the idea of those who have to live by the labor of their hands, attempting to cultivate a taste for music, or seeking the refining influences of such an association. We are

glad, however, to see such a spirit springing up—such a desire manifested to bring within the reach of the middling classes rational pleasures, which are too often believed to belong only to the rich. God, when
he painted the rose, and breathed its mysterious perfume upon the
violet, did not deny to the mechanic the senses to enjoy—neither did he
close his ear to the delights of harmony, nor strike music out from the
fascinations of his humble fireside.[25]

An ambitious enterprise was the Halifax Harmonic Society,
organized on October 26, 1842, by a group of 38 citizens. The aim
of the group was the cultivation of sacred music and it is said to
have had its own choir, orchestra, and soloists. The first work
studied was Haydn's *Creation*, but it has not yet been established
whether a performance took place. As is the case so often, the
impetus had been given by the arrival of a musical family, the
St. Lukes, in May of 1842. John St. Luke had been musical director
and ballet master at theatres in Bristol and in New York. In the
month after his arrival, his son and daughter, violinist and singer,
gave a joint recital. The indifferent reception given this recital
taught St. Luke that Nova Scotians cared little for the brilliant
glitter of Italian opera. The next recital, devoted to sacred music,
was received with great enthusiasm. As a result of this concert the
Harmonic Society was formed with John St. Luke as director.

The society continued its activities for six or seven years. Then
it went into eclipse until 1857. Upon its revival the society met with
enthusiastic support. So seriously were rehearsals taken that absen-
tees were fined, and those unable to sing but interested in music
were invited to attend rehearsals as patrons. Three public concerts
were given in the winter of 1858 at Temperance Hall.

Music in the rural areas and the small towns of Nova Scotia was
confined to the traditional songs and bagpipe tunes of the Scottish
fishermen and farmers, and the psalms brought by the devoutly
religious New Englanders. An exception was Lunenburg, a predominantly German settlement richly endowed with musical talent.
Here a Harmonic Society was formed on December 5, 1828, to
promote the singing of sacred music. Twenty-four men joined as
charter members; apparently choral singing was not considered
proper for women, who were admitted as visitors only. The group
met on Friday evenings throughout the entire year. After a few

[25]*Nova Scotian*, May 18, 1837, p. 154.

years it appears to have merged with the St. John's Singing Society, organized on December 17, 1830, which was active for at least three years.

A few decades later, Miss Blakeley tells us, musical societies were established in Antigonish and Pictou. In Antigonish the services of a Herr Kästner, former bandmaster of the 43rd Regiment, were enlisted to direct the Musical Society, which was founded in 1844. Kästner started with a band of 15 players but in time more instruments were added. He instructed each player in his particular instrument, wrote arrangements for the band, and taught music in the town. A concert given for Kästner's benefit in 1846 aroused such curiosity that people travelled distances of forty miles to enjoy the new experience.

Pictou was a flourishing community in the years after 1830. Two amateur concerts were given there in March 1842, and a Philharmonic Society gave a series of concerts in the winter of 1856–7 at the Pictou Academy. The society is mentioned as early as 1852.

In Barrington a Harmonic Society was founded in 1861 "to promote the knowledge of music by rehearsals, public concerts and lectures." It flourished until 1870.

A few native musicians of Nova Scotia must be mentioned for the reputation they gained as performers or teachers. Arnold Doane's championship of good music left a lasting impression in Halifax. Jacob Cunnabell studied and taught music in the United States for a number of years, and R. G. Halls wrote the music for a song celebrating the centenary of Halifax in 1849.

Teachers and musicians from Europe about the middle of the century included E. C. Saffery, Señor Louis G. Casseres, and Gaetano Francesco Farrugia from Malta, who achieved local fame with his Agnes Waltzes.

SAINT JOHN, N.B.: Saint John, N.B. was a flourishing port and a rapidly expanding ship-building centre throughout the nineteenth century. The names and activities of various musical societies revealed by J. Russell Harper's research present a lively panorama of musical life.

In 1824, when the population had reached 8,000, a Phil-Harmonic Society was founded. From then on musical societies appear to have been a permanent feature of the city's cultural life.

Most of these groups were devoted to choral singing. Secular music was cultivated by the Catch and Glee Club, formed in 1833 by an Irish immigrant, and church music by Stephen Humbert's Sacred Music Society, founded in 1840. Another Sacred Music Society was organized in 1837 by a member of St. Andrew's Kirk who was dissatisfied with the minister's limited toleration of music (see p. 39). The group aimed to study choral music of greater challenge than provided by psalms and hymns. It was active for at least eight years. Under one of its conductors, Professor Weisbecker, a former regimental bandmaster, concerts were presented with selections from Handel, Haydn and Mozart.

Concerts were also given, though rarely, by visiting troupes. The Herrmann troupe, which raised great enthusiasm in Halifax, performed in Saint John in 1832, featuring music by Mozart, Beethoven, Rossini and Weber. The St. Luke family resided temporarily in Saint John, teaching dancing and music, before moving to Halifax after a farewell concert in May 1842. During Christmas week 1841 they gave three concerts. In the following months St. Luke trained a local choir and, with the help of his children and an orchestra of 22 players, presented a concert in March. The programme included eight numbers from Haydn's *Creation* and a violin concerto by de Bériot. In 1853 the famous violinist Ole Bull gave a concert in Saint John.

The intensity of musical life cannot be measured by concerts alone. Music-making was fostered by bandmasters and other immigrants who settled in Saint John as music teachers. One of these, Arthur Corry, who came from Ireland about 1822, set up his own Musical Academy and his pupils regularly gave recitals.

TORONTO: The beginnings of music in Toronto have a romantic colouring. On Friday, February 19, 1796, Mrs. Simcoe entered in her diary: "We dined in the woods on Major Shanks' farm lot . . . ; a band of music stationed near. . . . Jacob, the Mohawk, was there. He danced Scotch reels with more ease and grace than any person I ever saw, and had the air of a prince." And on Friday, July 1, of the same year she wrote: "A large party from the garrison to dinner. A boat with music accompanied them; we heard it in the evening until they had passed the town. It sounds delightfully."[26]

[26]Major Shanks's farm lot was near the present Trinity Park. The party moved from the present Exhibition Grounds through Toronto Bay up the Don River to Castle Frank.

Around 1818, when Toronto, or York as it was then called, had a thousand inhabitants, the town's one instrumental artist was a man by the name of Maxwell. His violin was heard wherever private or public entertainment demanded music. At St. James Church Mr. Hetherington, "a functionary of the old country village stamp," acted as clerk and leader of the music. After announcing the psalm tune he would play it on his bassoon, ornamenting the song of the congregation with grotesque improvisations and discants. When it was decided to have a permanent choir, two groups were organized to compete for the position. One of the groups used the accompaniment of string bass, clarinet, and bassoon; it emerged the winner. The value of a church choir thus demonstrated, Hetherington was granted in 1819 an allowance of £ 20 for instruction in church music.

Mrs. Anna Jameson has given us an outspoken opinion on musical conditions in Toronto in 1837 in her "Winter Studies and Summer Rambles":

If the sympathy for literature and science be small, that for music is less. Owing to the exertion of an intelligent musician here, some voices have been so far drilled that the psalms and anthems at church are very tolerably performed; but this gentleman received so little general encouragement that he is at this moment preparing to go over to the United States. The archdeacon is collecting subscriptions to pay for an organ which is to cost a thousand pounds; if the money were expended in aid of a singing-school, it would do more good.[27]

A musician brought specially from England to play this "magnificent" organ at St. James Cathedral was Edward Hodges (1796–1867), the holder of a Cambridge doctorate of music, whose first performance, in September 1838, "electrified" the audience.[28] He did not find conditions to his liking and after several weeks accepted an invitation to go to New York City. As his son wrote in a letter of November 10, 1838, "The times were so bad, business so dull, everything is stagnant in the way of work, that Papa made up his mind not to stay any longer."[29] Thus within two years, Canada lost

[27]Anna Jameson, *Winter Studies and Summer Rambles in Canada* (New York, 1839; Toronto, 1923), p. 69 (1923 ed.). This passage was written on April 1, 1837.

[28]Thomas Arthur Reed, "Church Music in Canada," typewritten copy in the University of Toronto Library.

[29]Quoted in F. H. Hodges, *Edward Hodges* (G. P. Putnam, 1896), p. 111.

two good musicians to the United States. A precedent was set which was to be followed by many a Canadian musician.

Actually, the organ installed in 1838 was not the first in St. James Cathedral. In 1834 W. Warren was organist and edited the music of *A Selection of Psalms and Hymns* for the use of the diocese of Quebec (then including both the present provinces of Quebec and Ontario). Among the successors of Warren and Hodges it is interesting to note a woman organist, Mrs. Gilkison (sometimes spelled Gilkinson), who filled the position from at least 1842 until her resignation in June 1848. The reason for her resignation is not hard to guess: her salary was reduced from £100 to £75 in 1846 and to £50 two years later.

NEW VIGOUR IN MUSICAL LIFE: Towards the middle of the nineteenth century, musical life gained considerable vigour. Concerts became more ambitious both in the number of participants and the choice of programmes. Choirs, bands and orchestras were bold enough to attempt the performance of an entire oratorio, opera, or symphony chosen from the classical repertoire. Musical societies were now an accepted feature of urban life, even though they were usually short-lived as years of boom and depression alternated frequently, as fire gutted the local theatre or destroyed the church organ, and as epidemics of such diseases as cholera decimated the membership. Musical life was also more intensively mirrored in the newspapers and periodicals; instrument-building flourished; and musical instruction was accepted into the curriculum of institutions of higher education.

These developments coincided with the advance of political maturity marked by the institution of responsible government. They were fostered by the coming of the steamship and railway, which made the visits of great artists possible; in addition, the wave of immigration from Europe after the revolutions of 1848 brought many individuals who gave impetus to musical life in Canada.

QUEBEC: Only with the middle of the century did the "German period" wane in Quebec's musical life, and henceforth French musicians, native or immigrant, dominated the scene. Antoine

Dessane (1826–73) has been called the "father of music in Quebec," a title which he does not deserve even if we ignore the efforts of his predecessors. Nevertheless, no musician as learned as Dessane had yet lived in Quebec, and few have had such a lasting effect on the musical enterprises and organizations of the city. Dessane was born in France and studied at the Paris Conservatoire, then directed by Cherubini. He associated with César Franck, a fellow student. After passing his examinations in cello and organ with brilliant results, Dessane toured Italy, Austria and Germany and gained wide experience in chamber music as a player in the quartet of the composer George Onslow.

Disturbed by the revolution of 1848, Dessane accepted an offer as cathedral organist (1849–65) in Quebec, where he lived for the remainder of his life with the exception of a few years spent in New York. The presence of a man who carried with him the traditions of one of the great European music schools proved a very beneficial influence. With great energy and idealism, Dessane promoted concerts and musical societies and conducted courses of study reflecting the spirit of the Conservatoire. At his own home he held *soirées* which were attended by local and visiting celebrities.

As far as can be judged today, Dessane's output as a composer surpassed in quantity, seriousness and craftsmanship that of all his predecessors and contemporaries in Canada. As an organist, his first concern was church music. He wrote at least four masses, three of them labelled *solennelle*, and many shorter liturgical works. The longest of his orchestral works is the Suite for Large Orchestra (1863). The list of Dessane's compositions also includes some chamber and even dance music: his quadrille on five Canadian airs was published by L. Brousseau in Quebec. Several of the manuscripts are preserved at Laval University. From 1869, the year of Dessane's return from New York, there dates a pedagogical work, a theory of orchestration. It would be interesting to know whether this was written for his students in New York or for those in Quebec.

Towards the end of the 1840's the Société Harmonique regained vigour. The admission fee for concerts was four dollars per family, and with the support of leading citizens, the organization flourished artistically and financially. Concert programmes reflected a high level of musical sophistication. For instance, on January 23, 1857, the concert conducted by one Roschi (or Rotschi) included performances of Mozart's complete G minor Symphony, a Beethoven trio, and the "Prometheus" Overture, besides works by Mendelssohn, Rossini, Auber, and other composers. Regimental band musicians participated in this concert as they did in many others. In the same season, movements from Beethoven and Haydn symphonies and overtures by Mozart, Rossini and Weber were performed. In spite of this achievement, the society ceased its activities near the end of 1857 and the next attempt to revive it in 1861, for which Dessane gathered some sixty instrumentalists, proved a financial failure. A revival of the society in 1870 will be described later.

A notable chamber music organization was the Septette Club, which made its debut in 1857 under Dessane, just after the collapse of the Société Harmonique. It was one link in a chain of musical organizations which led directly to the present Orchestre Symphonique de Québec. The Septette Club performed parts of Beethoven's second and sixth symphonies in 1857 and 1858 respectively.

Noteworthy musicians active in pre-Confederation Quebec City included Alfred Paré (1829–1916), singer and violinist in the Septette Club and later in the Septuor Haydn; the conductors Ziegler and B. Schott, the latter reputedly a brother of the famous music publishers; and Damis Paul (1827–1913), organist and pianist in Quebec for 17 years. Paul worked in Montreal before coming to Quebec; and in later years he went to the United States to live.

Célestin Lavigueur (1830–85) was music teacher at the Quebec Seminary for thirty years, a violinist of esteem, and a composer of some of Canada's earliest operettas. Their titles, for example La Fiancée des bois and Les Enfants du manoir, suggest a Canadian scene. The latter, for which Lavigueur also wrote the libretto, was almost completed at the time of his death. One of his songs, "La Huronne," achieved wide popularity. Lavigueur was a gifted musician, but unfortunately he lacked the kind of disciplined training which at that time was available only in Europe.

Emmanuel Blain de St.-Aubin (1833–83), a native of France, came to Quebec in 1857. He excelled as a singer but also won a reputation as a voice teacher and songwriter. Later he carried on these activities in Ottawa.

MONTREAL: In Montreal R. J. Fowler, newly arrived from England, opened the first Philharmonic Society in 1848 with a concert of orchestral and choral selections and vocal solos. Like many later societies in this bilingual city, the Philharmonic attempted to unite French and English elements.

In 1852 cholera struck Montreal and it was not until 1855 that public life resumed its normal activities. From then on concert events began to multiply, but for a number of years no single musical society dominated the scene. A prominent conductor was Henry Prince, a local music dealer and writer of dance music, whose name appears at an event with the characteristically grandiloquent title of "Grand Military Concert of Vocal and Instrumental Music," played by the "Volunteer Militia Rifle Band" in September 1857.

On August 24, 1860, Montreal witnessed a musical celebration of unprecedented proportions. The occasion was the visit of the Prince of Wales, later King Edward VII, for the opening of Victoria Bridge. Fowler conducted the Montreal Musical Union, said to have consisted of four hundred voices; Frederick Herbert Torrington was concertmaster; Adelina Patti and the future Mme Albani were among the singers. The "Grand Musical Festival" consisted of three parts. It began with a concert of sacred music, next featured a large composition written especially for the occasion, and ended with a "Professional Concert." The work written in honour of the Prince of Wales was a cantata with words by W. Edouard Sempé and music by Charles Wugk Sabatier. Its movements were as follows: Part I, "Le Départ," consisted of Overture, Recitative, Full Chorus, Female Solo, Prayer, Recitative and Soldiers' Chorus; Part II, "L'Arrivée," consisted of a Female Chorus, Sextet, unison entry of the full chorus, Recitative and Final Chorus.[1]

The event was a memorable one, not only as a feast of music and patriotism, but as a test of endurance and patience. As the programme was a long one in itself, the opening had been set for seven o'clock. At the last moment it was learned that the Prince would be late in returning from a trip up the St. Lawrence valley. The concert was then postponed until eight. By this time some 6,000 people had assembled in the elegant and majestic Ball Room, but the Prince and his company were not among them. It was announced that the royal party would still be late, but the first part

[1] *La Minerve,* Aug. 9, 1860.

of the concert was begun anyway. Selections from Haydn's *Creation* were "Executed with a great deal of precision and spirit, and . . . repeatedly and loudly applauded." Then followed four parts of a mass not identified in the newspaper review. Now the time had come for the performance of the specially written cantata. But there was no Prince! The intermission was scheduled to be twenty minutes; at the end of one hour the audience had grown so impatient that—prince or no prince—Sabatier, who was to conduct his own work, "made the first emphatic waves of his baton of office. The stirring notes of the overture resounded through the building, and everyone settled themselves to hear the long-talked-of Cantata." Half-way through the first recitative the performance was interrupted by a false alarm about the Prince's arrival. "The next piece had a name of good augury—it was "L'Arrivée"—and sure enough, at the moment when the preliminary flourishes of the *Maestro's* baton were once more dividing the atmosphere, several excited flaps given from a white pocket handkerchief, in the gallery near the royal box, again raised anticipation on tiptoe." His Highness had arrived, and after the strains of "God Save the Queen" were heard once more, the cantata proceeded. "When this was over and the cheering had subsided, it was twenty minutes to 11 o'clock." The cantata was over, but the Prince had not heard all of it. Consequently, it was repeated from the beginning in a spirited performance, even though in the audience the "capacity for attention [was] . . . all but exhausted . . . so that persons were seen asleep or nodding, throughout the room." No wonder that the Prince and many of the audience retired at the end.[2] The show must go on, however, and the Professional Concert took its course. It offered excerpts from the operas of Rossini, Donizetti, Bellini and Verdi. Finally the programme was cut short, and when Signorina Patti ended with "God Save the Queen" the clock had struck one o'clock in the morning.[3]

Charles Wugk Sabatier (1820–62), the composer of the cantata, was of German origin but was educated in France. A strong anti-Bonapartist, he fled from Europe after 1848. The story is told that shortly after his arrival in Montreal he noticed in his hotel a statue of Napoleon III and immediately hurled it out of the window,

[2]The Prince asked to read the score and was "loud and frequent" in his expression of applause. N. A. Woods, *The Prince of Wales in Canada and the United States* (London, 1861), pp. 140–1.

[3]Montreal *Herald*, Aug. 30, 1860.

cursing the fact that even in Canada he could not be free of the tyrant. In spite of this he must have found conditions to his liking for he spent eight years in Montreal and four in Quebec. He was the first genuine piano virtuoso to settle in Canada, and apart from his performances he gained a considerable reputation as a composer of dance music and operatic fantasies, so fashionable at that time. These works were written for band or piano, and a few were published in Montreal. Sabatier helped to found, in 1860, the first Canadian musical periodical, L'Artiste, of which only two numbers appeared.

Though Sabatier was a richly talented musician, his intemperate manner of life led to his early death at the age of 42. One of his distinctions, doubtless, was the fact that he was the first "Bohemian" among our musicians. It is also of interest that he was one of the teachers of Calixa Lavallée. Today he is chiefly remembered, however, for a patriotic song which has had a great vogue in French Canada, "Le Drapeau de carillon."

Frederick Herbert Torrington (1837–1917), the concert-master at the "Grand Musical Festival," came to Montreal as a young man in 1857. He soon gained a front-rank place, both as violinist and as organist, and introduced to Montreal many musical classics. He contributed to musical life for twelve years and then left for Boston. We shall discuss Torrington's place in Canadian music more fully when we meet him in Toronto in the last quarter of the century.

Among the Canadian-born Montreal musicians who gained maturity before Confederation was Joseph-Julien Perreault (1826–66), a priest who was also choirmaster at Notre Dame Church for two short periods and who wrote a number of church compositions. His Messe de Noël is based on Christmas songs and was published after his death. It has been rearranged by Eugène Lapierre, who has done much to revive old French-Canadian music.

Jean-Baptiste Labelle (1828–91), was born in New York State, but came to Canada in or before 1843. He studied with the Austrian pianist Leopold von Meyer and with Sigismund Thalberg. From 1849 until 1891 he was organist at Notre Dame Church but in 1857 he found time for a concert tour through the United States and South America. He was also the conductor of one of Canada's earliest orchestral groups, the Société Philharmonique de Montréal (1863), a well-balanced group of about 29 players. Labelle won a reputation as the composer of several operettas, a cantata celebrating Confederation, and one for the Papal Zouaves regiment which left Canada for Rome in 1868. His collection of Gregorian chants, *Le Répertoire de l'organiste*, went through several editions. His best known song is "O Canada, mon pays, mes amours," the text of which was written in the turbulent year 1834 by the French-Canadian statesman Sir George-Etienne Cartier, and which was originally sung to an air by an anonymous composer.

SAINT JOHN, N.B.: An ambitious enterprise in Saint John, N.B., was the Harmonic Society. Its Minute book has been preserved and thus we are able to follow in detail its brilliant though short history. Formed on November 8, 1854, for the "mutual cultivation of taste and skill," the group began with 23 singers, but rehearsal attendance soon swelled to an average of 35 men and 20 women. After several weeks of irregular rehearsals, a conductor and organist was hired for the fee of $75 per year. This was Professor Theodoric Wichtendahl, who began a systematic course of instruction and after three months presented the choir in its first concert. Both secular and sacred music was studied, for among the first music purchased for rehearsal was an *Opera Chorus Book* and Handel's *The Messiah*.

Great success came with the 1855–6 season. At least seven concerts were given. Halls were packed, and on some occasions hundreds had to be turned away from the doors. Parts of *The Messiah* were performed, and *The Creation* was chosen for study during the next season. Unfortunately, however, petty squabbles arose between the conductor and the executive of the society. Eventually Wichtendahl was censured for lack of exertion, as the orchestra which he had been expected to form did not materialize. He resigned early in 1857. Two concerts given in April under his successor Signor de Angelis appear to have been the last of the society. Ironically, the society collapsed just after it had received a charter. Membership decreased, the society's organ had to be sold, and after August 1857 the Minute book remained blank.

TORONTO: The earliest attempts to form musical organizations and to present concerts in Toronto were made by a man who was not primarily a musician but a classical scholar, the Rev. John

McCaul (1807–86), President of King's College (later the University of Toronto). A keen amateur pianist and composer of some published anthems, Dr. McCaul was the impresario of many musical enterprises in Toronto. Born in Dublin, he came to Toronto in the late 1830's and immediately established himself as a leader in musical circles. Several years later he thought it opportune to organize two concerts. He persuaded James P. Clarke, then organist in Hamilton, and James Dodsley Humphreys, singer and organist, to conduct. A European violinist living in New York, M. Bley, was invited to act as concertmaster. The concerts took place on October 23 and 24, 1845, under the auspices of King's College. Admission was $1.50 for the two, and a net sum of $50.00 was made.

The concerts were extraordinary both for the variety of content and for the excellent taste they reflected. The programmes, which are preserved in the music division of the Toronto Public Libraries, list the overtures to *Coriolanus, Prometheus, Anacreon* and *St. Paul*, choral selections by Haydn, Handel, Rossini and others, besides such unusual music—considering the time and place—as a madrigal by Morley, a trio from *Cosi fan tutte*, Schubert's *Impatience*, and a Beethoven quintet for strings and two horns. Programmes of such discerning taste were rarely provided in Canada at this time.

A decade after Toronto's first literary and artistic societies, the Toronto Choral Society was organized on April 7, 1845. It enjoyed the patronage of another educational institution, Upper Canada College, through its principal F. W. Barron; it aimed at the cultivation of sacred music. Later, it merged with the Philharmonic Society, organized in 1846 by Dr. McCaul and John Ellis. The latter was an amateur cellist and music patron who helped to found and played in many of the instrumental groups in Toronto. With Bley as conductor, the Philharmonic's first concert took place on April 23, 1847. After a short eclipse, the society started afresh in 1848 and gave one concert in 1849 and two in 1850, bravely tackling such works as the overtures to *The Marriage of Figaro, Der Freischütz, Semiramide, Anacreon* and *The Italian in Algiers*. The conductor was George W. Strathy (1819–90), a Scot who was said to have met Liszt during his student days in Europe, and who later became professor of music at Trinity University in Toronto.

To trace the many revivals and eclipses of the Philharmonic Society is beyond the scope of this book. As far as can be ascertained, its dates were 1846-7, 1848-50, 1854-5, 1857 and 1872-94. The man most frequently associated with the society's concerts in its earlier history was James Paton Clarke (1808-77), the first British musician in Canada whose name can be found in standard musical reference books. Clarke was born in Scotland, and at the age of 21 led the psalmody in St. George's Church in Glasgow. When he came to Canada, he settled at first as a farmer, probably for the lack of a suitable musical position. Clarke had already won a considerable reputation when Dr. McCaul called him to Toronto in 1845, and in that year he collected and edited the *Canadian Church Psalmody*, which included eight anthems and hymns of his own composition. His career in Toronto was a brilliant one. He is said to have become music instructor at King's College in 1845,[4] and two years later he was appointed the second music teacher at an Ontario normal school (in Toronto). He was also the first person in Canada to receive the Bachelor of Music degree (1846), for which he wrote an eight-part anthem, "Arise, O Lord God, Forget Not the Poor," and in 1856 the University of Toronto conferred upon him the first doctoral degree in music awarded in Canada.

A number of Clarke's songs were printed in *The Anglo-American Magazine* during 1852 and 1853, and at the same time there appeared a larger work, *Lays of the Maple Leaf, or Songs of Canada*, made up of a number of songs and choral pieces extolling the beauty of the "fair forest land" and its emblem, the maple leaf. Curiously enough, the main phrase in one of the songs foreshadows "The Maple Leaf Forever":

Soprano.

These pieces have a charming simplicity and are influenced by folk song and the *Magic Flute* rather than the then fashionable drawing-room music.

In 1848 Clarke was appointed organist at St. James (Anglican) Cathedral but after fire destroyed the church he went to St. Michael's (Roman Catholic) Cathedral. He is spoken of as a "conscientious and earnest musician, clever composer, and an able

[4]See Baker's *Biographical Dictionary of Musicians* (4th ed. by N. Slonimsky; New York, 1958) and H. Charlesworth, *More Candid Chronicles* (Toronto, 1928), p. 52.

and successful teacher of the pianoforte. During the later portion of his career he composed a number of chamber trios and quartets of an original and pleasing character. . . ."[5]

Other pre-Confederation organizations in Toronto were as short-lived as those already mentioned, whether because of lack of personnel or public support or because of petty rivalries. These groups included the Toronto Vocal and Musical Society (1851–3), the Metropolitan Choral Society founded in 1858, and, finally, the Musical Union founded in 1861. All these groups introduced good music, especially oratorios. The greatest single event was a complete performance (after twelve weeks of study) of Handel's *The Messiah* on December 17, 1857 by the Sacred Harmonic Choir, in a hall filled to the doors. This is considered to have been the first complete oratorio performance in Upper Canada, but the conductor, John Carter, who came to Toronto in 1856 as organist of St. James Cathedral (1856–78), is said to have conducted an earlier performance in Quebec where he had come in 1854 as organist of the Anglican cathedral. *The Messiah* was repeated in Toronto in 1858. In June of that year, the Rev. G. Onions led a performance of *Judas Maccabeus*, and by coincidence we know the distribution of instruments matched against 160 voices: 20 violins, 2 cellos, 3 double-basses, 3 flutes, 3 clarinets, 2 trumpets, 1 bass horn, a choir of trombones, cymbals, and drum. Some of the players were borrowed from a military band. The Musical Union, founded by Carter, studied such works as *The Creation, Il Trovatore, Martha, Judas Maccabeus* and *The Messiah*. In the mid 1860's musical societies ran into bad times, and for almost a decade Toronto, then a city of about 50,000, was without a concert-giving choral society.

Two persons of great influence in musical circles were the Bavarian Jewish immigrants Abraham (d. 1860) and Samuel Nordheimer (1824–1912). Abraham came to Kingston, then the capital of Canada, in the early 1840's as music teacher to the family of Governor-General Sir Charles Bagot. In Kingston he organized a musical society and with his brother Samuel founded the music business of A. & S. Nordheimer. A few years later the firm moved to Toronto where it rapidly expanded into a prosperous importing house for sheet music and pianos and established a publishing

[5]"Music in Toronto: Reminiscences of the Last Half Century," Toronto *Mail*, Dec. 21, 1878.

activity of its own. It operated on a scale larger than any other music supply house in the country, having opened a Montreal branch in the period under discussion and, later, agencies or branches in many other cities. In the late 1880's, the Nordheimers set up their own piano factory.

Undoubtedly the Nordheimers' business activity paved the way for Toronto's position as the centre of music publishing in Canada. In addition, their contributions to Canadian musical history included such diversified activities as opening concert halls in Toronto and Montreal and inducing many artists to perform or settle in Canada. Samuel acted as president of the Philharmonic Society and supported many other musical enterprises. He became a prominent banker and financier as well as German consul for Ontario, while Abraham's son Albert (d. 1938), who was trained as a musician, for many years chaired the music committee of St. James Cathedral and acted as Dutch Consul.

HAMILTON: By the middle of the century Hamilton had become the second largest town in the province of Upper Canada with a population of 10,000. An important event in the early musical history of this industrial centre was the concert on March 13, 1855. The orchestra played an overture and Haydn's "Surprise" Symphony (or parts of it) under a man with the distinguished-sounding name of St. George B. Crozier, Baron Le Poer.[6] Hamilton matched Toronto's musical pace in the performance of Haydn's *Creation* on May 26, 1858, by the Hamilton Philharmonic Society with a chorus of ninety and an orchestra of twenty-five under Edward Hilton. Two years later *The Seasons* was performed, and for more than a decade this society continued to present oratorios. Among other societies in Hamilton in this period was the Cecilian Glee Club which flourished from about 1860 to 1866.

The vitality of musical life in Hamilton is demonstrated by the following figures: in 1858, when the population had reached nearly 20,000, there were two piano dealers, two music stores (also selling pianos), five music teachers and one organ-builder—certainly not a bad showing for a town of its size.

[6]To this another title may be added "Inspector of Revenue." Crozier must have given valuable services to music, for in 1872 he received a Doctor of Music degree from Victoria University in Cobourg, Ontario. He was the third person to receive the degree from a Canadian university.

VISITING ARTISTS: The musical activities so far described were those of resident amateurs and professional musicians. However, there were occasions when Canadians could hear a visiting artist of real genius. On October 21 and 23, 1851—before there was a railway to bring her—Jenny Lind sang in St. Lawrence Hall, Toronto, to a thousand people, each of whom paid at least $3.00 admission. The artist enraptured her audience, not only by her singing, but also by her charm and skilful rapport. Thus the review in the Toronto *Globe* was concerned with everything except the music. In the eloquent style characteristic of old newspapers the critic reported:

. . . [And] surpassing, perhaps, the desire to hear the music, was the eagerness to see a person who has made such generous use of the gift committed to her, and dealt out her charities with so princely a hand. . . . She is, indeed, a noble woman. And wonderful as her voice undoubtedly is, the magic, we suspect, is with herself.[7]

Here follows the programme of Miss Lind's farewell concert on October 23:[8]

Part I

Fantasia on themes from *La Sonnambula* by Bellini, arranged by Belletti	clarinet solo	Signor E. Belletti
Romanza, "Una furtiva lagrima," from *L'Elisir d'amore* by Donzietti	voice	Signor Salvi
Prayer, "Und ob die Wolke," from *Der Freischütz* by Weber	voice	Md'lle Lind
Fantasia on themes from *Masaniello* by Auber, arranged by Thalberg	pianoforte	Mr. Otto Goldschmidt
Recitativo, "Ah mie fedeli," and aria "Ma la sola," from *Beatrice di Tenda* by Bellini	voice	Md'lle Lind

Part II

Fantasia, "Le Tremolo," Caprice on a theme by Beethoven by De Bériot	violin	Mr. Joseph Burke

[7]Toronto *Globe*, Oct. 23, 1851.
[8]After Mrs. Raymond Maude, *The Life of Jenny Lind* (London, 1926), p. 169.

Cavatina, "Raimbaut," from *Robert le diable* by Meyerbeer	voice	Md'lle Lind
Reverie by Goldschmidt	piano forte	Mr. Otto Goldschmidt
The Bird Song by Taubert	voice	Md'lle Lind
Cavatina, "In terra ci divisera," from *Illustri Rivali* by Mercadante	voice	Signor Salvi
John Anderson My Jo', Scotch Ballad	voice	Md'lle Lind
The Echo Song, Norwegian Melody	voice	Md'lle Lind

Other world-famous artists who appeared in the fifties or early sixties included Henriette Sontag, a German soprano who sang in Toronto on January 2, 1854, the year of her death; Sigismund Thalberg, the famous "long-fingered" pianist, once the rival of Liszt, who played operatic fantasias and other virtuoso pieces in Quebec on June 30 and July 1, 1857, and also in Toronto; Ole Bull (1853, 1857); Henri Vieuxtemps (*ca.* 1858); young Adelina Patti, who sang in 1855 and 1860, and Louis Gottschalk, an American pianist who created a great stir in Quebec City in 1862. These visits were made easier by the invention of the railway and the steamship, but the chief factor was the country's proximity to the United States, which had long since surpassed Canada in population as well as commercial and cultural development. It is in this period that we can find the roots of the star-worship characteristic of North American audiences. The belief that a foreign artist is necessarily greater than a native one was often justified at that time. Unfortunately, it persisted as a myth to a much later day, when Canadian artists ranked with the best of other countries.

Touring ensembles also made side-trips to Canada and their exemplary performances became an inspiration for Canadian groups. The Germanians, an orchestra of Berliners who had gone to the United States in 1848, gave hundreds of concerts in the United States in a short span of years. This excellent group was a strong factor in the growth of American culture. At least two Canadian tours were arranged. It is said that the Germanians won their first laurels on their trip to Canada in 1850:

The Canadian tour was triumphant. Nine concerts were given in the Theatre Royale, Montreal, within two weeks, as wives of English officers vied with Canadian ladies in throwing bouquets which, between the blossoms, often contained billets-doux poetically expressing those feelings that romantic melodies aroused in their hearts. So extensive was the flower-bestowing that baskets were needed to transport bouquets at the close of the concerts. The players were favorites socially as well as musically; officers of the XIX Regiment entertained them, and a large picnic commemorated their departure. Quebec, Kingston, and Toronto were visited. In the latter city Parliament was in session; hence five concerts were attended by Lord Elgin and his family.[9]

A French singing group, the Montagnards Basques, toured the province of Quebec in 1856. They found an echo in the formation of several local choirs, foremost among them La Société Musicale des Montagnards Canadiens, of Montreal, who appeared before the public in the early 1860's. The memory lingered on and bore late fruit in La Chorale des Montagnards (ca. 1885–ca. 1891) under Arthur Renaud. This group of 25 singers made a point of dressing in a picturesque French peasant costume: grey socks, culottes and jackets, and a grey felt hat with a red feather.

OPERA: Another type of entertainment which appeared in the mid-nineteenth century grew largely outide the musical societies. The oldest report of opera performance, after Quesnel's Colas et Colinette and Grétry's Richard Cœur de Lion, comes from Quebec. Here, in May 1846 the Société des Amateurs Canadiens performed Le Devin du Village,[10] the little opera written by the philosopher-musician Jean-Jacques Rousseau nearly a hundred years earlier. Like the composer, the conductor of this memorable performance was of Swiss birth; in fact, Napoléon Aubin (1802–90) served as Swiss Consul in Montreal.[11]

Then as now, the performance of opera was a hazardous undertaking, and usually music lovers had to content themselves with excerpts. A number of "opera meetings" were held by the Toronto Vocal and Musical Society in the early 1850's. In Montreal, Jean-Baptiste Labelle organized a "Grand Concert Opératique" at the

[9]H. Earle Johnson, "The Germania Musical Society," Musical Quarterly (Jan. 1953). See also p. 109.

[10]Alfred Loewenberg, Annals of Opera, 1597–1940 (2nd ed.; Geneva, 1955). Loewenberg gives the date as May 26, LeVasseur as May 16.

[11]He was also a journalist and newspaper editor, but perhaps his most important achievement lay in a different field altogether: he was the organizer of gas-light inspection for confederated Canada!

Mechanics Hall in November 1857. Amateurs and professionals participated in instrumental and vocal selections from the works of Bellini, Donizetti, Adam, Schubert, Meyerbeer and others.

In the history of Toronto, the year 1853 marks the beginning of opera. "Here is something good at last! The WHOLE OF THE FIRST ACT OF LUCRETIA BORGIA!" exclaimed the February issue of the *Anglo-American Magazine*. The performance was given by local singers and chorus with piano accompaniment under the direction of Mr. R. G. Paige. Toronto's first operatic venture was reviewed in the same periodical's March issue (p. 334):

... the opening overture was very good, and seemed to give general satisfaction. With the opening part of the opera from "Bella Venezia" to "Vieni! la danza invitaci," we were not satisfied; we did not think that Mr. Strathey [Strathy] seemed at home in his duties, and although he is most undoubtedly a thorough musician, we are afraid that he rather threw the first chorus into confusion from his want of experience as an accompanyist and director. The Brindisi, however, made amends, and we can with justice assure the singers that we have heard it at the Broadway opera house, with Bishop as a prima donna, and Bochsa as conductor, when it was neither as correctly nor as spiritedly executed. Any little defects were, however, speedily forgotten when the first notes of Lucrezia's opening cavatina, "Com' è bello, quale incanto," were heard.

Torontonians did not have to wait long before they could hear a full-length opera performance. On July 8 of the same year the Artists' Association Italian Opera Co. with a "magnificent orchestra" gave a performance of Bellini's *Norma* at the Royal Lyceum. The conductor was Luigi Arditi, a well-known conductor of opera and composer of the still popular waltz-song "Il Bacio". Admission charges ranged from 2s. 6d. to 7s. 6d. The reviewer of the *Anglo-American Magazine* was very pleased with the performance (Aug. 1853, p. 222): "Thanks to Mr. Nickinson, Torontonians have been gratified with a sketch of an Italian Opera. A very good sketch it was, and one from which they could realize all the beauties of the composer." He noted that the singers and the orchestra sounded too loud in the small hall, and after praising the choruses he summed up: "We shall not attempt to criticise, *that an Entire Opera has been performed in Toronto is a great fact*, and one worthy of a corner in a note-book" (my italics). The review ends with a delicious little sermon:

A word now to the audience: Frequent applauding may evince much good nature, but at the same time it has the sure effect of making artists careless, as it must convince them that the applauders do not really know what or why they are applauding. Frequent interruptions are particularly inadmissible in an Opera, and we were as much amused at the first chorus girl being applauded, instead of Norma, as we were disgusted with the interruption in the midst of the "Deh! con te."

According to F. E. Dixon, a Torontonian who wrote his musical memoirs many years later, "three operas were performed, Norma, Lucia and Lucrezia and I went to all three."[12] His memory must have deceived him, for according to a contemporary report, the troupe stayed in Toronto for only one night.[13] The same report, however, stated that the "Montreal papers speak of them [the Italian Opera Co.] with enthusiasm," and elsewhere it is said, in July 1853, that "the Quebeckers and Montrealers have had an opera troupe already amongst them."[14] Printed programmes of these performances have not been discovered so far.

In 1855 Dessane produced the first act of Boieldieu's *Dame Blanche* in Quebec, employing local soloists. As the plot is laid in Scotland it was thought proper to dress not only the singers but also the instrumental players in Scottish Highland costumes.

The following are a few historic opera performances of the 1860's: the first Toronto performance of *Der Freischütz* on May 14, 1860, by the visiting Cooper Opera Troupe; the *Barber of Seville* in Quebec on June 10, 1864; the concert performance of *Il Trovatore* in 1866 under Toronto's John Carter; and Adélard J. Boucher's presentation of nine numbers each from *La Somnambula* and *The Bohemian Girl* in 1867.

This brief survey shows that full-scale performances of grand opera were yet rarely achieved. Of costumes, stage scenery, orchestra, entirety, one or more had to be compromised in most performances. The major share of opera was provided by travelling

[12]F. E. Dixon, "Music in Toronto: As It was in the Days That are Gone Forever," *Daily Mail & Empire*, Nov. 7, 1896.
[13]*Mackenzie's Weekly Message*, July 7, 1853.
[14]*Anglo-American Magazine* (July 1853).

companies from outside Canada. On the other hand, we cannot show enough admiration for those rare local attempts that were made in this most demanding branch of music; they are expressions of the Canadian pioneer spirit at its best.

CONCERTS: THEIR PROBLEMS AND PROGRAMME CONTENT: We have surveyed musical activities and personalities at the period when concerts first became part and parcel of urban life in Canada. To complete the description, we must tell more about the formidable problems of these pioneer enterprises and the type of music they cultivated.

First of all, let us stress how difficult it was to arrange even a single concert, let alone carry on a musical society for a number of years. Conductors often had to work with completely untrained singers and, for a concert, neighbouring towns and villages (sometimes across the United States border) had to be scoured to discover performers on missing instruments. These players would arrive, with luck, in time for the dress rehearsal. Sometimes no church or public hall was available and concerts had to be held in dance rooms, skating rinks, and other makeshift places. Small-town gossip and personal envy could make work unpleasant for a leader or disrupt an entire organization. Official endowment being unknown, costs had to be met by admission or subscription fees, and sometimes a conductor or impresario risked and lost his personal savings. On many occasions, however, musicians contributed their services free of charge for the benefit of some charitable purpose. Typical examples were the Promenade Concert in Toronto in 1852, given in aid of Negro fugitives from the United States, and a concert given in 1855 for the benefit of victims of the Crimean War.

Concerts, other than oratorio and opera performances, were not yet specialized into the choral, orchestral, chamber, and solo types that we know today. The majority of musical organizations were choirs; instrumentalists were assembled hurriedly for each concert. Most concerts, in fact, displayed all the musical talent that happened to be available at the moment. A typical concert might feature an augmented church choir, an orchestra of from 15 to 50 players built around the core of a local brass band, the local music teacher performing first on the violin then on the cornet, a talented lady amateur and her daughter attempting an operatic duet, and on rare occasions a famous guest artist. Good performers were scarce and everybody who was willing to face an audience was welcome to have a try. At many concerts amateurs alternated with professionals, making for a very uneven quality of performance.

This unevenness is not always apparent from reading contemporary reviews, "written with a simplicity and naïveté, which suggests the efforts of a modern rural paper to do justice to some artistic efforts of the local inhabitants, written probably by the local clergyman's wife or some other lady of cultural pretensions. . . . Something good had to be said of everyone although the compliments at times appeared slightly strained."[15] And so we read about "extremely difficult pieces performed with marked success" or an artist who "played with quiet ease and grace characteristic of that gentleman's performance, and elicited hearty applause from his hearers." These samples from a Montreal newspaper are typical of many written in equally non-commital and florid style.

Even the great visiting artists shared the programme with lesser attractions, a custom not confined to Canada. The pianist Thalberg, for example, shared his Quebec recitals with Mlle Theresa Parodi, Miss Amalia Patti, and Signor Nicola (all singers), Herr Mollenhauer (cellist), and Monsieur Strakosch (conductor). Before the advent of the twentieth century few, if any, concerts in Canada were devoted to the performance of a single artist.

Those concerts that boasted an orchestra included in a typical programme overtures and sometimes symphonic movements. Overtures heard in Canada before 1860 include those to *The Marriage of Figaro*, *La Clemenza di Tito*, *The Magic Flute*, *Prometheus* (judged a "most difficult" work at a Montreal performance), *Leonore* (No. ?), *Coriolanus*, *Der Freischütz*, *La gazza ladra*, *A Midsummer Night's Dream*, *William Tell*, *An Italian in Algiers*, *Semiramide*, and a few others that are now forgotten. A few reputedly complete performances of symphonies have already been mentioned: Haydn's "Surprise" Symphony in Hamilton, his "Toy" Symphony (now attributed to Leopold Mozart), and Mozart's Symphony in G minor in Quebec. Beethoven's First or Second Symphony was played in Toronto in 1854 under James P. Clarke. Excerpts from the "Surprise" Symphony and from Beethoven's First, Second, and even Fifth Symphonies were heard relatively

[15]D. C. Masters, *The Rise of Toronto, 1850–1890* (Toronto, 1947), p. 94.

often. In Toronto the funeral march from Beethoven's "Eroica" was performed in 1855, and in 1852 the Germanians, in their five hundred and twenty-fifth concert on the continent, played the finale of the Fifth. With astute judgment a critic noted that the movement had more massive grandeur than Verdi's overture to *Nabucco* and Rossini's dramatic *Siege of Corinth*, which were also on the programme.

It is doubtful that any of these works (except those played by the Germanians) were presented in their original instrumentation, certain instruments being rare or lacking altogether. Whatever resources were available were employed—and rightly so, if it was thus made possible to introduce a great piece of music. For example, the overture to *A Midsummer Night's Dream* was performed in Toronto by eight hands on the keyboard, that to *La gazza ladra* by twelve!

The remainder of the concert, or indeed entire concerts of a lighter type (Fig. 5), consisted of a hodge-podge of marches, familiar airs, operatic fantasies, instrumental solos, vocal quartets and the like performed in rapid succession. Just as today, the lighter concerts were often called Promenade Concerts. Sensationalism, instrumental stunts and vocal acrobatics were a big part of the attraction, and artists who could perform on several instruments won special admiration. As a young man Calixa Lavallée, for example, played the piano, violin and cornet in the same concert.

It is easy for us to smile at these programmes with their mixture of styles and circus-like array of entertainers, but we must not forget that even in Europe taste sank to a low ebb in the years after Beethoven's death. To mention one instance only, the "Appassionata" Sonata was virtually unknown at public concerts in Vienna and Berlin when Clara Wieck performed it in the late 1830's.[16] Indeed, the hodge-podge programmes may not necessarily indicate lack of taste. The ability of the musically naïve to enjoy a popular tune as much as a symphony when the two are juxtaposed may really be a virtue, and perhaps we should regret that modern audiences, sophisticated and snobbish by comparison, have lost this ability.

Almost every programme in Canada did contain a good share of music by Handel, Haydn and Mozart, and even though the operatic

[16]John N. Burk, *Clara Schumann* (New York, 1940), pp. 119, 147.

FRENCH SOCIETY

LES ENFANS DE PARIS.

THE

First Concert

—OF—

THIS SOCIETY

WILL BE GIVEN

In the Victoria Theatre.

FRIDAY EVENING, AUGUST 16th, 1861.

PROGRAMME:

PART I.

1. QUADRILLE—*Ludine*,.................................C. D'ALBERT
2. CHORUS—*Introduction of the Chalet Opera*,.......A. ADAM
3. EXIL ET RETOUR—*Chorus*,..........................MONPOU
   SOLOS BY A YOUNG LADY HONORARY MEMBER AND MR. FELIX.
4. WALSE—"*Mountain Daisy*",.........................C. D'ALBERT
5. SOUVENIRS DE JEUNE AGE—*Preaux Clers*,............HEROLD
   BY A YOUNG LADY HONORARY MEMBER.
6. LES ENFANS DE PARIS—*Patriotic Chorus*,...........A. ADAM

PART II.

7. QUADRILLE—*Italian Campaign*,......................C. D'ALBERT
8. SCENE, CHORUS AND SOLOS—*Chalet Opera*,...........A. ADAM
   BY MRS. SANDNIK AND MR. FELIX.
9. OH! MON FERNAND—*Favorite*,........................DONIZETTI
   BY A YOUNG LADY HONORARY MEMBER.
10. LA FILLE DE LA NUIT—*Chorus*,.....................JOURDAIN
11. LE POSTILLON DE BESANÇIN—*Chansonnette*,..........BERAT
    BY MR. FELIX.
12. GARIBALDI GALOP,..................................C. D'ALBERT

CONDUCTOR, - - - - - - - - M. G. SANDNIK.

The Concert will commence at half-past Eight o'clock, precisely.

music of Bellini, Rossini and Donizetti ruled the day, Beethoven, Mendelssohn and Weber were not at all unknown. Oratorio became so familiar to audiences that in 1866 a Montreal critic uttered a sigh of relief when for once a concert of sacred music presented something other than *The Messiah*, *The Creation* and the (spurious) Twelfth Mass of Mozart.[17] Nor should we forget that most of the music heard was new to the audience, except to a few recent immigrants of middle-class background. Masterworks could best be introduced alongside the lighter fare. Torrington did not hesitate to play operatic medleys on his church organ, but Bach's "St. Anne" Fugue was also in his repertory. It is no mean testimony to this pioneer's courage and to the taste of his audience that he gave the opening performance on a new organ in Montreal in 1861 with a programme consisting of works by Mozart, Mendelssohn, Cherubini, Haydn and Handel.

In these general remarks about concert programmes we have not distinguished between the various regions of Canada. One may well ask whether any characteristic differences in taste between the English and French Canadians can be detected at this early stage. There are indeed signs of the British love of oratorio and choral singing and of the French inclination towards opera and song; yet Toronto concerts were dominated by operatic music, whereas oratorio was frequently heard in predominantly French Montreal. Of greater significance is the distinction in musical temperament noted by a neutral observer, the German geographer Johann Georg Kohl, who visited Canada and the northern United States in the 1850's. He wrote from Buffalo:

Wir hatten einen jungen, sehr liebenswürdigen französischen Cana-dier, einen ganz ausgezeichneten Pianospieler bei uns. . . . Er spielte so vortrefflich, so voll Feuer, so rauschend, so energisch. . . . die Amerikaner wie die Engländer lieben in der Musik nicht das energische und laute, weit mehr das zarte und stille—wenn auch falsche Genre.[18]

[17] Review of concert of sacred music by St. James Street Methodist Choir, Montreal *Gazette*, March 8, 1866.

[18] Johann Georg Kohl, *Reisen in Canada* . . . (Stuttgart, 1856), pp. 456–7 (published in English in 2 volumes as *Travels in Canada*, trans. Mrs. Percy Sin-nott, London, 1861). Since the English version does not give an accurate transla-

FIGURE 5. An early concert programme from Victoria, B.C. From Provincial Archives, B.C.

MUSIC IN THE HOME AND MUSIC AS A CAREER: Although concerts were well attended, cultivation of serious music in the home was far from universal. Of those well-to-do people who owned a piano or parlour organ few took its study seriously. They liked to play "pretty pieces" but would not take the time for intensive study. Playing an instrument was admitted as a pleasant pastime and a definite asset for marriageable daughters—on the same plane as baking or embroidery. A musical career was generally discouraged and frowned upon. When Emma Lajeunesse left North America to study in Europe, an attempt to raise funds for her through a concert or by some other means resulted in failure. In the singer's words:

The French-Canadians . . . had the old-world traditional misgiving of a public career, and especially that dislike for any one belonging to them to go on the stage itself, a feeling which was then very much still alive in Canada, although the idea was already beginning to die out in other countries. Consequently all help, as they then honestly thought in my best interests, was witheld from me in that quarter.[19]

This attitude did not prevent Canadians from giving the singer a most royal welcome when she visited her native country decades later as the world-famous Mme Albani!

MUSIC EDUCATION: Most of those talented musicians, such as Emma Lajeunesse, who did have the courage to pursue a musical career, had to seek instruction abroad. In Canada the facilities for even elementary musical education were very slight. Private teachers were few and for a beginner it was hard to distinguish an expert from a quack. Elementary schools, with a few exceptions, offered no systematic training in music.[20]

In the 1840's, however, music began to assume a regular place in the education of the middle classes, and music teachers were engaged by many of the "higher ladies academies." The Adelaide

tion of this passage I have retranslated it as follows: "We had a young, very amiable French Canadian with us, a quite extraordinary piano player. . . . He played so excellently, so full of fire, so brilliantly, so energetically. . . . the Americans, like the English, do not love in music the energetic and noisy, far more the tender and subdued, even though false *genre*."

[19]Emma Albani, *Forty Years of Song* (London, 1911), p. 173.

[20]For one of the exceptions see A. P. Haig, "Henry Frost, Pioneer," *Canadian Music Journal*, II (Winter 1958), p. 35.

Ladies' Academy in Toronto, Misses Dunn's school for ladies in Cobourg, and the Burlington Academy in Hamilton offered instruction in piano, harp, guitar, and vocal music. In Sackville, N.B., music was taught from 1854, when a Ladies' College was established at Mount Allison. In the far west St. Ann's Academy, founded in New Westminster, B.C., in 1865, provided thorough training in the fundamentals of piano playing. In the early seventies a sixteen-year-old girl performed Beethoven's "Pathétique" Sonata, a testimony to the appreciation of good music that was fostered there.

In Toronto's Upper Canada College for boys, singing and instrumental music were optional subjects as early as 1847. The Quebec Seminary had music on its curriculum even before then. In the boarding school of that city's Hôpital Général, girls were taught music for several decades prior to 1857 by the organists of Quebec Basilica. From that year until the closing of the school in 1868, the nuns of this institution took charge of music lessons.

The first university to pay attention to music was King's College of Toronto. We have already mentioned the report that James P. Clarke became music instructor there in 1845. However, the university calendars of the time do not list his name. On the other hand, calendars of Trinity University of Toronto list George Strathy as Professor of Music from 1855 on. The University of Toronto gave Clarke a Doctor of Music degree in 1856; Trinity followed suit and bestowed one on Strathy in 1858.

MUSIC PUBLISHING: Progress in music education paved the way for a modest activity in music publishing. Previously the needs of the few people skilled in instrumental playing or sight singing were supplied by sheet music and books imported from London, Edinburgh, Paris, or Boston, or by ruled manuscript books in which the individual music-maker wrote down his favourite tunes. By the middle of the century, private schools and music teachers turned out sufficient numbers of pupils skilled in reading and performing music to encourage music dealers to venture into the local production of sheet music.

Strictly speaking, this was not the beginning of music publishing in Canada. For fifty years, collections of religious music, instruction books and song books had been published. A few of the earliest music books of historical significance have already been described. Since no bibliography exists on this subject, a brief checklist of all known books containing music published in Canada before 1850 has been given in the Appendix (p. 273).

Individual pieces of music were first printed as part or appendix of literary journals. The Montreal *Literary Garland* printed songs, waltzes, galops and quadrilles in 1839–40 and after 1846, much of the material being supplied by W. H. Warren; the Montreal newspaper *La Revue canadienne* issued a monthly *Album littéraire et musical*, beginning in June 1846; the Quebec *Le Ménestrel* of 1844–5 contains several pieces by Charles Sauvageau, and a waltz by Johann Strauss; in Toronto the *Anglo-American Magazine* printed a number of pieces by James P. Clarke and others in 1852–3. The music sections of these magazines were very much alike: one, two, or sometimes three pieces per issue, the music consisting of songs, dances, marches, and other short piano pieces by Canadian or foreign composers. It was carefully chosen to appeal to a wide public and thus gives an idea of the "pretty pieces" that people liked to hear.

Publishing of separate pieces of sheet music came into its own about 1850. From a bibliographical point of view, this music can be divided into three main types: music printed in the United States and associated with Canada by virtue of a dealer's imprint, a title, or a dedication; music, originally published abroad and reprinted in Canada; and finally, the genuine home-grown product, music written, printed, and published in Canada. The first type is characteristic of the earliest period, but the second grew to be the largest; it comprised the fashionable dance music of the day, popular songs, and operatic excerpts, all by foreign composers. These reprints were issued in such series as Nordheimer's "Collection of Popular Songs and Ballads." The purely Canadian publications were in the minority. Their number until Confederation may be estimated at one hundred.

The firms pioneering in this field were not exclusively music publishers but usually importers and dealers in instruments and sheet music of other publishers. The names most frequently met with are Adélard J. Boucher, J. W. Herbert, John Lovell (a printer and book publisher), Henry Prince, and Eusèbe Sénecal in Montreal; L. Brousseau in Quebec; F. W. Clear in Saint John, N.B.;

and A. & S. Nordheimer (see p. 100) in Toronto, with branches in other cities.

INSTRUMENT-BUILDING: In the early decades of the century musical instruments were usually imported from England or other European countries. The beginning of instrument-building in Canada, according to the present state of research, can be dated fairly closely to about 1820. At first there were a few modest workshops, but by the time of Confederation piano- and organ-making had developed into lively industries. There were several good reasons for this growth, apart from the increase of population and thus of musical activities. Importing instruments was costly and difficult, and the frequency of church fires made the quick repair or replacement of organs desirable. Furthermore the Canadian climate was too severe for many European instruments. On the other hand, wood was in ample supply in Canada, and among the immigrants, especially those from Germany and the United States, were a number of skilled instrument-makers eager to turn their craft to good use in the new country.

Organs varied greatly in size and cost. Archdeacon Strachan of Toronto collected subscriptions in 1837 for a £1,000 organ—certainly a large imported instrument—while a "sweet-toned organ with four semi-stops and dulciana"[21] of about one-tenth that value provided music in a church at Galt. It was built by the firm of Hager and Vogt in Preston, one of two organ firms in that town about the middle of the century.

We can name only a few of a number of instrument-makers who enjoyed fine reputations in pre-Confederation days.[22] The first man known to have built organs in Canada was not a professional craftsman but a bandmaster, Richard Coates (1778–1868). We have already met him in our description of music at Sharon (see p. 73). A native of Yorkshire and through his mother, a relative of Sir Joshua Reynolds, Coates was trained both as a painter and as a musician and he served as bandmaster in the British army at the Battle of Waterloo. He came to Canada in 1817 and after living in Toronto for over a decade (apparently as a painter, for he is associ-

21[A. W. H. Rose] *The Emigrant Churchman in Canada*, ed. H. Christmas (London, 1849), pp. 183–4.

22For details on organ-building in nineteenth-century French Canada consult Gérard Morisset, *Coup d'œil sur les arts en Nouvelle-France* (Quebec, 1941).

ated with "the early dawn of the fine arts in York"[23]) and acting as music master for the Children of Peace, he turned to farming and also operated a sawmill near Oakville. Being mechanically gifted, Coates built such things as a telescope to watch the boats on Lake Ontario, a "Pulmotor" to rescue people from drowning, and a pleasure yacht. Although he did not establish an organ factory, he is reported to have built at least seven pipe-organs, some barrel-operated and some with keyboard. Three of them are reported to have been built for the Children of Peace, one for St. Jude's Church in Oakville (about 1857), and another for his own use, which is still owned by one of his descendants.[24]

There were also professional organ-builders in Upper Canada, a number being of German origin. It was in Montreal, however, that organ-building was first established as an industry. Jean-Baptiste Jacotel, an organ-builder from Paris, established himself in Montreal in 1821 but concentrated on repair work. After his death his son Jean-Baptiste and his son-in-law Auguste Fay continued the business, importing most of their organs from Europe or the United States. In later years the two men separated. Jacotel continued to work until 1845, Fay until 1864. A more productive firm was that of Samuel R. Warren from Boston. Established in Montreal from 1836, Warren had built some 350 organs by 1869, ranging from small chapel organs with a few solo stops to large church organs known for their "orchestral" mixtures of stops. Outstanding examples were the organs of Notre Dame Church in Montreal and St. James Cathedral in Toronto. Warren's Quebec-born apprentice Louis Mitchel opened shop in 1861, gaining fame with a number of excellent organs which had been commissioned for Quebec, Ottawa and other Ontario cities, Chicago, and various towns in New England.

Pianos were popularized by such firms as George W. Mead (Montreal), T. D. Hood (Montreal), Laurilliard (Saint John, N.B.), Richard Owen (Quebec), and others. Some of their pianos —varying in size and shape, but usually smaller than the modern upright—can now be seen in Canadian museums. In Halifax H. & J. Philips from Hamburg, built their first piano about 1846 for

[23]Henry Scadding, *Toronto of Old* (Toronto, 1873), p. 336.
[24]Much of the information on Coates was supplied by his great-grandson, Mr. Ernest G. Lusty of Rodney, Ontario. See also H. C. Mathews, *Oakville and the Sixteen* (Toronto, 1953).

Lieutenant-Governor Sir John Harvey. The founder of Canada's most widely-known piano firm, Theodore Heintzman (1817–99), was apprenticed in Berlin and New York, where he worked in the same shop as Charles Steinway. He came to Toronto in 1860 and turned out his first piano there by hand in his workshop. In 1866 he moved to larger quarters and shortly after built a new factory and warerooms. The development of Heintzman's firm will be traced in a later chapter.

In the 1860's the leading manufacturer of pianos seems to have been John Fox of Kingston, who employed "in all about one hundred hands" and produced about five hundred instruments a year. Several changes of management occurred, and after 1871 the firm continued its rise under the name of Weber & Co. With Fox and Heintzman, Ontario took the initial lead in piano-building from Quebec province. As agents for Steinway and other piano makers the firm of A. & S. Nordheimer had by Confederation become the largest importer of pianos. Its headquarters were in Toronto but it maintained a number of branches in other cities.

As makers of stringed instruments the Lyonnais family of Quebec achieved wide reputation. Pierre-Olivier Lyonnais (1795–1850) learned their construction in the 1820's from the bandmaster Schott, whose regiment was stationed in Quebec, after an accident had confined him to bed. He produced some eighty violins, violas, and cellos himself. Later, his nephew Joseph Lyonnais and other members of the family continued the craft. Augustin Lavallée (1816–1903), a man of a varied career, was for some years an instrument repairman. After 1852 he began to build stringed instruments at St. Hyacinthe. Together with two of his descendants he is said to have built over one hundred violins. There must have been many other makers of stringed instruments, of amateur or professional standing, but the manufacture of instruments other than organs and pianos never developed into a major industry.

A few statistics may serve to demonstrate the growth of instrument-building. The Montreal Directory of 1843–4 lists 4 piano and organ manufacturers; in 1848 (but also in 1842) there were 6 firms. The 1851–2 census lists for Upper Canada 4 piano manufacturers but no organ-builders, for Lower Canada 13 piano- and 3 organ-builders. Ten years later, the number of piano manufacturers in Upper and Lower Canada had risen to 64, that of organ-builders to 5. One must keep in mind here that the methods of counting may not have been too consistent in various regions and that the numbers may include individual craftsmen as well as business proprietors. While most instruments were made for domestic sale, a modest amount of exporting was also done, amounting to $5,500 in the year 1868.

CONTEMPORARY STATISTICS ON MUSIC: Since we are dealing with statistics, let us finish this chapter with those in the 1851–2 census (the first in Canada) which concern music. For comparison the 1861 figures are added in brackets. In Upper Canada 92 (133) musicians and 19 (10) music sellers were counted, whereas Lower Canada had only 18 (102) musicians and 5 (5) dealers. 25 (41) of the musicians lived in Toronto, 36 (18) in Hamilton, 7 (68) in Montreal, and only 4 (9) in Quebec City. The obvious distortion of this picture must be blamed on inconsistent methods of inquiry. Perhaps varying distinctions were made in each town between professional and part-time, military and civilian, musicians. It is hard to accept as correct figures which state that Hamilton had five times as many musicians as Montreal. Certainly, in the production of native musical talent, French Canada with its older history was far ahead of Upper Canada, where few outstanding musicians were born before the 1860's.

7 / Progress in Eastern Canada

THE BACKGROUND: OBSTACLES AND CHALLENGES: For the Canadian economy as a whole the period from the year of Confederation (1867) to the outbreak of World War I was one of expansion and growing prosperity, interrupted briefly by interludes of depression or crisis. Under its new Dominion status the country (theoretically at least) no longer consisted of three separate sections—the Maritimes, Lower Canada and Upper Canada—but was a united federation of provinces. Political maturity grew through the practice of self-government. With the spanning of the Prairies by railway, homesteaders quickly peopled the empty west. By 1886 uninterrupted rail travel from Halifax to Vancouver was a reality. Attracted not only by the promise of free land but also by the lure of gold and other mineral discoveries, thousands of new settlers came from the older provinces, from the United States, and from the crowded or despotically governed lands of Europe and East Asia. Between 1867 and 1914 Canada's population grew from 3½ to 7½ million. With the development of industry, many of the older towns in the east doubled their population within a few decades and entirely new cities mushroomed throughout the west.

Musically too, this was a period of great progress. The appearance of Canadian-born musicians of rank side by side with the great stream of immigrant musicians, the existence of larger and more stable musical societies, a vigorous concert life, the formation of bands and orchestras, regular visits of opera troupes and occasional productions with local talent, a modest output of composition, the establishment of conservatories and music journals, the development of piano and organ factories, and the propagation of the European standard concert repertoire among a rapidly growing musical public—these were Canada's important musical achievements in the late nineteenth and early twentieth centuries.

As in trade, industry and politics, these developments did not come about without conscious effort, or without meeting resistance. The largest obstacle in the path of musical progress was the utilitarian and commercial outlook of a large section of North American society. Of course, the main problems at this stage of Canadian history stemmed from the need for material and political development rather than that for cultural attainment. Some of the settlers achieved the desired goal of quick prosperity, but for most pioneers the struggle for existence was difficult and absorbing. The very real physical hardships and the practical problems involved in building a new country naturally called forth austere views emphasizing practical talents and skills rather than artistic accomplishment. Material success was the goal. It was not surprising that art was considered the pursuit of idlers and eccentrics by people who were raised in such a thinly populated and isolated country or who came from a working-class or rural environment in Europe. How could such people, talented though they might be by nature, be expected to form a taste for good music when they so rarely had a chance to listen to the performance of great artists or to see the spectacle of opera?

As has been pointed out earlier, opposition to art was also nourished, if for different reasons, by some religious sects who sternly objected to worldly music-making and restricted church music to a minimum. However, this attitude was far from general.

The very formidable hurdle music encountered was the lack of financial patronage. Serious music has depended at all times and places on such patronage. In Europe the sponsorship of art had passed in the nineteenth century from the nobility to the middle class and to government at its local or national level. In Canada, although there were instances of wealthy businessmen or dignitaries sponsoring the studies of a promising young artist, giving money for the construction of a concert hall, or underwriting the deficit incurred by a symphony orchestra or opera company (see the following chapters), private or institutional patronage remained an isolated phenomenon. Prior to the establishment of the Canada

Council in 1957 governments—municipal, provincial or federal—have rarely taken up the administrative or financial support of the arts to an adequate degree (although the province of Quebec in more recent years has been making considerable material contributions to musical education and performance).

The rising urban middle class did create a demand for entertainment and thus encouraged the formation of large-scale musical enterprises. Paradoxically, at the same time it retarded the growth of these enterprises by its unwillingness to subsidize them sufficiently. Many orchestral and choral societies, musical periodicals and schools were launched with great *éclat*, only to fail from lack of financial support. The collapse of organizations, of course, was sometimes due to inner weakness, such as poor leadership or premature ambition, but generally speaking music would have made more rapid progress had official and private sources been available and willing to underwrite inevitable deficits. A Montreal critic complained in 1868 about the "very indifferent taste evinced for *good music* by the higher social and better educated classes of this city"[1] and his feelings have been echoed by writers in other cities.

Notwithstanding these adverse conditions music advanced surprisingly fast and came to a genuine flowering in the early years of the twentieth century. The years from Confederation to World War I, more than any other period in Canadian history, were the time when the seeds for the love of great music were planted, when musical organizations were established, and when the great classical symphonies and oratorios received their first performances in Canada. Credit for this achievement belongs to individual professional musicians and countless amateurs whose love of music refused to succumb to discouraging conditions.

To understand their achievement more fully, let us consider the situation in which a musician newly arrived from Europe found himself.

> Ils exercent pour moi leur hospitalité;
> De ce je ne me plains. Mais, las! point de musique.[2]

[1] Review of a "Grand Concert of the Montreal Amateur Musical Union," Montreal *Evening Telegraph*, Feb. 5, 1868.
[2] Joseph Quesnel, "Épitre à M. Généreux Labadie" (1804), printed in J. Huston, ed., *Le Répertoire national*, I (Montreal, 1848).

These words of Quesnel describe the impression of many a new-comer to Canada. A European was bound to miss the rich concert life, the stimulating circle of accomplished musicians and sophisticated amateurs in which he had moved. Instead he faced provinciality and philistinism and met few people who shared his tastes. He might react to the new scene in various ways. Impatient with the crudeness of musical life and disappointed with the lack of recognition he might soon depart, probably to seek fortune in the United States where success seemed more easily attainable. This was the course taken even at a much later time not only by many immigrants, but also by native musicians. Other musicians would in despair give up music as a profession and turn to more lucrative trades.

There remained another path: to make the most of existing conditions, sacrificing glamour to the quiet satisfaction of pioneering. The very lack of musical refinement was an inspiration for hard work aimed at stimulating a love of good music in a community where much natural talent was to be found. Canada owes its musical progress to such idealists, rather than to those musicians who were interested merely in cashing in on the rapidly growing demand for music lessons and in catering to sensationalism.

It is well to remind ourselves at this point that music in Canada has no primitive origins (for Eskimo and Indian music has had little influence on the art in general), but is the transplantation of the highly civilized culture of the European homelands, modified by a different environment. How well old-country traditions took root depended largely on the salesmanship of the individual musical pioneer, who had to create his audience and often his job as well. Apart from musical talent his most essential qualification was interest in the people around him, interest in making them like and demand good music. He had to accept rather than despise their low level of taste in order to lift it to a higher one. Musicians like Torrington and R. O. Pelletier did not shrink from playing medleys and light overtures on church organs, while giving the masterpieces of Bach due recognition. A pioneer's work demands a certain degree of compromise as well as endless patience and willingness to do much for little remuneration.

The typical pioneer musician earned his living as a bandmaster or organist-choirmaster and supplemented his income by teaching.

Having gathered around him a circle of pupils and music lovers, he might proceed to organize a musical society, preparing concerts with his group and inviting outstanding artists to visit and participate. The pioneer musician discovered that formation of such organizations—not only choirs and instrumental groups, but also conservatories and periodicals—was the best means of promoting music. In a new country musical organizations play an especially important role. Whereas in Europe musical culture is rooted in the home and proceeds to organized music-making, in a colonial environment the process is generally reversed: as cultivated homes are few, the higher forms of music-making are often introduced into people's lives "from outside," through the efforts of an "organization." Music appreciation among the wide public is the result rather than the cause of musical societies which are initiated by a few professionals and enthusiasts.

Naturally, most musical societies were choirs. It takes less time to become a chorister than to develop instrumental technique. Moreover, choral singing was fostered in the churches and was, as well, a tradition with British immigrants. To establish a well-balanced orchestra presented greater difficulties because of the scarcity both of trained players and of certain instruments, such as French horns, bassoons and violas.

Most pre-Confederation musical organizations were short-lived and both financially and artistically unstable. In the 1860's and 1870's, however, there appeared a number of well-rehearsed societies which flourished for decades and became the focal point of musical life in their respective cities. Montreal's Mendelssohn Choir (founded about 1864) and Philharmonic Society (1877), Toronto's Philharmonic Society (1872), and Quebec's Union Musicale (1866) and Septuor Haydn (1871) are examples. The stability of these groups was partly a result of a larger population, which increased the audience and enabled musical directors to exercise greater choice in the selection of performers. Last but not least, the calibre of musical leaders themselves had grown.

In our description of musical organizations, limited as it will have to be to the more important ones, we shall again proceed by regions, as these were still very much isolated from each other culturally as well as geographically. Even though musical development was strikingly similar in many places, each region was a little musical world in itself, with its own celebrities and institutions. Exchanges of artists between cities were very rare and there were few, if any, nationwide movements or organizations.

QUEBEC: To begin with Canada's oldest centre of musical activity, let us review the Union Musicale of Quebec. On November 22, 1866, this society presented its opening concert, which included Haydn's Imperial Mass and the spurious Twelfth Mass attributed to Mozart. The instrumental players were, as was the custom, mostly borrowed from regimental bands; the chorus, the backbone of the society, was reinforced with singers from other groups. If the income of $43 seems modest, the total figure of $29 for expenses seems almost unbelievably low. Ernest Gagnon (see pp. 178, 180–3) was chosen director of the Union, and Ephrem Dugal (1835–1905), one of the co-founders, acted as president for forty years. Dugal also led the choir of St. Jean-Baptiste Church, where he achieved excellent results.

For many decades the Union Musicale was the chief vehicle for the performance of large-scale works in Quebec. It presented masses and oratorios, especially those by such French masters as Gounod, Dubois and Franck. In 1915 it performed Franck's *Beatitudes*. The secular music of Félicien David also enjoyed great popularity. Two of his symphonic odes were performed as was his opera *La Perle du Brésil*, the last in 1878. The conductor on this occasion was Nazaire LeVasseur (1848–1927), a friend of Antoine Dessane who was actively associated with the Septuor Haydn, the Union Musicale and the Société Ste-Cecile. The Société was founded by Dessane in 1869 and it must have been closely allied with the Union Musicale. It aimed at the performance of good music in concert hall and church and included many of the best musicians and amateurs of Quebec. In his later years LeVasseur, who modestly referred to himself as an amateur, wrote a series of very informative essays on the musical history of Quebec, a history then stretching over three hundred years.[3] His intimate knowledge of Quebec musicians added much colour to his writing. At various places in this book indebtedness to LeVasseur has been acknowledged.

The Union Musicale established its own band in 1870 when it purchased eight brass instruments, but it continued to borrow

[3]N. LeVasseur, "Musique et musiciens à Québec," in *La Musique*, (1919–22).

players from other organizations whenever a performance called for orchestral accompaniment. The nearest approach to an orchestra in Quebec was the Septuor Haydn, an excellent chamber ensemble which continued the tradition started by Frederic Glackemeyer and Judge Sewell and broadened by the Quintette Club and the Septette Club (1857–ca. 1871). The Septuor took great pride in a music library which was based on that of Glackemeyer. Founded in August 1871, the ensemble consisted of string quintet, flute, and piano. In over thirty years of existence it gave hundreds of concerts in Quebec City and throughout the province, performing classical chamber music as well as orchestral music specially arranged for the Septuor. "Cette vaillante société,–la plus artistique, assurément, de toute la Puissance du Canada" was the way the Septuor was described by Boucher & Pratte's *Musical Journal* in February 1882.

The leader of the Septuor during its entire life-span was one of those pioneers whose spirit and devotion have raised music in Canada to the level it enjoys today. Arthur Lavigne (1845–1925), though a native of Montreal, was for many years a leading figure in Quebec's musical life. As a young man Lavigne, together with Adélard J. Boucher, opened a music store in Quebec in 1868, which was to become an important meeting place for musicians. He published many compositions, both his own and those of other composers. He produced the first printed copies of "O Canada." Together with some of his colleagues, he also founded Canada's oldest institution of music education, the Quebec Académie de Musique (see p. 188).

In 1869 Lavigne and three Montreal musicians took part in the giant musical celebration of the National Peace Jubilee in Boston, and in 1872 all but one of the members of the Septuor Haydn went to Boston to the still larger World's Peace Jubilee to join an orchestra of 2,000 and a chorus of 20,000. In order to popularize good music, Lavigne invited to Quebec many artists, some of the finest American orchestras, and even an opera company. A remote echo of the Peace Jubilees was the great festival in Quebec in October 1883, organized by Lavigne. Several bands combined to form a huge orchestra; there were also choirs and guest soloists. The event not only made musical history but marked the first occasion in Quebec when a great hall was lit by electricity.

One of Lavigne's chief ambitions, a Quebec orchestra, was

realized in 1903, when the Septuor Haydn disbanded and the Société Symphonique de Québec was formed with Lavigne as president and Joseph Vézina as conductor. Lavigne's contribution to music was rewarded towards the end of his life by a doctorate and a professorship in the music faculty of Laval University.

The Société Harmonique (see pp. 78, 92) was revived once more in 1870 by Dessane and Frederick W. Mills, an organist, to cultivate vocal and instrumental music. Edouard Glackemeyer, who was by this time one of the oldest music enthusiasts in the city, was its honorary president. His election came exactly half a century after his father had become president of the first Quebec Harmonic Society. The first concert of the new series took place in February 1870.

An outstanding family in the musical life of Quebec has been that of the Gagnons; three of its members have held the post of organist at the Basilica since 1864. The work of the first, Ernest Gagnon, will be discussed later in connection with the collection of folk songs. Ernest's younger brother Gustave (1842-1930) was a pupil of a brother-in-law, Paul Letondal, before continuing his studies in Paris, Leipzig and other European cities. Both brothers taught at the Laval Normal School and the Quebec Seminary. Gustave Gagnon's compositions include a *Marche pontificale* (1886) written for Cardinal Taschereau and piano music in a lighter vein. Since his retirement in 1915 his son Henri (b. 1887) has been organist at the Basilica.

JOSEPH VEZINA AND BAND MUSIC: The discussion of another outstanding Quebec musician touches once again a medium prominent in nineteenth-century Canada—that of band music. When the British regiments and their bands departed after Confederation and were replaced by a Canadian volunteer militia, a crisis arose in band music, for local resources were inadequate to fill the gap immediately. Fortunately some of the bandmasters and players of the British bands stayed in Canada and became the nuclei for the newly created Canadian bands. Soon however, Canadian musicians too became active in organizing and training bands. In Montreal for instance, Edmond Hardy founded L'Harmonie de Montréal in 1874 and conducted it for over half a century, while two years later Ernest Lavigne, brother of Arthur, created the popular Fanfare de la Cité.

In 1867 young Joseph Vézina (1849–1924) joined the military band of the 9th Battalion (Voltigeurs). Only two years later he was appointed bandmaster. Thus by coincidence the musical career of Canada's first great bandmaster began in the very year which marked a turning point in the history of band music. The son of François Vézina, musical director of the St. Jean-Baptiste Society, Joseph grew up in a thoroughly musical atmosphere. Although he went to Europe in 1866, his trip does not seem to have had musical studies as its object, and theory lessons with Calixa Lavallée lasted only for half a year. We can therefore say of Joseph Vézina not only that he was one of the first distinguished musicians who had no training outside Canada, but also that, more uniquely, he was largely self-taught. His favourite instrument was the baritone horn, but he was able to play and teach most wind instruments, and piano and organ. These skills were coupled with a wonderful gift for remembering whole compositions after only one hearing and an inborn talent for conducting.

Like most French-Canadian musicians Vézina worked in the service of the Church, first as organist at St. Patrick's and later as choirmaster at the Basilica. The greatest share of his prodigious energy, however, was given to band music. During the last three decades of the century he organized, trained, and conducted band after band in or near Quebec, and even found time to write many compositions for this medium. His longest associations were with the "B" Battery Band of Quebec Citadel and the Harmonie de Notre-Dame de Beauport.

When in 1903 Vézina assumed leadership of the newly formed Société Symphonique de Québec he was no stranger to orchestral conducting. On many festive occasions—patriotic celebrations, winter carnivals, or visits from royalty and other high personages—Vézina had conducted large instrumental and choral groups, often numbering performers by the hundreds. The most historic of these occasions was St. Jean-Baptiste Day 1880 when massed bands gave the first performance of "O Canada" under Vézina's baton.

Vézina led the Société Symphonique until the year of his death. Vigorous to the last, as late as 1923 he conducted Gounod's *Redemption* with a chorus of 350 and an orchestra of 100. The great services to music of this tireless worker were recognized by Laval University in the bestowal of an honorary doctorate in 1922. It was not, however, until thirty years after his death, that he was listed in a standard work of musical reference, the 1954 edition of *Grove's Dictionary of Music and Musicians*. Vézina's considerable output as a composer will be surveyed in another chapter.

MONTREAL: Numerous musical societies were organized in Montreal during the decade of Confederation. Three English-language groups were noteworthy: the Montreal Oratorio Society, conducted at one time by the German musicologist Gustav Schilling and at another by the organist R. J. Fowler; the Amateur Musical Union, founded in 1868 by Torrington and later conducted by Adélard J. Boucher, and comprising an orchestra of about 20 strings, about 8 wind instruments, a piano, and an organ; and the Mendelssohn Choir, a group with an average of over 100 voices. Of these organizations, only the last enjoyed a long and uninterrupted history. It was founded about 1864 by Joseph Gould, a highly gifted amateur who conducted the choir until it disbanded in 1894, the very year when a choir of the same name was founded in Toronto. The Montreal choir held several concerts each year with the collaboration of guest artists. It specialized in contemporary *a cappella* part-songs but also sang accompanied works, achieving the reputation of being one of the continent's finest amateur choirs.

In the same period, two French-language choral groups were founded by François Benoit: the Société Musicale des Montagnards Canadiens and Les Orphéonistes de Montréal (1864), a male choir of 30 voices. Adélard J. Boucher (1835–1912), the leader of the Amateur Musical Union, also organized Montreal's Société Ste-Cecile (1860). He further contributed to the improvement of musical taste and knowledge by founding his own music-publishing firm and by promoting operatic concerts and editing musical periodicals.

The need for a large choral and orchestral society was supplied by the Philharmonic Society of Montreal (1877–99) which, in the 87 concerts given during its existence, performed a greater number of large-scale works than any contemporary Canadian group. The Philharmonic Society was an outgrowth of a three-day Montreal Musical Festival which was held in 1877 and which included a performance of *The Messiah*. Its first conductor and president was Dr. P. R. McLagan, who was later active in Winnipeg musical circles. From December 1880 until its end the society was led by Guillaume Couture, to whom it owed its high standard and fame.

Having been a choirmaster in his native Montreal from the age of 13, Guillaume Couture (1851–1915) was an experienced musician even before 1873, when his sponsor, the Abbé L. A. Sentenne, p.s.s., enabled him to go to Paris to continue his studies. Couture delighted his teachers by his talent and diligence. In one year of hard work with Théodore Dubois of the Conservatoire he mastered a theory course which normally was completed in two or three years. Romain Bussine, his voice teacher, took him into his home as a boarder and gave him free tuition. Couture's compositions were printed in Paris and performed by the Société Nationale de Musique (founded in 1871 by Saint-Saëns and Bussine to perform works of living French composers). A *lauréat* of the Conservatoire, Couture returned to Montreal in 1875.

During a second visit to Paris (1876–7) the young musician was fortunate in obtaining a position as choirmaster at Ste-Clotilde Church where César Franck was organist. Few Canadians—certainly none in his time—had such close association with famous musicians as did Couture. He was an intimate of Franck and Saint-Saëns, and knew Messager, Massenet and Delibes. Had he chosen to settle in Paris, his name might have become famous in French music. He preferred to return to Montreal, however, where he plunged into varied activities. A career as choirmaster in several major churches culminated in his appointment to that office at St. James Cathedral. He applied himself earnestly to sacred composition, organized operatic, choral and orchestral societies, and wielded a profound influence as a private and classroom teacher of theory and voice. His pupils included such outstanding musicians as Lynnwood Farnam, Achille Fortier, Henri Gagnon, George Alfred Grant-Schaefer, Léo-Pol Morin, and Rodolphe Plamondon.

Couture's greatest talent was choral conducting. Under him the Philharmonic Society developed into a first-class organization numbering over 200 voices. In the earlier years, Couture formed a Société des Symphonistes of nearly 50 instrumentalists for the purpose of accompanying the choir. Maintaining a regular orchestra in those days was difficult, however, and he later preferred to invite orchestras from Boston or New York to take part in the concerts of the Philharmonic Society. The vocal soloists too were usually foreign artists.

The list of works which received their first Montreal or first Canadian performance under Couture reads like a catalogue of great choral-orchestral literature. Highlights of the society's career include Mendelssohn's *Elijah* (1884) and St. *Paul* (1886), Cherubini's Requiem (1885), Schumann's *Paradise and Peri* (1885), Haydn's *Seasons* (1887), Mozart's Requiem (1888), and Beethoven's *Mount of Olives* (1893) and Ninth Symphony (the last under a guest conductor, Emil Mollenhauer, in 1897). The repertoire also included extended choral compositions by Bennett, Berlioz, Bruch, Dubois, Dvorak, Gounod, Handel, Massenet, Saint-Saëns and Sullivan. In Paris, Couture had become an ardent admirer of Wagner and a later visit to Bayreuth strengthened his devotion. The Philharmonic Society presented concert performances of *The Flying Dutchman* (1895) and *Tannhäuser* (1896) with foreign singers in the leading roles and a few Montrealers in minor roles.

It was the taste of the time rather than the difficulty of performing the music that restricted instrumental programming largely to overtures and other short pieces. Nevertheless a number of classical symphonies and concertos were heard, including Beethoven's Sixth Symphony and Schubert's "Unfinished" Symphony. Couture's introduction of so many masterworks in so many styles is one of the greatest single contributions to Canadian culture. The extent and variety of his repertoire has been matched among Canadian conductors only by Sir Ernest MacMillan.

Couture's approach to music has been described as intellectual rather than imaginative or poetic. As a conductor he insisted on rigid musical discipline. Léo-Pol Morin considered him "un éminent musicien, le plus instruit, le plus intelligent, le plus cultivé de son temps. Il fut même le premier grand pédagogue en notre pays."[4] Having adopted the musical standards of Paris, Couture was an outspoken critic of mediocrity and charlatanism. His acrid pen made enemies and involved him more than once in newspaper polemics. But Couture rose far above the negativism of simply attacking musical ignorance. He was able, by applying his many talents, to raise the musical standards of Montreal from a provincial to a cosmopolitan level.[5]

A contribution in a different field of music was made by the violin virtuoso Frantz Jehin-Prume (1839–99), a representative of

[4]Léo-Pol Morin, *Papiers de musique* (Montreal, 1930), p. 79.

[5]Couture's compositions will be discussed in chap. XII together with those of a number of other Montreal musicians engaged in composition.

Frederick Herbert Torrington
(*Collection Miss Molna O'Connor*)

Joseph Quesnel
(*Public Archives of Canada*)

Ernest Gagnon
(*Public Archives of Canada*)

Augustus Stephen Vogt
(*Collection Miss Molna O'Connor*)

Emma Albani

Guillaume Couture
(*Collection Jean Papineau-Couture*)

Calixa Lavallée
(*Public Archives of Canada*)

Pages from *Le Graduel romain*, Canada's first book of music

Programme for the first Toronto performance of *The Messiah* in 1857. (*Collection of Toronto Public Libraries*)

The first organ built by Coates for the Children of Peace at Sharon, Ont.

Concert programme from Saint John, N.B., 1843. (*New Brunswick Museum*)

ST. JOHN SACRED MUSIC SOCIETY.

Concert of Sacred Vocal and Instrumental Music,

by the Saint John Sacred Music Society, at the Hall of the Mechanics' Institute, on *Wednesday* evening 8th February, 1843, commencing at half past 7 o'clock.

PART 1st.

HYMN,	Ode to the New-Year.
Treble Solo and Chorus,	I'll wash my Hands in Innocency,
CHORUS,	Glory to God in the Highest.
TREBLE SOLO,	I hear thee speak of the better land,
ANTHEM,	The Last Day,
Tenor SOLO,	Lonely, how can I lonely be,
Anthem,	The Lord is King.
TRIO,	Onward, onward, men of Heaven.

PART 2d.

Hymn,	The Good Shepherd,
Treble Solo and Chorus,	Peace troubled soul.
Chorus,	Awake the Trumpet's lofty sound.
Bass Solo and Chorus,	Thou art King of Glory O Christ,
Tenor Solo,	In cold misfortune's cheerless day,
Treble Solo and Chorus,	Watchman tell us of the night,
Duett,	Of stars the fairest pledge of day,
Chorus,	Lift up your heads O ye Gates.

☞ During the interval between the First and Second parts of the Concert, a Collection will be taken up in aid of the Funds of the Institution.

N. B.---Mr. Weisbecker will preside at the Piano Forte.

Saint John, February 1, 1843.

Dance at the Château St. Louis in Quebec. Water colour by G. Heriot, 1801.
(*Public Archives of Canada*)

A typical orchestra of the turn-of-the-century period, the Ottawa
Amateur Orchestral Society. (*Public Archives of Canada*)

the famous Belgian school of violinists which included Vieuxtemps, de Bériot and Ysaye. Showing great talent from early childhood, Jehin-Prume received his first lessons from his uncle, the violinist François Prume. At the age of ten his playing at a public concert aroused the admiration of Meyerbeer and Spontini. He completed his studies in violin and theory at the Conservatoire Royal of Brussels with such masters as de Bériot, Léonard and Fétis. In 1855 began a virtuoso career which carried the young violinist through many countries of Europe. His crowded years brought many triumphs and gained him such distinctions as the title "Violinist to the Belgian King."

In 1863 Jehin-Prume was appointed as concertmaster to the Imperial Court of Mexico. After the collapse of the Mexican Empire only two years later he turned northward. The New York *Times* lauded his playing for a sweetness and delicacy such as had never been surpassed in the United States. In New York an invitation reached him to spend a vacation fishing in Canada. It came from Jules Hone (a former student of François Prume), who had recently settled in Montreal. Jehin-Prume accepted, but the vacation turned into a concert tour of Canadian cities from Quebec to London. On the occasion of his triumph in Montreal he met a young singer, Rosita del Vecchio (1848–81), whom he married in 1866. This chain of events explains how the internationally known violinist came to settle in Montreal, a city then far from the main stream of music.

Although the Jehin-Prumes made Montreal their home they gave many recitals throughout the province of Quebec (with their good friend Calixa Lavallée) and in Ontario, Manitoba, and the United States. They also toured Belgium and other European countries. In his later years Jehin-Prume devoted more time to teaching, an occupation which he disliked and in which he was less successful.

Jehin-Prume delighted Canadian audiences with virtuoso playing such as few people had heard before. In 1871 he appeared as both conductor and soloist in six Montreal concerts in which, among other works, he introduced the violin concertos of Beethoven and Mendelssohn, Beethoven's "Pastoral" Symphony, and a Mozart string quartet. Never had so much fine instrumental music been concentrated in a series of programmes in Montreal. In many recitals Jehin-Prume also featured his own compositions for violin and orchestra or piano.

In 1877, Jehin-Prume helped Lavallée in the production of Gounod's *Jeanne d'Arc* and for some time acted as concertmaster of the Montreal Philharmonic Society. Chamber music was also an interest close to his heart. In 1891 or 1892 he founded the Artistic Association, a chamber ensemble of four string players and a pianist. During five seasons this group presented over 30 excellent recitals of chamber music. These activities prove that Jehin-Prume was interested in more than displaying his own virtuosity. He was not only one of the greatest performing artists who have settled in Canada but a vigorous champion of classical orchestral and chamber music.

Several other Montreal musicians, such as R. O. Pelletier and Alexis Contant, will be discussed in the survey of nineteenth- and early twentieth-century composition in chapter XII. Mention should be made here of two musicians whose main contribution was made through teaching. Paul Letondal (1831–94), a blind musician who came from France in 1850, had received a solid grounding in piano technique and musicianship as a pupil of Friedrich Kalkbrenner. He was able to pass on Kalkbrenner's methods to his own pupils, who included Calixa Lavallée, Gustave Gagnon, Salomon Mazurette and Letondal's own son Arthur. The piano was Letondal's chief instrument, but he was an expert also on the organ and cello and in the craft of composition.

Dominique Ducharme (1840–99), pupil in Montreal of Letondal and Sabatier, completed his studies in Paris with Marmontel and Bazin. In Europe he also gained entry to the circles of Saint-Saëns, Liszt, and Rossini. After his return to Montreal he occupied the position of organist at Gésu Church for thirty years. Although he had a distinctively beautiful touch as a pianist, he shunned public appearance and did not develop his performing talent to full capacity. As a teacher, however, he was much respected, and he introduced, under the influence of Paderewski, some of the technical facets of Leschetizky's piano teaching. His best-known pupils were Emiliano Renaud and Alfred Laliberté.

CALIXA LAVALLEE: Nearly all the Montreal and Quebec musicians just surveyed had French names. German musicians, so conspicuous in the early nineteenth century, now rarely occupied positions of musical leadership. Instead immigrants to French

Canada more frequently came from France and Belgium. Even more significant, the proportion of foreign-born musicians decreased. For the first time a whole group of excellent native musicians came into prominence, and Canada even began to export musicians to other countries. No previous decade produced anything resembling the large number of musicians born between 1841 and 1851; few later decades rivalled this period in fecundity. Gustave Gagnon (b. 1841), Romain-Octave Pelletier (1844), Arthur Lavigne (1845), Joseph Vézina (1849), and Guillaume Couture (1851) were active in Montreal or Quebec. Arthur Dumouchel (1841), Salomon Mazurette (1848), and at least one Anglo-Canadian, Samuel Prowse Warren (1841), established fine reputations in the United States; the soprano Emma Lajeunesse (1847) rose to fame in Europe as Mme Albani. The list is completed by a man whose work cannot easily be reviewed under the heading of any one city. Calixa Lavallée (1842–91) was active in both Montreal and Quebec, and the impact of his work was felt far and wide in Canada and the United States.

Many Canadians still picture the composer of "O Canada" as an obscure music teacher who dashed off a patriotic song in a short hour of inspiration. Undoubtedly Lavallée is remembered today chiefly for this single composition. In his lifetime, however, his reputation was not based on "O Canada": on the contrary, he was asked to write a patriotic song precisely because he had already acquired fame as a composer and conductor. Lavallée was considered Canada's "national musician" years before the song was written, and he did not live to witness its subsequent popularity. The detailed obituary devoted to Lavallée by the New York *Times* did not even mention "O Canada." Only after 1908, when the now generally accepted English translation was written, did the song start its sweep over the entire country.

It is significant that Canada's two most famous musicians of the nineteenth century, Calixa Lavallée and Emma Lajeunesse, both had French and British ancestors. On his father's side, Lavallée's ancestors can be traced back for two hundred years in French Canada. His mother was partly of Scottish descent, though unable to speak English. Born in Verchères on December 28, 1842, Calixa spent his youth in an intensely musical atmosphere. His father, Augustin Pâquet dit Lavallée, had originally been a woodcutter and blacksmith. A versatile man, he developed into an instrument repairman, bandleader, and music teacher. During the last period of his life he was also known as a violin-maker (see p. 117). When Calixa was still a boy, the family moved to St.-Hyacinthe, where his father worked with the organ-builder Joseph Casavant and led the band of the Société Philharmonique. Here the boy had a fine chance to try out different instruments. While Augustin remained an amateur performer all his life, he encouraged his sons to take the study of music seriously. Two of them, Joseph and Charles became outstanding trombone- and cornet-players. Calixa showed such remarkable talent that at the age of eleven he played the organ at St.-Hyacinthe Cathedral. Two years later he gave his first piano recital at the Théâtre Royal in Montreal, where his family now made its home.

At that time there lived in Montreal a prosperous butcher by the name of Léon Derome who had an intense love of good music. He sought the company of musicians, sang in choral groups, and was always ready to subsidize artistic endeavour. Young Lavallée's talent impressed him so much that he offered to take the boy into his home to supervise his musical education. Derome remained a true friend and benefactor until the end of Lavallée's life, coming to his aid in times of sickness and misfortune.

The promise evidenced by the youth aroused the enthusiasm of Charles Sabatier and Paul Letondal, who gave him free music lessons. But the regular routine of lessons was not for Calixa; he was eager to learn through the practical experience of performing. Thus the basis of his musical education was broad rather than systematic. He specialized in the piano, but also became an accomplished violinist and a creditable cornetist.

An urge to travel which was never to leave him drove the youth away from home in the late 1850's to try his fortune in the United States. Soon he could proudly report from New Orleans that he had won first place in a competition, at which he performed on all his three instruments. His success won him an engagement as accompanist to the Spanish violinist Olivera on a concert tour to Brazil, the West Indies, and parts of the United States. Back from the tour the young man joined the Northern army during the American Civil War, enrolling as a musician and, later, as bandmaster of a Rhode Island regimental band. Perhaps this decision came because he had seen slavery at work in the South; perhaps he was motivated by the important role that bands then played in stirring up patriotic emotion among the people. Certainly, at this time Lavallée became conscious of the rousing effect of patriotic music.

A little over a year later Lavallée left the army as a lieutenant and returned to Montreal, where he gave piano lessons, took part in charity concerts, and played cornet in a theatre orchestra. *Les Beaux-Arts*, the Montreal music journal, complimented him in 1863 as "[un] musicien intelligent et de talent qui saura bientôt acquérir la confiance de la société montréalaise. . . ." However, Lavallée must have found this field of activity too narrow and his income too meagre, for in 1865 he moved to the United States for the second time. He taught in New Orleans and also undertook tours which took him from California to Massachusetts. About five years later he accepted the position of conductor and artistic director at the New York Grand Opera House. In spite of its name, the tradition of this theatre lay in minstrel shows rather than grand opera. Whatever the opera house lacked, Lavallée found in New York a stimulating environment where he could hear plenty of good music. However, his second American period came to an end in 1872, under peculiarly dramatic circumstances. On the eve of the first performance of Lavallée's three-act comic opera *Lou-Lou*, the owner of the Grand Opera House, the notorious James Fisk, was assassinated on the street and the theatre closed.

Disappointed, the composer returned to Montreal. The warm welcome he received there from friends and fellow musicians quickly raised his spirits. Montrealers found Lavallée a fully matured artist. A magazine article pronounced his musical personality a true expression of French Canada, "essentiellement national et, par conséquent, populaire."[6] In 1873 a group of friends, led by Derome, helped Lavallée to realize an old dream: to extend his formal musical education through study in Paris. Their generosity assured Lavallée a monthly allowance of $80 during his stay abroad. To enable him to pay his return ticket a special concert was organized in Montreal by Adélard J. Boucher with the assistance of over 100 performers. The money was well invested. It enabled Lavallée to study piano and composition under such masters as

[6] L.-O. David, "Calixa Lavallée," *Opinion publique*, March 13, 1873.

Bazin, Boieldieu, Jr., and Marmontel. That the teachers were satisfied with their Canadian student is indicated by the performance of a Lavallée symphony by a Paris orchestra in 1874[7] and by a letter, signed "your teacher and friend, Marmontel":

Je compte sur vous pour transmettre à vos chers compatriotes les conseils que je vous ai donnés et que vous avez su apprécier. Faites aimer et comprendre la belle musique, faites estimer l'art et les artistes, et prouvez aux envieux et aux détracteurs que *vous avez un talent à l'abri de tout reproche*. Je compte sur vous et je ne doute pas une instant de votre honneur et de votre délicatesse.

Votre professeur et ami,
Marmontel.[8]

The musical life of Paris inspired Lavallée to intensify his efforts to foster musical development in Canada and equipped him with the requisite skills to achieve this purpose. He decided that henceforth all his energies must be devoted to the establishment of a national conservatory organized along French and Italian lines and combined with an opera school. He had voiced his firm belief in native musical talent in the newspaper *La Minerve*: "Il y a chez nous le talent et l'intelligence qui ne demandent que l'école."[9] But such a school required governmental or other subsidy. In order to win such support, Lavallée felt that he first had to give a practical demonstration of the potentialities of Canadian talent.

Lavallée's first step was to set up a joint studio with his friends the Jehin-Prumes. This has rightly been called an "embryonic conservatory." Next he began to rehearse Gounod's lyrical drama *Jeanne d'Arc* with an all-Canadian cast including a chorus of about 80 voices. Mme Jehin-Prume was the leading singer. One week of performances took place in Montreal in April 1877; two more weeks followed in November. The venture was a great success, both as an

[7]Eugène Lapierre, *Calixa Lavallée* (rev. and enlarged ed.; Montreal, 1950), p. 165: "Pendant le séjour à Paris, un orchestre symphonique donna, en première audition, une symphonie de C.L. Le chef qui la mit à l'étude et la révéla au public parisien s'appelait Maton. Les recherches poursuivies avant la guerre pour retrouver la partition n'ont rien donné." Lapierre does not say where he read about the performance. An intensive search through Paris concert programmes by Dr. W. Amtmann of Ottawa did not produce a record of this symphony. On page 96, Lapierre has a footnote stating that Maton conducted a symphony by Lavallée in 1874.

[8]Quoted in Lapierre, *Lavallée*, p. 97.

[9]*Ibid.*, p. 214.

exhibition of Canadian talent and, more specifically, as evidence of Lavallée's gift as musical director. Confident of finding support Lavallée travelled to Quebec to lay his plans for a music school and permanent opera company before the Minister of Education and Public Works. His reception was cold, to say the least. Nevertheless, Lavallée persevered by bringing his performance to the provincial capital. In the spring of 1879 he conducted Boieldieu's *La Dame Blanche*, first for two weeks in Montreal and then for several days in Quebec. Again the public responded warmly and newspaper reviews acclaimed him enthusiastically. Official quarters, however, continued to give nothing more than vague promises.

Lavallée now moved to Quebec. He led a vocal quartet, participated in chamber and orchestral music, and held the position of organist-choirmaster at St. Patrick's Church. In spite of his disappointments he still willingly gave his energy to public causes. When the city prepared for the official reception of a new Governor-General, the Marquis of Lorne, and his wife, the Princess Louise, the festival committee encouraged Lavallée to compose a cantata of welcome. He was told to spare neither means nor effort for this grand occasion. Full of enthusiasm he set about writing the music and assembled nearly 300 musicians from the choirs and bands of the city and brought instrumental players from other Canadian and American cities to augment the orchestra. The celebration took place on June 11, 1879. The climax of the cantata, to words by the poet Napoléon Legendre, was a simultaneous rendition of "God Save the Queen," "Vive la canadienne," and "Comin' thro' the Rye"—a feat of contrapuntal composition which created a sensation. The combination of these songs symbolized the friendship between the French and British elements of Canada.[10]

Triumph went hand in hand with humiliation. Lavallée was now considered Canada's greatest musician, yet the festival committee, who had encouraged him in this labour and offered guarantees against expenses, failed to induce the authorities to pay him several hundred dollars to cover the deficit. Public acclaim and words of thanks from Princess Louise were obviously considered reward enough for a musician. "Le gouvernement Joly a reçu la

[10]A similar feat was accomplished in 1953 by Claude Champagne who combined Lavallée's "O Canada" with "God Save the Queen" in his *Paysanna*, an orchestral work commissioned by the C.B.C. for the coronation broadcasts in that year.

Princesse. Mais c'est moi qui ai payé le violon," Lavallée is reported to have exclaimed bitterly.[11]

In the years after Confederation it became apparent that Canada needed a national song which would express the aspirations of the young Dominion and help to weld together the different sections of the population. Anglo-Canadians sang Alexander Muir's "The Maple Leaf Forever" (1867), but because its text refers to the British victory at Quebec in 1759 this song has never been accepted by French Canadians. They sang "Vive la canadienne," "Un Canadien errant," "A la claire fontaine," and other folk songs on patriotic occasions. "Sol canadien, terre chérie" (1829), with words by Isidore Bédard and music by T. F. Molt, was probably the earliest deliberately written "hymne national." Sabatier's "Le Drapeau de carillon," J. B. Labelle's "O Canada, mon pays, mes amours," and Lavigueur's "La Huronne" enjoyed popularity for a long time. Even Sir Arthur Sullivan wrote a Dominion Hymn, "God Bless Our Wide Dominion" (1880), but it never gained wide acceptance. To these songs one could add a long list of national anthems by amateur (and occasionally professional) composers such as are still turned out year after year.

The immediate occasion that gave birth to Lavallée's "O Canada" was the Fête Nationale des Canadiens-français held in Quebec in 1880 concurrently with the St. Jean-Baptiste Day celebrations. In January of that year it was proposed to hold a competition for a national hymn, to be first introduced on St. Jean-Baptiste Day. It soon became apparent that there was not enough time left for a competition. Instead Lieutenant-Governor Theodore Robitaille invited Judge Adolphe B. Routhier to write the words of the hymn and Lavallée to set it to music. Needless to say, Lavallée assumed this task with great eagerness. He prepared a number of sketches for Routhier's "O Canada, terre de nos aïeux" which, evening after evening he submitted to the criticism of Arthur Lavigne, Jehin-Prume and other friends gathered in his home at 22 rue Couillard. Several ideas were rejected; but after a period of a week or two in February or March Lavallée invented a tune which was greeted with unanimous enthusiasm. The story goes that in this exciting moment Lavigne took the copy of the music to rush with it to the Lieutenant-Governor without realizing that Lavallée had not even

[11]Lapierre, Lavallée, p. 169.

signed his name to it. It was April when the music committee which was set up to organize the musical part of the Festival, and which was headed by Ernest Gagnon, presented the formal invitation to Lavallée to submit the national hymn. On St. Jean-Baptiste Day the music was first heard, as the climax of a *Mosaïque sur des airs populaires canadiens* which Joseph Vézina had arranged for the celebration. The performance took place at a "grand banquet national" in the Pavillon des Patineurs in Quebec.[12]

Many attempts at an English translation have been made in subsequent years.[13] The one now chiefly used was written by Judge Robert Stanley Weir in 1908. It should also be pointed out that the song is now rarely heard in the original harmonization with the constantly repeated bass notes in bars 8–13.

Even the writing of "O Canada" did not bring Lavallée closer to the fulfilment of his plans. He must have felt that there was nothing more he could do in Canada. His eager and tireless devotion to the cause of fostering Canadian musical performance and appreciation had been blocked by lack of official co-operation. Nothing lay ahead for him in Canada but the routine of an organist-choirmaster or private music teacher. It must have been a bitter decision when, at the age of 38, he turned again to the United States.

The chronology of events during the following years is not clear. It is known that Lavallée moved to Boston and for some time played piano on a Fall River–New York steamer in order to support his family. However, before long his talent was recognized in Boston, a city where a decade earlier he had been warmly applauded for the performance of a Mendelssohn piano concerto. He was appointed organist and leader of a choir of 100 voices at the Roman Catholic Cathedral. An appointment followed as theory and composition teacher at the Petersilea Conservatory, and during an extended absence of the director, Lavallée was left in charge of this school. An important episode during the early Boston years (the date is variously given as 1881 and 1883) was a tour as accompanist

[12]Blanche Gagnon, in "Notre Chant national," *La Musique* (1920), p. 103 gives a conflicting account of the creation of "O Canada" which relates that Lavallée wrote the melody first and that Ernest Gagnon took it to Judge Routhier, asking him to write words for the music. Lapierre and other scholars discount this story.

[13]The Toronto Public Library has on file some 25 English texts. Some consist of one stanza only, others of the complete poem. Some are translations, others are free adaptations.

and solo pianist with the famous Hungarian soprano Etelka Gerster. Lavallée also increased his activity as composer. Many of his works for band, piano, the stage, and other media were published in Boston. His comic opera *The Widow* was performed in 1882 in Springfield, Illinois, New Orleans, Chicago, and other American cities and met with a warm reception. *Tiq*, subtitled *Settled at Last*, a "melodramatic musical satire" about the Indian question and its solution by the United States government, followed in 1883. Out of gratitude to the city that was so kind to him, Lavallée dedicated a symphony for orchestra and chorus to Boston. No trace of this work has been found.

In short, as church musician, teacher, performer, and composer the Canadian exile found manifold employment for his talents and much of the recognition he had missed at home. In response, he now identified himself with American music, just as he had formerly made the cause of Canadian music his own. American composers could not have found a more enthusiastic champion of their music than this Canadian. As a member of the programme committee of the (U.S.) Music Teachers National Association, he created a sensation in music circles: he organized for the eighth annual M.T.N.A. meeting in Cleveland a concert of exclusively American music—generally considered the first of its kind. It took place on July 3, 1884, with a group of singers and instrumentalists; Lavallée presided at the piano. Such well-known composers as Foote and Chadwick were represented on the programme. The concert was only the first of several of its kind organized by Lavallée.

For the term of 1887 Lavallée was elected president of the M.T.N.A. Among American musicians this was considered an extremely high honour. In January 1888 Lavallée represented the organization at the third annual conference of the National Society of Professional Musicians, an educational conference in London. One of his tasks was to impress the fact of North American musical progress upon English musicians, a progress which was then not widely enough appreciated. He also introduced American compositions to England, but declined to submit one of his own to the Birmingham Triennial Festival, declaring that he was a native of Canada and not an American composer. He did write one *pièce d'occasion* for England, an *American March*. Before his departure he was honoured at a special dinner given by the Lord Mayor of London.

On his return to Boston he paid a brief visit to Montreal—the last as it turned out. His health, long frail, became worse. After a lengthy illness, during which he was once more visited by his life-long friend Léon Derome, he died in Boston on January 21, 1891. Sir Adolphe Routhier has stated that he died "in poverty bordering on wretchedness."[14] Surely this condition had come about because his failing health had greatly reduced Lavallée's earning capacity and not because he lacked recognition during the last years of his life.

Over forty years passed before Lavallée's body was transferred to his native country. On July 30, 1933, it was placed in Montreal's Church of Notre Dame. From the same year dates a revival of interest in the man and his music. The first sign of this renewed interest was an all-Lavallée concert given in Montreal on July 13 by the Canadian Grenadier Guards Band under Captain J. J. Gagnier. In August, the music journal Le Passe-Temps produced a special issue on Lavallée. Above all, our knowledge of Lavallée has been enriched by the scholarly fervour of Dr. Eugène Lapierre, whose biography of our "musicien national du Canada" was first published in 1936. Lapierre assembled the documents on Lavallée's life, traced many of his forgotten compositions, and fostered their performance.

The importance of Lavallée's work in Canada clearly lies in attitude and intention rather than achievement. We must agree with D. J. Logan's statement that "others preceded him and were more effective than he as a formative force in promoting musical education and taste in Canada."[15] Lavallée's direct influence on Canadian musical life, as a leader of societies or as a teacher, was relatively small. His plans for a conservatory and opera company were not realized. It is idle to speculate what their fulfilment would have meant for Canadian music; certainly education and performance would have taken great strides. Lavallée's hopes for government support of music may have been naïve and idealistic in the Canada of 1880; but his clear recognition of the needs of Canadian

14The [Canadian] Home Journal (Dec. 1907).
15D. J. Logan, "Canadian Creative Composers," in Canadian Magazine, XLI (1913), 489.

music, and the subsequent identification of his personal career with these needs denotes greatness. He always put public service before personal success and found the highest satisfaction in creative work.

This idealism is the keynote of a personality which has been variously described as enterprising, restless, generous, and whimsical. A man who so often moved from place to place, who was active now as choirmaster and conductor, now as teacher and pianist, and who was ever eager to throw himself with full energy into some new scheme—such a man might well be regarded as restless and adventurous. Yet was such a life not dictated by circumstance rather than by character? Was it not the inescapable life of a Canadian of that period who sought to employ his rich talent to the fullest extent?

Accusations of Bohemianism and disorganized working are refuted by the following quotation:

The many readers of this account [biographical sketch in Freund's *Music and Drama,* 1889] were probably surprised to learn what a busy, serious, and artistic life this accomplished musician had led; for he was a man of original thought and progressive methods—a great deal more of a man than the musician who merely passes his life in the old grooves of mind and action content with winning for himself a local reputation and the means of subsistence.[16]

Strange though it appears, we have to accept the fact that this consciously Canadian musician, the composer of "O Canada," was able to identify himself with equal enthusiasm with the musical hopes and aspirations of the United States. His patriotism was not narrow; he felt himself a North American citizen in the widest sense. But in spite of the recurring pattern in his life—disappointed hopes in Canada followed by success south of the border—he kept close ties with Canada to the last. Only a year before his death he became collaborator on a new Montreal journal, *Le Canada artistique.* He also kept in close touch with French Canadians in New England: "His patriotism, too, was shown in his relations to the French-Canadian organizations of Fall River and other cities. He was in a sense their prophet, and his relations with all their leaders were very intimate."[17]

Lavallée was one of the most versatile of all Canadian musicians.

[16]From obituary in New York *Times,* Jan. 31, 1891.
[17]*Ibid.*

He was equally adept at light and serious, secular and sacred, music; his compositions embrace every *genre* of music from song to orchestral music. His wide practical experience as a performer on different instruments stood him in good stead as composer, teacher, and conductor. "As a pianist he ranks among the foremost in the country. His execution is brilliant, facile, graceful and clear; his *technique* wonderful, and his *répertoire* extensive."[18]

Coupled with his purely musical gifts was an administrative talent which would have been equal to the task of carrying out his Canadian dreams and which did find employment in the United States:

By instinct he was a man of administrative ability, and he delighted to appear at musical conventions, and come into contact with the leading minds in the musical profession. He was ambitious of establishing a national school of music and musicians; and he obtained from our composers a large number of new works which he hoped to produce, so that the public could judge of the extent of our native talent.[19]

Because Lavallée's activities were scattered over so many cities and so many branches of music, it was difficult for his contemporaries to obtain more than a fragmentary view of his achievements. The exception was the famous Canadian choral conductor Augustus Stephen Vogt, whose opinion of Lavallée was given to Dr. J. D. Logan in these words:

I became acquainted with Lavallée in the 80's of the last century, when I was in Boston as a student of music, and he impressed me as a man of extraordinary ability—not merely as a clever executant of the piano, and not merely as an adroit deviser of pretty melodies and sensuous harmonies, but as a genuinely creative artist, a pure musical genius.[20]

TORONTO: As we turn to the cities of Ontario we discover a more dynamic social climate, pervaded by commercial zest and technology. The rapid material development of Ontario—then still frontier territory—was in sharp contrast to the conservatism of the French-speaking province steeped in the traditions of a pre-industrial Canada. An important native-born group of musicians was

[18]F. O. Jones, *A Handbook of American Music and Musicians*, (New ed.; Buffalo, 1887).

[19]New York *Times*, Jan. 31, 1891.

[20]Logan, "Canadian Creative Composers," p. 489.

active in Quebec at this time; in Ontario the foreign-born dominated the musical scene. The immigrant, while not more talented than the Canadian musician, often surpassed him in quality of training, width of horizon and organizing experience. Thus Ontario was able, in spite of its youth, to develop musical societies approaching or equalling in quality those of the older province. Less interested in opera, Ontario cities showed great sympathy with the British traditions of choral singing and especially of oratorio.

Musical life in Toronto in the decades before 1900 revolved around the Philharmonic Society, which had been revived in 1872 by two leaders of earlier musical activities, Dr. James P. Clarke and the university president John McCaul. For the opening concert in October 1872 *The Messiah* was chosen.[21] The following year, the aging Dr. Clarke retired as conductor, and under his successor Frederick H. Torrington oratorio performance grew into a tradition.

We have already met Torrington as a young man who had made a name for himself as a violinist and organist in Montreal, where he had settled after coming from England. He was an energetic and somewhat despotic musician with a love of doing things on a large scale. Toronto afforded him many opportunities to indulge this tendency. When he arrived in 1873 to become organist and choirmaster at Metropolitan Church, musical life in the city had been very quiet for a decade, as several societies had collapsed in the early 1860's. The new conductor of the Philharmonic Society welded what had been a loose group of massed church choirs into a disciplined chorus of 200 singers. In 1874 Torrington presented the Canadian *première* of *Elijah* and two years later that of *St. Paul.* A chorus of 500 singers was employed when Gounod's *Redemption* was performed in 1882, the year it was composed. The society was strong in oratorio but, unlike its Montreal counterpart, never ventured into opera. It shared with the Montreal society the disadvantage of having its orchestra determined by the availability of players rather than the requirements of the score. Over the years there was some improvement. The Society had twenty string players in 1872; at the end of ten years these had increased by only six. Only two years later, however, the strings increased to

---

[21]Oddly enough the choir of 152 singers included more men (98) than women (54). The orchestra of amateurs and professionals included 12 violins, 3 violas, 3 cellos, 2 basses, 2 flutes, 2 clarinets, 1 bassoon, 1 horn, 2 trumpets and 2 drums.

45 players and the orchestra had a total of 69 players. Under these conditions instrumental music fared rather badly at first. Symphonic music was commonly restricted to the performance of single movements, although there were complete performances of Haydn's "Surprise" Symphony and Beethoven's "Emperor" Concerto before 1884. This restriction was not the fault of the conductor, for in the view of one of his players he was "a fine drill master for both orchestra and chorus—thorough in every detail, even to having the bowing marked so that all the violin players would bow exactly alike."[22]

The Philharmonic's largest enterprise was the great Festival of 1886, which consisted of three evening performances and one matinée. All Toronto's musical resources were drawn upon. There were 1,000 choristers, 1,200 children's voices, and an orchestra of 100. Lilli Lehmann and Max Heinrich, two famous singers, were the guest artists. The festival suffered from several weaknesses: lack of symphonic music, insufficient orchestral rehearsal, and an apparently undue emphasis on the spectacular. In her memoirs Lilli Lehmann summed up the whole affair as "extremely ludicrous. . . . An elderly local conductor knew so little about the Mozart scores that I called him, in English, in the presence of the committee a veritable 'ass,' after my aria from the *Entführung*, and he did not take umbrage but tried to excuse himself. I know that it was not ladylike of me, but I felt that I must say it."[23]

On the other hand one must appreciate the tremendous enthusiasm which the festival inspired, an enthusiasm that gave birth to such projects as the formation of a regular orchestra and the building of a concert hall. As a matter of fact, several orchestras were formed in succession under such names as "Torrington Orchestra" or "Orchestral School." These were short-lived and tended to lapse, to be succeeded after a year or two by a new one. Neither the orchestras nor the Philharmonic Society continued to function after the concert hall became a reality. Massey Music Hall, for which over $100,000 was given the city by Hart A. Massey, a manufacturer and philanthropist, was opened on June 14, 1894, with a performance of *The Messiah*. The construction of this

[22]Herbert L. Clarke, *How I Became a Cornetist* (St. Louis, 1934), p. 10.
[23]Lilli Lehmann, *My Path through Life* (New York and London, 1914), p. 357.

hall with its admirable acoustics, ushered in a new era in Toronto's musical life, and new organizations continued where the Philharmonic Society left off. One of these was the Festival Chorus led by Torrington, who remained active until his seventy-fifth year. In 1912 he led farewell performances of two of the oratorios he had conducted so often: *The Messiah* and *St. Paul*. Torrington's achievements also included the foundation of the Toronto College of Music, and he was honoured by being awarded an honorary doctorate from the University of Toronto.

Another musician who stamped a deep mark on musical life was American-born Edward Fisher (1848–1913). After studying in Boston and Berlin, Fisher began his Canadian career about 1875 as musical director of the Ottawa Ladies' College. A few years later he moved to Toronto, where he founded the St. Andrews Choral Society which was later expanded into the Toronto Choral Society (1879–92). This group of about one hundred singers gave subscription concerts in which oratorios such as *The Seasons* and *Samson* and shorter choral-orchestral works were performed. Fisher helped to organize the Canadian Society of Musicians and the Canadian Guild (now College) of Organists. He became musical director at the Ontario Ladies' College in Whitby; like Torrington, he founded a conservatory—the Toronto Conservatory of Music—and received an honorary doctorate.

Chamber music was heard sporadically in public. At most periods there was a string quartet of some degree of accomplishment. Perhaps the earliest was led by F. Griebel, the foremost Toronto violinist about the middle of the century. However, most chamber ensembles were transitory and played more often for pleasure than in professional engagements. Nothing short of remarkable was the career of the Toronto Quartette Club which presented twelve fortnightly "Monday Popular Concerts" in the 1885–6 season. The ensemble, consisting of Henri Jacobsen, John Bayley, Arthur E. Fisher and Ludwig Corell, presented classical chamber music interspersed with solo numbers by guest artists. Present-day concert managers would find it hard to believe that at least one concert of chamber music drew a crowd of 1,300. An entire Mozart string quartet was on this programme, and his clarinet quintet on another. In the following season, the same players, under the name Chamber Music Association, presented six concerts which included a number of Haydn and Beethoven quartets. It is also reported that all the

Mozart and Beethoven piano trios and quartets were heard in the early 1870's, but these performances may have been in a private circle.

Two of the string quartet players made wider contributions to music in Toronto. Arthur Elwell Fisher deserves mention for his energetic promotion of higher music education in the 1880's and 1890's. An Englishman, he obtained a diploma from Trinity College, London, and came to Canada as organist and choirmaster. He taught voice, piano and violin, prepared candidates for the bachelor of music examinations at Trinity College in Toronto and eventually became himself an examiner in music for the University of Toronto. His beneficial influence as educator was also felt through his outspoken writings in the *Musical Journal* and his work on the executive of the Canadian Society of Musicians. He was also a prolific composer.

John Bayley, bandmaster of the Queen's Own Rifles Band from 1879 to 1901, was described by Herbert L. Clarke as "a finished musician of high order; he was a remarkable organist . . . and one of the best clarinetists I have ever heard in my life."[24] This opinion carries weight, coming from the famous cornet soloist of the Gilmore, Victor Herbert, and Sousa bands, who had received the basis of his musical education and first professional experience in Toronto.[25]

HAMILTON: Like so many other Canadian cities, Hamilton owes much of its musical development to a number of families with whom music-making was a natural need and who included both amateur and professional musicians. Such were the families of George Robinson and Albert Stares. Most active, perhaps, was the family of Thomas Littlehales, manager of the Hamilton Gas Light Company. Their home, "Harmony Hall" was known far beyond the city boundaries as a meeting-place for music lovers. On Sunday afternoons, musicians, their instruments under their arms would drop in for a session of classical chamber music. Together with their friends, the Littlehales children formed a musical society, the Jubal Club. The experience in singing and instrumental playing

[24]Clarke, *How I Became a Cornetist*, p. 17.
[25]Of the many other pioneer musicians in Toronto we can mention only the flautist J. Churchill Arlidge, the voice teachers Francesco d'Auria and W. Elliott Haslam, and the organist T. C. Jeffers. Alexander T. Cringan is discussed on p. 186.

gained there helped its members in later years to make important contributions to concert performances in the city.

In oratorio performance the Sacred Harmonic Society (who performed *The Creation* and *The Seasons*), the Hamilton Choral Society (*The Messiah, Elijah*) and the Hamilton Philharmonic Society succeeded each other in the years between 1877 and 1890. The conductors included Torrington (who commuted from Toronto), Clarence Lucas, F. Jenkins and John Edmund Paul Aldous (1853–1934). The last was a leading musical figure in Hamilton for many decades. A graduate of Trinity College, Cambridge, he settled in Hamilton in 1877 as organist at Central Presbyterian Church. He was active as leader of choral and orchestral groups and director of music schools.

KITCHENER-WATERLOO: MUSICAL CENTRE OF THE GERMAN MINORITY: As communities grew and the number of churches using choirs and organ music as part of the service increased, Canada came to be regarded by European musicians as a desirable place to work. But because church positions were so closely linked with the religious traditions of Great Britain or France, they were naturally filled with musicians trained in the traditions of these countries. As musicians holding church appointments had the greatest opportunity and encouragement to lead musical societies, we have one explanation why German musicians, formerly so prominent in eastern Canada, now occupied a less conspicuous place in musical societies and bands. Instead they assumed a pioneer role in instrument-building and, like musicians from other Continental countries, were chiefly engaged in teaching.

The German musical contribution to Canada, however, was not restricted to the work of individual professional musicians. Since the early decades of the nineteenth century, a region of western Ontario has been a centre of German immigration from Germany, eastern Europe, and Pennsylvania. The most important town in this district was named Berlin in 1833 but its name was changed to Kitchener in World War I. Here and in the neighbouring town of Waterloo developed the first centre of organized music-making by a national minority group in Canada.

The most popular form of musical entertainment in the early days was the playing of brass instruments. No family celebration, no picnic, and no election campaign was considered complete without the stirring sounds of a brass band. In the beginning these bands were informal family and neighbourhood groups; about 1860 organized bands appeared, and in 1865 they merged in the Berlin Musical Society under William Kaiser. The Kitchener Musical Society, as it is now called, still sponsors band music. About 1875 reed instruments were added, and in 1878 the society had a band of 22 members and a quadrille band of 6. An orchestra of 9 was also being organized.[26] Four years later, Waterloo formed a Musical Society of its own. Among the leaders of these various groups, Noah Zeller (ca. 1852–1914) had the longest record as conductor and teacher.

A musician of excellent training whose influence dominated the local scene for many years was Herman Theodore Zoellner (b.1854), who settled in Berlin in 1880. He taught music privately, and for 25 years in public schools, besides playing the organ at New Jerusalem Church. He organized the Berlin Philharmonic and Orchestral Society, which comprised all elements of the population, non-German as well as German. Its repertory was essentially the same as that of the Anglo-Canadian groups in other cities. *The Creation* was performed in 1883 and subsequent years brought Mendelssohn's *Hymn of Praise* and *St. Paul* and Rossini's *Stabat Mater*.

German traditions asserted themselves more distinctively in the singing societies patterned after those of Germany. Singing was first cultivated by an athletic society—the Turnverein. It was founded in 1861, about a month later than the first known German musical society in Canada, in Victoria, B.C. The Turnverein devoted two evenings each week to singing. About 1865 a Liedertafel ("song-table," a male-voice choir) was founded in Waterloo. It flourished until World War I.

The German community's most typical musical expression was the Sängerfest ("singers' festival"). About a dozen such festivals were held during the last quarter of the nineteenth century, not only in Berlin-Waterloo but also in Hamilton and some American cities, including Detroit. Choral societies from various German communities would visit on these occasions. The emphasis was on musical co-operation rather than on competition. Nearly as important as the music were the festivities: torchlight parades, good food and drink, and the atmosphere of *Gemütlichkeit*. The earliest

[26]Perhaps 9 string instruments, in combination with which the band could perform as an orchestra.

festival was the Friedensfest ("peace festival") at the termination of the Franco-Prussian war in 1871, but more details are known about the three-day Sängerfest in August 1875.[27] For weeks preparations had taken place to decorate streets with coloured lanterns and festoons. Visitors arrived from far away, and neighbouring towns declared a public holiday so that people could travel to Berlin and enjoy the excitement of the concerts, speeches and parades, the food and the free beer donated by local brewers. The singing societies present included the Concordia of Berlin, the Liedertafel of Waterloo, the Harmonia of Toronto, the Germania of Hamilton, the Liederkranz of Preston, and several from the United States. Chicago and Montreal (which had had a German singing society since 1871) sent delegations.

Kitchener and Waterloo maintained their musical reputation throughout later years but its specifically German character disappeared. With a revival of German immigration about 1950, some of the old musical traditions may come to life again. The first Sängerfest in over half a century, held as part of Kitchener's centennial celebrations in 1955, may prove to be the starting point of a new series of festivals.

LONDON: Although London's distinction as one of the most active musical centres in Ontario dates from recent decades, London was a musical city even in the nineteenth century. Performances of Handel's Dettingen Te Deum (1884) and Sullivan's oratorio Prodigal Son (1885) are believed to have been the first in Canada.

Among pioneer musicians there were W. T. Erith, teacher of singing and piano from London, England (active ca. 1860); W. J. Birks, conductor of the Arion Club (founded 1884); and W. Waugh Lauder, musical director at Hellmuth Ladies College (1883–5), a pianist of rank. The brothers Sippi were of Italian ancestry but raised in Ireland.[28] Dr. Charles Augustus Sippi came to Canada in 1865. From medicine, he turned to teaching at Hellmuth College and then to a musical career—managing the London branch of the A. & S. Nordheimer music company and playing the

27W. H. Breithaupt, "The Saengerfest of 1875," 22nd Annual Report of the Waterloo Historical Society, 1934 (Kitchener, 1935).

28Emilio Goggio, "The Italian Contribution to the Development of Music in Ontario," Canadian Review of Music and Art (Oct.–Nov. and Dec.–Jan. 1945–6); "Italy's Contributions to Growth of Music in Ontario," Toronto Globe and Mail, May 14, 1955.

organ at Memorial Church. As co-founder of the Ontario Music Teachers' Association (1885, later Canadian Society of Musicians) and its first president, he fought to raise the standard of public-school and private music teaching. His brother George B. Sippi, an authority on sacred music, was organist and choirmaster at St. Paul's Cathedral for 37 years. As director of diocesan music he assembled an important music collection which has since become a part of the University of Western Ontario Library.

OTTAWA: Although Ottawa was established as the capital of Canada in 1858, its growth never offered serious rivalry to the older cities of Montreal and Toronto. In fact, Ottawa's population did not exceed 100,000 until the second decade of the twentieth century. A Philharmonic Society is recorded about 1870 as meeting for weekly practice during the winter months under H. R. Fripp. Ten years later it was revived by John W. F. Harrison with about 100 singers. An Englishman, Harrison (ca. 1847–1935) acted as organist at Christ Church and musical director at the Ottawa Ladies' College and was later associated with the Toronto Conservatory of Music for many years. In the 1880's the Ottawa String Quartette Club presented concerts of the prevailing mixed type, combining light and serious music, and in the last decade of the century an Amateur Orchestral Society flourished. The leader of the string quartet was François Boucher, a violin virtuoso and son of the music publisher Adélard J. Boucher.

A name frequently found in contemporary publications is that of Gustave Smith, music professor at the Ottawa College. A Frenchman in spite of his name, Smith came to Canada as a young man about 1857, having attended the Paris Conservatoire. At first he was active as a music teacher and organist in Montreal but by 1870 he had moved to Ottawa where he occupied similar positions. Smith was not only a composer of church and secular music, much of which found its way into print, but also one of the most prolific Canadian critics and writers on music and other subjects. Early in his Canadian career he wrote two textbooks, Le Parfait Musicien (1859) and Abécédaire musical (1861).

PETERBOROUGH: To obtain a well-balanced view of music in this period, the musical resources of at least one Ontario town with a population below 10,000 should be surveyed. About 1890 the town of Peterborough had a Fire Brigade Band of 24 (on occasion converted into an orchestra), an amateur orchestra of 14 which supplied music free of charge to church services and on other occasions, and two choral societies connected with churches. Finally, there was Bradburn's Opera House, erected in 1875. The fact that it occupied the third floor of a building would seem to indicate that the "Opera House" was really a simple auditorium with a stage, serving all kinds of entertainment from dances to vaudeville and election meetings, but rarely, if ever, living up to its name.

HALIFAX: Ever since the Halifax Philharmonic Society presented *The Messiah* in March 1869, the city has had an annual measure of oratorio (most often *The Messiah* and *The Creation*) and opera. Minstrel shows were staged frequently in the sixties and seventies and a strong tradition was established in light opera. For example, *The Mikado* was given in 1887, only two years after it had been composed. Among the earliest performances of grand opera in Halifax were those of *Il Trovatore* and *Martha* in the summer of 1871 by the Brignoli Grand Opera Company.

Halifax has always benefited from being the port of arrival for many European immigrants and visitors. From 1840 to 1867 all Cunard steamers called at Halifax. In this era many artists gave their first North American concerts in Halifax (or Quebec), testing the audience's reaction there before facing the more exacting critics of New York and Boston.

Great encouragement was given to music in 1877 with the opening of the Academy of Music—not, as the name suggests, a music school, but a concert hall. Seating 1,500 spectators, it was built through the initiative of prominent citizens. The opening concert was given by the Philharmonic Union under Charles H. Porter, with guest artists from Boston. Soon the Academy became the centre of musical life. Here local organizations gave concerts and performances of light opera, and outside groups such as the Boston Symphony Orchestra and the Westminster Choir came as visitors.

Two musical influences dominated the Maritimes at this time: those of New England and Germany. Sometimes these influences merged, since the Americans who settled in eastern Canada had taken advanced training at German conservatories. Young musicians from the Maritimes would study in Boston, and performing artists from New England would visit Canada. One of these,

Charles Henry Porter (1856–1929), was the leading spirit in many musical enterprises in Halifax from the 1870's until the early years of the twentieth century. A native of Naugatuck, Connecticut, he studied in Leipzig before settling permanently in Halifax. Before going to Leipzig Porter was organist and choirmaster at St. Matthew's Presbyterian Church, Halifax. On his return he resumed this position. He also became the conductor of the Orpheus Club, a male choir which together with guest artists presented several concerts each year. He was the first principal (1887–1900) of the Halifax Conservatory of Music and was active as an organizer of music festivals. In addition, Porter was also a prolific composer, but eventually he turned to a business career.

Another New Englander, Arthur Bird (1856–1923), spent the years 1877–81 in Halifax; like Porter he applied German methods of music teaching. He was organist at the same church and also conducted a male chorus, the Arion Club. Later he returned to Germany where he gained reputation as a composer with Brahmsian tendencies. In the early 1880's Porter's brother Samuel, an organist, led the Haydn Quintette Club. This was the most important instrumental group in Halifax, since it was still impossible to finance a full orchestra. Heinrich Klingenfeld, violin teacher at the Conservatory who arrived from Munich in 1885, enlarged the Haydn Quintette Club with bandsmen and student players to present a number of orchestral concerts. He was succeeded in 1893 by Max Weil, a native of Philadelphia educated in Leipzig. German influence was further strengthened by Ernst Doering, who was brought to Halifax as cello teacher at the Conservatory. Together with Charles Porter and Klingenfeld, he formed the Leipzig Trio about 1890.

SAINT JOHN, N.B.: The Saint John Oratorio Society, organized in 1882 by Thomas Morley, produced the great Handel, Haydn, and Mendelssohn oratorios. At first a local orchestra was employed, but later instrumentalists and leading singers were imported from Boston. After the lapse of the Oratorio Society, the Euterpian Club under James Ford did some fine work in *a cappella* singing but unfortunately its career too was short.

FREDERICTON: A LOOK AT CHURCH MUSIC: Time and again our description of musical life leads us through the portals of the church into the realm of sacred song and organ music. In Fredericton we encounter a personality rare since the days of the missionaries and parish priests of New France: a clergyman who combined his religious vocation with the activities of a skilled musician.

John Medley was born in London, England, in 1804 and came to Canada in 1845 as Anglican Bishop of Fredericton. His first major project was the building of a cathedral. On a trip to England in 1848 to secure aid for this, he procured a small organ for St. Anne's Chapel. However, Christ Church Cathedral, although consecrated in 1853, had no organ until about 1860. For nearly half a century, until his death in 1892, the Bishop (later Metropolitan) took a profound and active interest in church music and helped to improve its quality. His biographer William Ketchum describes the state of church music in Fredericton at the time of the Bishop's arrival:

Church music was little understood or attended to. In some instances objections were made to chanting the canticles. The so-called hymns in use consisted of a very slim selection from the "metrical version of the Psalms, by Tate & Brady." All this must have been deeply felt by the Bishop, with his love for earnest, reverent services, and frequent communion; with his excellent taste in Church music. . . .[29]

To improve conditions, the Bishop, with a committee of his clergy, compiled a Diocesan Hymnal which served for a number of years until it was replaced by *Hymns Ancient and Modern*. The latter appeared in England in 1861 and maintained its popularity through many decades.

Medley enriched the repertoire not only with existing music but also with compositions of his own. These include about twenty anthems and many introits, chants, hymn tunes and services. Some of these were published in England by Novello; others found their way into printed collections of church music.

For 45 years, with occasional assistance, the Bishop conducted the Cathedral choir and was also his own precentor. For two years he had the help of an able musician, Major Alexander Ewing, composer of the well-known hymn "Jerusalem the Golden." An Englishman, Ewing was stationed in Fredericton from 1867 to 1869

[29]W. Q. Ketchum, *The Life and Work of the Most Reverend John Medley, D.D.* (Saint John, N.B., 1893), p. 64.

as commander of a regiment. He was appointed supplementary organist, joined the choir, and finally became conductor and teacher of a Choral Society with which he gave a number of enthusiastically received concerts.

One of the Bishop's colleagues recalled that "next to his Cathedral, perhaps, the Bishop loved his choir, though, as he has often remarked, nothing, not excepting his Diocese, ever caused him so much trouble as the management of this small, but musically refractory, body of people."[30] Ewing suggested a reason for this trouble: "Musical amateurs are proverbially 'kittle cattle,' and it required much tact and constant watchfulness to maintain efficient co-operation on the part of all its members, inasmuch as those who considered that they were not allotted their due share of 'solos,' were sometimes disposed to be recalcitrant (a phenomenon by no means peculiar to the amateur choir of Fredericton Cathedral)."[31]

In spite of these difficulties, the achievements of the choir were considered excellent. "No choir practice was considered complete until every anthem and introit, every chant and hymn was perfect."[32] As Ewing summarized it, ". . . it would have been difficult to meet with a better [musical] service out of England."[33]

The combination of talents embodied in Bishop Medley was rare in Canada, but it was echoed to some degree in his own city. His colleague, the Rev. John Black, Rector of King's Clear and missionary to the S.P.G., left at his death in 1871 a number of manuscript compositions. In 1874 these were published in Toronto in a collection entitled *Cantate Domino: A Hymnal and Chants for Public Worship.*

Much detailed information on the activities of choirs and bands in Fredericton is contained in Mrs. F. A. Good's paper "Some Random Notes on the Musical History of Fredericton" (1933).[34] The earliest dates mentioned by Mrs. Good concern the installation of an organ at the Methodist Church in 1845 and a concert in 1844 at the Legislative Building. The Concert featured orchestral overtures by Mozart and Beethoven, violin pieces by Spohr and Paganini, and vocal selections.

[30]Rev. F. Alexander, quoted by Ketchum, *John Medley*, p. 329.
[31]Alexander Ewing, quoted by Ketchum, *John Medley*, p. 327.
[32]Col. George J. Maunsell, quoted by Ketchum, *John Medley*, pp. 323–4.
[33]Alexander Ewing, quoted by Ketchum, *John Medley*, p. 328.
[34]Manuscript, made available to the author through the kindness of Mr. G. Alvah Good and Professor A. G. Bailey.

Although choirs other than church choirs occurred only sporadically, regimental and civilian bands were a permanent feature of musical life. They accompanied all important local celebrations and enlivened pleasure parties on river steamers. One of these bands, the Fredericton Brass Band was an offshoot of a Reform Club inspired by a temperance orator. It functioned until about 1930, when it became the York Regiment Band. (Ironically enough, the building of the Reform Club was later occupied by the Liquor Control Board.) Among the many musicians and amateurs conscientiously registered by Mrs. Good, at least two excelled the rest. Professor Cadwallader was for twenty years organist at Christ Church Cathedral and music teacher at the Normal and Model Schools. Cedric W. Lemont (1879–1954), a native son, began his career as organist and choirmaster. About 1899 he settled in the United States where he established a fine reputation as an organist, teacher and composer (see p. 226).

NEWFOUNDLAND: Although Newfoundland has been a province of Canada only since 1949, her history and geographical position have always linked her closely to Canada. For over three hundred years fishery has been the main occupation of Newfoundlanders and in recent days lumbering and mining have also assumed importance. Most of the villages are situated along the rocky coast and towns are few. The small amount of immigration, the difficulty of communication (much of it by ferry with the outside world and by coastal steamer within the province), and the retardation of industrial development have made this province the least susceptible to the influence of urban civilization and North American technological society.

Hence the musical importance of Newfoundland rests on the wealth of traditional and locally composed folk songs rather than the musical life of its cities. Most Newfoundlanders are of Irish or Southern English origin (with Scottish and French minorities) and it is among the former that folk singing has been kept alive most vigorously. In addition, a number of songs have been absorbed from the American mainland. On their sea trips and in the lumber camps Newfoundlanders came into contact with French Canadians, Nova Scotians and Americans as well as people from far-away countries with whom they frequently exchanged songs. Hence the

Newfoundland songs are closely related in subject and manner of singing to those of Nova Scotia and many are similar to the Appalachian versions of a common European heritage. In addition to the old-country love ballads and sea songs, of which different versions exist in various localities, there are many songs of local origin celebrating local events. One of the first collectors of Newfoundland folk songs, Elizabeth Greenleaf summed up her impression of the songs composed in Newfoundland as follows:

A complete collection of them would, I am sure, give a complete history of the island, from the early "gams" aboard the fishing vessels of all nations who came to fish the Banks and to dry their catch ashore, through the social movements like the emigration of the nineties, to politics, wars, sea disasters and everyday life, including folk-motifs, and of a tone quite different from the historical ballads composed by the ruling classes.[35]

In the capital, St. John's, and in towns like Carbonear and Harbour Grace, music was cultivated in the period under discussion by choirs and bands. A Choral Society in St. John's presented *The Messiah* in December 1884, and in the next year Gade's *Crusaders* was performed with the accompaniment of piano and harmonium. Music teachers included many of Irish ancestry, such as a group of nuns of aristocratic origin who at one time taught singing in schools. Among the more successful Newfoundland musicians were Georgina Stirling, an opera singer whose career led her to Europe, and Charles Hutton (1861–1949), who studied in London and became the leading musical personality in St. John's. Together with his wife, a trained singer, he gathered an ensemble of singers to prepare performances of *The Geisha* or *H.M.S. Pinafore*.

[35]Elisabeth Bristol Greenleaf and Grace Yarrow Mansfield, *Ballads and Sea Songs of Newfoundland* (Cambridge, Mass., 1933), p. xxxvii.

8 / Westward Expansion

THE OPENING UP OF THE WEST: In the cities and provinces whose musical history we have traced so far, the achievement of the late nineteenth century consisted chiefly in the intensification of older forms of music-making, such as church and concert music, and the addition of new features, such as professionalism, music publishing, and instrument-building, to the musical fabric. But music in Canada also expanded geographically. The nineteenth century witnessed the exploration and settlement of the prairie and mountain country between Lake Superior and the Pacific. The political result was the incorporation of four new provinces into Canada: Manitoba (1870), British Columbia (1871), Alberta (1905) and Saskatchewan (1905). By 1900 nearly 900,000 people had settled west of the Lakehead, a number equal to the population of all Canada seventy years earlier.

Once more we can trace the sequence of musical colonization: the beginnings in new surroundings, the efforts towards refinement, and the first achievements. In the west, however, the sequence is telescoped into the short space of a few decades; settlement did not begin in earnest until the last three or four decades of the century, and then it proceeded with great rapidity.

By 1850, exploration of the west already had a long history. The rivers and trails north of Lake Superior and west of Hudson Bay had long been known to the fur-traders and *voyageurs*. The extreme west of Canada had been discovered in 1778 by Captain James Cook, who approached from the Pacific Ocean, and it was first reached by land from eastern Canada by Alexander Mackenzie in

1793. Trading posts had also been established at the site of present-day Winnipeg and Edmonton and at other locations. Not until the 1850's, however, did a settlement grow to the proportions of a town. This was Victoria, capital of the crown colony of Vancouver Island. Most other towns in the West owe their existence to the construction of railway lines. Winnipeg was incorporated as a town in 1871, Calgary in 1884, Edmonton in 1892, Saskatoon and Regina in 1903.

The lure of gold and other minerals attracted an army of adventurers and fortune-seekers now to one region, now to another. Others were enticed by the promise of free land and settled down to farm or to establish cattle ranches. For all it was a life full of privation and adventure, bold hopes, frequent disappointment and occasional success. Civilized life was thousands of miles away, for even the prairie towns boasted little more luxury than one-room log houses on muddy, unpaved streets.

The newcomers were more varied in national and social origin than the first settlers in any of the older provinces. Quebec was settled by people from certain parts of France; Ontario by a variety of British people and a few minorities. The west, however, was settled by people from nearly all the European countries, and from eastern Canada, the United States and the Orient. This very variety accounts for the colourfulness of its musical life.

THE FIRST INSTRUMENTS: It would be logical to assume that the first pioneers in the west had to rely exclusively on their vocal cords to satisfy their musical appetites, for on a journey thousands of miles in length who would burden himself with such a luxury as a musical instrument? Nevertheless, many must have done so. The documents so far inspected contain many references to instruments, few to folk singing. (We are not thinking here of the canoemen and fur-traders in the service of the North West Company and Hudson's Bay Company: their musical habits properly form a part of the culture of eastern Canada.) The conditions of pioneer life on the prairies were not conducive to the preservation of folk song, chiefly because settlements were too isolated and settlers were of different national origins. The production of original folk song in the west has been small. Most local-colour songs were actually imported from the United States regions to the south, which had been settled earlier, and were common property of the mid west and west from Texas to Alberta with only slight regional variations. For example, "Red River Valley," the best-known song from the Canadian prairies was named after the Red River in Texas, not the one flowing into Lake Winnipeg.[1] Like other popular songs imported from the United States, such as "Bury Me Not on the Lone Prairie" and "The Tenderfoot," it dates from the late nineteenth century. Even songs with original Canadian words, such as the widely-known "Saskatchewan" or "The Alberta Homesteader" are sung to previously existing tunes.

On the other hand the west has been a magnet for a great variety of language groups. Even if song did not find fertile ground, the first and second generations of immigrants must have possessed an enormous fund of song: Scandinavian, Slavic, German, etc. Song collecting has not as yet probed very deeply, but further research may reveal many surprises.

Musical instruments did make the long journey together with the first settlers. Professor Dorland relates how a group of Highlanders set out from Fort Churchill in 1814 on their journey to the Red River settlement, marching six abreast, led by a piper, "the men in front pulling the sledges and tramping down a path for the women and children who followed behind."[2] At Red River Academy, a military station on the site of modern Winnipeg, the officers often had dances with bagpipes and fiddles, and a piano was brought to the settlement as early as 1833. In his book based on the diaries of *The Overlanders of '62*, Dr. Mark Sweeten Wade tells the story of a group of people from Ontario, Quebec, and England who were headed for the goldfields of British Columbia. They experienced incredible hardships on their way across the prairies and the Rocky Mountains, abandoning step by step their carts, animals and eventually much of their baggage. This was "the largest party of men that travelled across the Canadian plains and pierced the Rocky Mountains almost a quarter of a century before the advent of modern transportation facilities."[3] The main party of Over-

---

[1] It has been assumed that the song started out in New York in 1896 as "In the Bright Mohawk Valley." Yet there is some evidence that it was sung in Manitoba at the time of the 1885 Rebellion.

[2] Arthur G. Dorland, *Our Canada* (Toronto, 1949), p. 144.

[3] M. S. Wade, *The Overlanders of '62*, ed. John Hosie (Archives of British Columbia, Memoir no. IX) (Victoria, 1931), p. xi. See also Margaret Fairley, "Westward with Music," in *New Frontiers* (Summer 1956).

landers numbered 150 people as it left Fort Garry (Winnipeg) with 97 carts and 110 animals. In the group were four violinists, two flautists, and several players of brass instruments, clarinet and concertina. Others gathered to while away the hours of the evening by singing a few favourite songs. On July 16, 1862, on the way to Fort Edmonton, "a meeting was held in the centre of the correll, of all Musicians both Vocal & Instrimental [sic] for the purpose of getting up a musical Association, & accordingly an association was formed by some 32 joining themselves togather & . . . we played & sung a number of favourite Pieces & then retired for the night."[4] Nine days later the musical association presented a concert before a capacity audience at Fort Edmonton. Another concert was given on August 20 near the site of present-day Jasper. "The singing and instrumental sounds would surely be new and a surprise to the wild beasts and mountain sheep if in hearing," one of the travellers commented on the event.[5] A vivid picture was drawn by a member of the alternate party which had left Fort Garry a few days later. On June 30, 1862, he recorded in his diary, "One is playing cards, another crew cooking Ducks, an old schoolmaster with his stick looking on, now one is playing the fiddle, another the cornet à piston, another singing, cattle all around us quietly grazing, another baking, and last of all mosquitoes biting."[6]

While a violin, clarinet, or concertina added only little weight to a pioneer's baggage, it was a problem of a different sort to transport pianos around Cape Horn or on carts across the prairie plains and rivers and over mountain passes to satisfy the musical desires of pioneer settlers. Yet this is what was done. "The men detailed to York boats, Red River carts and Victoria-bound barques knew pianos as the most cumbersome, contrary and delicate devices civilization had thrust upon them."[7] Pianos were packed on mules at a rate of a dollar a pound from Quesnel to Barkerville, the centre of the Cariboo gold region. Dancehalls and saloons had grown up there overnight, and the hurdy-gurdy girls charged ten dollars or more a dance, "not the stately waltz, but a wild fling to shake the rafters and tire out the stoutest miners."[8] Nothwithstanding the

[4]Wade, Overlanders, pp. 70–1.
[5]Ibid., p. 97.
[6]Ibid., p. 81.
[7]James McCook, "Pioneers Preferred Pianos," Beaver (Winter 1954), p. 9.
[8]Agnes C. Laut, The Cariboo Trail (Toronto, 1916), p. 96.

forbidding costs and difficulties of transportation, pianos were essential amenities in this atmosphere. As James McCook put it, "on the prairies pianos and pemmican had a priority rating." "Part of the money, received from their first 'bumper crops' of 'Manitoba Hard' went for upright pianos."[9] Several dates for early pianos in Western Canada are: Victoria *ca.* 1851; Prince Albert 1880; Lethbridge 1887.[10] A piano that came to the site of Vancouver about 1860 is preserved at the local city archives.

The vogue for pianos was due largely to the pioneer women, for many prospective brides from England and eastern Canada made it a condition that they be provided with a piano in their homes. Women associated these instruments "with the dignity and conventionality of the older communities they had left. The fiddle would encourage rowdy reels but the piano soothed the savage breast and the accounts of early pianos doing duty reveal them chiefly as instruments of sentimentality and remembrance—sometimes even in the Yukon dancehalls—and tears ran through many a bold moustache as bachelors sang to the gentle tones of favorites such as the saccharine 'Molly Darling.' "[11]

VICTORIA: In comparison with the cities of Ontario, even the oldest city in western Canada seems young. If we compare the dates of the first musical organizations, however, we find that the difference in years is much smaller than is commonly supposed. Only fourteen years separate the establishment of the first musical society in Toronto from that in Victoria (1859). Whereas the cities of the east had grown slowly and gradually, the rise of Victoria was ushered in by a dramatic event. At the beginning of 1858 fewer than 500 people lived in Victoria. When the story spread that gold had been discovered on the mainland, about 20,000 people arrived within four months to make Victoria the supply centre and starting point of their expeditions. Along with the prospectors came a motley crowd of merchants and all kinds of adventurers, some honest, some unscrupulous. "Victoria was a frontier sort of town in the late '50's. There were saloons galore and music halls, where

[9]J. E. Middleton, "Music in Canada," *Canada and Its Provinces* (Toronto, 1914), xii, 650.
[10]A melodeon was in Morley, Alberta, about 1867.
[11]McCook, "Pioneers Preferred Pianos," p. 11.

it was said nice people didn't go. There was little entertainment for family life and so the families had to make their own."[12]

The roots of such home-made entertainment stretch back to the years before the gold rush.[13] The settlers at the Hudson's Bay Company's Fort Victoria included a number of well-to-do "Old Country gentlemen in the English sense of the word," men coming from a landed gentry class who were anxious to restore some of the cultured atmosphere of the homeland. Being fond of sports and amusements they went on riding excursions which would be followed by high tea or dinner and ended with dance and song. By 1853 the instrumental resources at such musical *soirées* boasted two violins, a piano (which had been shipped all the way around Cape Horn), a flute, and a tin whistle. Such music-making was enjoyed alike by settlers and Indians who crowded outside the palisades to listen.[14] Several other pianos and a cello were added in the mid fifties, and a barrel organ with three barrels of ten tunes each arrived from London in 1859.

Thus a solid basis had been established on which to counteract the influence of the saloons and music halls. Efforts to create worthwhile entertainment resulted in January 1859 in the organization of the Victoria Philharmonic Society. Under the presidency of a distinguished citizen, Matthew (later Sir Matthew) Begbie, the future Chief Justice of British Columbia, and under the direction of John Bayley, Inspector of Police and a trained musician, a number of concerts were presented. Of one hundred members, only ten to fifteen were active performers. The society did not flourish long, but four years later reports mention a decision to revive it. Meanwhile a German Singverein—the first in Canada—had come into existence in May 1861, and a French Society, Les Enfans de Paris, gave its first concert in August. The Singverein under its musical leader Professor Zinke became a strong community force as it attracted many non-German residents to its varied activities. These included "soirees and dances, concerts, picnics in Summer. Serenad-

[12]J. K. Nesbitt, "Old Homes and Families," Victoria *Daily Colonist*, Sept. 25, 1949.

[13]The most valuable among the various sources consulted on the musical history of early Victoria is Dorothy Blakey Smith, "Music in the Furthest West a Hundred Years Ago," *Canadian Music Journal*, II (Summer 1958).

[14]N. de Bertrand Lugrin, *The Pioneer Women of Vancouver Island, 1843–1866* (ed. John Hosie; Victoria, 1928), p. 200.

ing was popular in those days. On election nights, for instance, it was the custom to sing outside the victor's home. He came to the porch, made a speech, invited the serenaders into the house for 'a bumper.' "[15]

The society's reputation rested as much on its social entertainment and cuisine as on its musical programmes, all being considered excellent. "Welshmen, Englishmen, Scotsmen and Americans were singing night after night with the Germans," Nesbitt tells us. One of the conductors bore the undoubtedly non-German name of St. Clair. Eventually the Singverein grew prosperous enough to acquire a hall of its own where parties, concerts, and dances were held for a number of years.

Victoria attracted a great variety of musicians. A piano- and organ-maker, John Bagnall, established himself in 1863; William Seeley was an organist and organ repairman; celebrity was represented by Mme L'Hotelier who had been, in her youth, a prominent singer in Paris theatres (as Mlle Louise Balagny); and an amateur composer, Mr. Horne, one of the officers of *H.M.S. Ganges*, wrote a *Vancouver Island Waltz* (1860), the autograph of which has been preserved.[16] Music teachers were numerous, and no city in the British Empire was ever graced by the presence of so many "Professors of Music," for such was the title they invariably gave themselves.

In 1864 two brass bands amalgamated to form the Victoria Musical Society. A Glee Club was established in 1866 and later a Choral Society, again with Sir Matthew Begbie as president. Sir Matthew had a "very deep and powerful" bass voice which sounded grand even at the age of seventy and his solo performance had the "utmost taste and finish." He was also a faithful member of the excellent choir of St. John's Church. This church and others kindled interest in oratorio performances, which began with *Esther, the Beautiful Queen* in 1884 and established a tradition with Handel's *The Messiah*, first given on Easter Sunday of 1887. On this occasion a choir of two hundred voices was led by Enrico Sorge.

From about 1875 there were visits by concert companies and

---

[15]Nesbitt, "Old Homes and Families."

[16]Another local composer was Arthur Thomas Bushby whose *British Columbia March*, written for the New Westminster Rifle Corps, is reproduced in the *Canadian Music Journal*, II (Summer 1958). See also D. B. Smith's article in the same issue.

Italian and English opera troupes. In his memoirs Herbert Kent tells us that in the last quarter of the century "the old Theatre Royal on Government Street was very frequently secured for Operatic Companies, and, contrary to the order of things in late years, these organizations found it profitable to give three or four days, and in many cases, a week of Grand Opera."[17]

Local operatic effort began with the foundation of an Amateur Dramatic and Operatic Society about 1880. *The Beggar's Opera* was suggested as the first work to be given, but the lady proposed as leading singer refused to sing in such a "gross, vulgar and indecent" piece. Instead, Thomas Arne's *Love in a Village* was selected. The performance was directed from the piano by Professor Digby Palmer. In later years, many Gilbert and Sullivan comedies and grand operas such as *Martha* and *Il Trovatore* were attempted, so large were local musical resources.

In 1878 a Victoria Amateur Band was organized and for years met in weekly practice of classical music. Its name was soon changed to Victoria Amateur Orchestral Society when string players joined the group. It was conducted by Professor Schaffer and later by Coote M. Chambers (an accountant by trade); the concertmaster was Thomas Wilson, a music teacher. Victorians were exceedingly proud of this organization of some 30 players which provided musical entertainment for about 15 years.

FROM VANCOUVER TO WINNIPEG: Our survey of the musical beginnings in the new regions of western Canada will end with observations about a few selected towns only, since the pattern of development was much the same everywhere. The first record of music usually concerns individuals who entertained themselves and their neighbours by singing or playing an instrument. Thus, years before Vancouver was given its present name (*ca.* 1885), there was music in the settlements on the same site. A shoemaker amused himself with his bagpipe, and the violin and flute of one Crazy George were much in demand. The minister at Burrard Inlet is said to have used an accordion at church service, but a small organ was at Hastings Sawmill as early as 1876, when it was carried to the dock to welcome Lord Dufferin with the strains of "God Save

[17]Herbert Kent, "Musical Chronicles of Early Times," Victoria *Daily Times*, Dec. 14, 1918.

the Queen." In Regina, founded in 1882, the situation was similar. When Lieutenant-Governor Dewdney "asked Sir John A. Macdonald for permission to buy a piano for Government House, he remarked that there was 'over the average number of musical people in Regina.'"[18]

Strange were the ways of the first musical groups. In 1862 the Bishop of Columbia received a chime of eight bells as a gift from an English lady. The bells were installed in a specially built tower of New Westminster's Holy Trinity Church in 1865. Luckily a soldier of the Royal Engineers, stationed at a nearby camp, was an expert in the art of bell-ringing. Under his guidance, the members of the Bell Ringers' Club were initiated into this branch of music:

Wild clangings and clashings jarred the atmosphere for a few weeks, to which several highly-strung citizens made strong objection. Complaints were vain. The disturbance went on, for efficiency in swinging a three-ton bell, making its clapper strike just at the critical moment and at no other time, couldn't be gained without months of practice. Gradually, however, order and sequence evolved from maddening chaos.[19]

The bells became a beloved institution in New Westminster:

Without doubt our bells are the pride of the town. No such heavenly and *homely* sound can be heard elsewhere on the North Pacific Coast. It is no sentimental exaggeration to say that, at their first peal, more than one sturdy colonist, estranged for many a long day from the dear old sound, burst into tears.[20]

All but the tenor bell were rendered useless in the great fire of 1898.

Even odder was the Coal Harbor Bachelor's Quadrille Club (Vancouver) which in 1885–6 held a New Year's Dance at which "the music was made by beating sticks upon boards. A few aristocrats had instruments made by stretching skins over barrel hoops, but their softer melody was not discernible in the hubbub made by hammering lumber."[21]

[18]Earl G. Drake, *Regina, The Queen City* (Toronto, 1955), p. 29.

[19]Henry Morey, "Musical Pioneers of the Far West Did Much to Promote Growth of Art," Vancouver *Daily Province*, Oct. 26, 1927.

[20]*Columbia Mission Report* (1868).

[21]Vancouver *Weekly Herald*, Jan. 15, 1886, p. 3. This and much of the following information on early Vancouver was obtained through the courtesy of Mrs. J. G. Gibbs, Vancouver City Archives.

The Royal Engineers, planners of cities and builders of highways, included a number of soldiers with musical training, young energetic people with a love of dancing, music and drama. In the early 1860's they built the Theatre Royal, a pioneer institution in British Columbia. The theatre had an orchestra, which provided music for dances, dramatic and musical evenings, and various social and official functions in New Westminster. It was led by Private William Haynes, a skilled violinist. The men in uniform were the pioneers of entertainment in other settlements as well. In 1870, the year marking the creation of the province of Manitoba, members of the First Ontario Rifles supplied the first theatrical and musical performance to the two hundred inhabitants of Winnipeg.[22] Again in Regina the North West Mounted Police presented musical and dramatic shows supported by their own band.

Another impetus to music-making came from the Church. The story could not be told more graphically than in the words of the correspondent of the *Musical Journal* who reported from Birtle, Manitoba, in 1888:

On his arrival here in 1882 your correspondent found only one miserable little melodeon and two pianos in the whole place. In 1883 our Methodist friends advanced a step and invested in a very fair reed organ, the English Church people shortly after following suit. The same year witnessed a large increase in the town, not only of musical instruments, but of talent. In 1884 the Presbyterians, following the good example of the other churches, purchased a good reed organ. The town could then boast of seven organs and eight pianos. Towards the end of this year we organized the "Birtle Musical and Dramatic Club." From then till the spring of 1887 things went on smoothly, new organs and fresh talent appearing every month or two. Early in the spring of 1887 the Presbyterians . . . substituted a small but good "pipe organ" for the reed organ they had hitherto used. They now claim to have the only pipe organ in the country west of Winnipeg. It was built by Messrs. Polton and Baldwin of Winnipeg and is valued at $1000. At present it has only the one manual with four stops. . . . I have no hesitation in saying that in another year or two there will be an addition to it in the way of a "swell organ" which will give them an A 1 instrument for a small church.[23]

[22]Alexander Begg and Walter R. Nursey, *Ten Years in Winnipeg* (Winnipeg, 1879), pp. 17–18.
[23]*Musical Journal* (Toronto, April 15, 1888).

With the foundations thus laid by individual music lovers, military establishments, and churches, amateur organizations of various types made their appearance only a few years after the foundation of each settlement. In Winnipeg musical "firsts" followed each other in rapid order. A reed organ with five stops was played in 1873; a pipe organ was in use in neighbouring St. Boniface two years later. By 1876 a Glee Club and a city band had been established. Within the first ten years of its history Regina had a Musical Club (*ca.* 1882), a Musical and Literary Society (1886), a brass band of 14 instruments financed by the community (1886), a Glee Club and a Musical Society (1888), a Choral Society which met in weekly rehearsals to provide "free instruction in vocal music and to assist at charitable entertainments" (1889),[24] and a Minstrel Club (1891), not to speak of several church choirs and the North West Mounted Police Band. In Vancouver funds to establish a brass band were raised by subscription early in 1887, in time to greet the arrival of the first transcontinental train with the sounds of "See the Conquering Hero" and other appropriate tunes. The next year people were invited to join the Vancouver Musical Club, the only condition for admission being that "members must have voices of some kind."

Within a decade or two, musical organizations of a more mature character took the place of the many feeble and short-lived groups. The new groups were comparable in seriousness of purpose to the large musical societies of Montreal, Quebec, and Toronto, though hardly matching them in musical resources. A newly arrived Anglican bishop, Acton Windeyer Sillitoe inspired the formation of the New Westminster Choral Union (*ca.* 1880), the first important musical organization in the West outside Victoria. It cultivated oratorio and introduced *The Messiah* and other works in New Westminster. It also travelled to neighbouring settlements, by stage coach or sleigh to sing in improvised concert halls where "cultured citizens sat next to roughly dressed loggers."

In the early 1880's when the railway had reached Winnipeg and the town's population had risen to 7,000, a German immigrant by the name of Joseph Hecker founded the first Philharmonic Society on the prairies. Unfortunately Hecker soon departed to the United States, and the society's successor, a choir organized by

24Drake, *Regina*, p. 59.

Dr. P. R. MacLagan from Montreal, was not active for long. Instrumental music was cultivated by the Apollo Club. Light opera was very popular. A performance of *Iolanthe* by the Hess Opera Company from England opened the Princess Opera House in 1883. When fire destroyed the theatre 16 years later, it had a long record of performances by the local Operatic Society.

In Regina too Gilbert and Sullivan enjoyed great popularity. A Musical and Dramatic Society staged *The Pirates of Penzance* in 1899 but eventually ran into difficulties when it was realized that the payment of fees for performing rights had been forgotten. The work of the society was continued, however, by the Regina Philharmonic Society. It was organized by Frank L. Laubach (*ca.* 1858–1923), a professional musician from Scotland, who was the undisputed leader in musical affairs from 1904 until his retirement in 1922.

The Vancouver Philharmonic Society made its appearance in 1890, joined by the Orchestral Society in a performance of overtures, songs, choruses, and other music by such composers as Gounod, Bizet, Mendelssohn, and Schumann. The number of singers exceeded 100, and in 1895 the orchestra numbered 40 players. The most prominent pioneer musicians here were the English-born brothers George J. and Fred W. Dyke, who as choirmasters, orchestra leaders, violinists, and teachers participated in musical activities from their beginnings in 1886. George (*ca.* 1865–1940) in particular has been credited with opening the first music-supply store and the first music school (with five teachers) and with arranging the first visits of world-renowned artists to Vancouver. In 1913 he moved to Victoria, where he was active as a music critic and concert manager.[25]

With these varied musical resources the budding young com-

[25]The following musicians accomplished important pioneer work in Vancouver in the early decades of the century. John David Alvin Tripp (1867–1945), who was born in Dunbarton, Ontario, was the first piano student to graduate from the Toronto Conservatory of Music. He became a teacher there after continuing his studies in Europe. He helped to establish the Conservatory examinations in western Canada and in 1910 moved to Vancouver where he achieved great reputation as a pianist and teacher. Jean Robinson (Mrs. Walter Coulthard, 1883–1933), a graduate of the New England Conservatory, settled in Vancouver in 1904. She created a sensation there by introducing Debussy's piano music. Active in all fields of music, she helped in the formation of the Vancouver Women's Musical Club and the British Columbia Music Teachers' Federation.

munities were able to enjoy a variety of musical shows. Performances were, moreover, not restricted to local talent. The new railway lines carried not only individual artists but entire companies to the distant provinces. In 1899 a small troupe from New York's Metropolitan Opera House presented *The Chimes of Normandy* in Regina and probably in other towns; in the same period Godfrey's British Military Band created a sensation. The Emma Juch English Opera Company—soloists, chorus and orchestra comprising over 125 people—was engaged for $10,000 to open the Vancouver Opera House on February 9, 1891. The opera performed was *Lohengrin*, in which "Miss Juch was indescribably charming as Elsa, and has won all Vancouver by her wonderful genius of voice and acting as well as by her gentle character and amiable traits."[26] The opera house was constructed by the Canadian Pacific Railway at a cost of over $200,000. After the performance Miss Juch stated that she had never sung in a more perfect building.

Mme Albani, Canada's famous *prima donna* made her first tour of the West in the winter of 1896–7, singing in various towns from Port Arthur to Victoria. Her performances were a combination of concert and opera, although it was sometimes difficult to secure proper stage equipment: "At one place—it was Calgary, I think—nothing like limelight or electric light was forthcoming for the light effects in the Garden Scene of 'Faust,' and we had to fall back upon the big lamp of a locomotive, which the railway people lent us, and which did duty for the moon."[27] In spite of such handicaps, Mme Albani's appearance was regarded as a holiday occasion everywhere. Dances and other amusements were organized and people came from their homesteads and ranches dozens of miles away to enjoy the festivities.

FACTORS OF GROWTH: The strongest impression created by this account of musical beginnings in western Canada is surely that of the amazing speed and variety of development. Just as it had taken Upper Canada only a short time to establish musical societies approaching or equalling those of the older regions, so the newly opened west in its turn appeared eager to catch up with the rest of the country in a few decades. Several theories have been ad-

26Vancouver *World*, Feb. 10, 1891.
27Emma Albani, *Forty Years of Song* (London, 1911), p. 236.

vanced to explain this phenomenon. One points out that the settlers included a large number of well-educated people. J. E. Middleton has stated that "the West had a better start in music than the older provinces. Prairie pioneers coming mainly from Ontario had the taste produced by a hundred years of progress."[28] In reference to the pioneer women of Vancouver Island, de Bertrand Lugrin writes:

Among the first few scores of women to come to the colony there were many who were real musicians. They had been educated in England and taught what was best. They were familiar with the classics, and had learned only what was worth knowing. Many of them brought pianos with them, and the civilizing and harmonizing influence of music soon began to make itself felt among those who had never known anything except the war chants of the Indians, the savage music of the native dances, or the rare song of the voyageurs.[29]

The same writer stresses elsewhere that these women were very well acquainted with the popular operas of the period. To counterbalance the hardships of life and the influence of cheap and vulgar entertainment was a challenge for the better educated pioneers. The need for music under pioneer conditions was emphasized by an anonymous Toronto writer in 1874 who admitted that the Canadians had "been so much engaged in the utility of life . . . as to have had but little time to spare for its beauties." But "the more intense his 'struggle for existence' the greater the need for some resting place from the sordid cares and small worries of his daily life."[30] This "theory of compensation," as it might be called, is also demonstrated by de Bertrand Lugrin, again in connection with the ladies of Victoria. He says that they took a great part "in developing and upholding the finer things of life under most strenuous and harsh conditions. . . . They realized that the great solace for distress, discomfort and hardship is music. . . ."[31] While couched in somewhat sentimental phrases and one-sidedly stressing the middle-class element, these quotations nevertheless describe an important factor in the musical growth of the West.

Added to these social forces was the geographical fact of isolation.

[28]Middleton, "Music in Canada," XII, 650.
[29]Lugrin, *Pioneer Women*, p. 199.
[30]"Music in Canada," *Nation* (Toronto), May 7, 1874.
[31]Lugrin, *Pioneer Women*, p. 226.

Even though professional troupes undertook occasional tours of the prairies and coastal regions, the West was still "a hundred dollars from anywhere"—a hundred dollars at least from any centre of professional art. The West certainly had to rely upon its own musical resources to a greater degree than did the older provinces. It is no accident that competitive music festivals, with their emphasis on amateur activity, were found a most congenial expression of western conditions and have remained the centre of musical life ever since their beginning in 1908.

One advantage which the new provinces enjoyed in establishing their musical life was the development of the phonograph—the beginnings of both almost coincided in time. When the first phonograph appeared in Regina in 1891 it may not have exercised any powerful influence on musical taste, but during the next decades it rapidly developed into a major source of musical entertainment. According to a Toronto composer and pianist, W. O. Forsyth, in the West "the influence of the Gramophone is not the unhealthy and distracting one many suppose, or would have us believe. Nearly every one owning one of these instruments possesses some good records which reproduce the performances of famous singers and instrumentalists. . . ."[32]

Although other factors that contributed to the rapid musical development of the west might be mentioned, one conclusion becomes obvious from those theories already discussed. While elaborate facilities for music-making may be lacking under the hard conditions of pioneer life, the need for music and the capacity for its enjoyment are intensified rather than thwarted. Music is not a luxury but a natural mode of human expression.

[32]W. O. Forsyth, "The Winsome, Wonderful West," *Canadian Journal of Music* (Sept. 1914).

OPERA: The present chapter rounds off our survey of music in late nineteenth-century Canada with a discussion of the highlights of concert life and various peripheral activities. At first let us dwell on two of the most complex forms of musical entertainment: opera and festivals.

One of the first impressions of visitors to Canada in the mid twentieth century is the lack of opera houses and the rareness of opera performances. It comes as a great surprise to discover on old city maps that almost every Canadian city, large or small, had a "Grand" or "Royal" opera house about the turn of the century. Montreal and Toronto had such institutions from *ca.* 1875. In the next decades not only the larger cities but many small towns followed suit—Walkerton in Ontario, Indian Head in Saskatchewan, St.-Jean (Richelieu) in Quebec, and even Dawson City in Yukon Territory. Closer investigation quickly dispels the illusion that Canadian cities vied with each other in the production of opera. The Grand Opera Houses of Canada had little but the name in common with the famous theatres of Europe. Few, if any, maintained their own permanent troupe, although some employed a small orchestra on a regular basis. What then was the function of these halls? They echoed to the sounds of vaudeville, musical comedy, stage plays, and the noise of political and other rallies. Only a small part of the entertainment was real grand opera. Such inflation of names, whether applied to amusement halls, music schools, or orchestral or operatic groups, was characteristic of the period. It was difficult then, and it sometimes still is, to distinguish from their names between a *bona fide* opera company and an amateur operetta club working with piano accompaniment.

Today these opera houses have been converted into movie theatres or have made room for offices and stores. One opera house still open is the Victoria Opera House in Cobourg, Ontario. Opened in 1860 it was at first only a banquet hall, and the court room upstairs was only later converted into a theatre.

If we consider that in the middle of the twentieth century Canadian opera lovers depend largely on radio, television, and phonograph performances, we realize that our Canadian grandparents were, after all, not too badly served with this form of spectacle. Though grand opera was rarely performed by native singers, the public had more opportunity than they have today to hear performances of travelling companies. Canada benefited from its nearness to the United States, for many troupes would never have come, had it not been easy to extend their United States visit to Canada. The majority of the singers were of Italian, French, or English origin, frequently recruited in North America. The troupes ranged from minstrel-show companies with brass bands to genuine opera companies, such as the Strakosch Italian Opera, the Kellogg troupe or the Hess English Opera Company.

There must have been some good and much bad in these operatic performances. The orchestral accompaniment was often mutilated by the absence of the rarer instruments. Prima donnas of widest fame and "most celebrated tenors" were featured prominently in advertisements but excused in the last moment as being indisposed. In reality they had never come with the company. Little is known about the participation of Canadian musicians in the chorus and orchestra.

The frequency of performances varied from year to year but undoubtedly surpassed present-day production in most cities. Within only a few months in 1880 Toronto was visited by four or five different companies. In the season 1889–90, 26 different operas, 10 of them grand operas, were performed in Toronto. The following season had no less than 91 performances of 24 works, among them only four grand operas: *Lohengrin, Les Huguenots, Carmen* and *Rigoletto*. The figures decrease a little for the season of 1891–2, but they are still impressive. Fifty-seven performances of 19 operas were given, among them four major works: *Faust*, *Cavalleria Rusticana* (whose world *première* had taken place in 1890), *Tannhäuser* and *Carmen*. It is interesting to note that the earlier Wagner operas were familiar to Canadians long before those by Mozart.

Operatic productions using Canadian talent were rare. Montreal achieved most in this field, because the French-Canadian love of opera was as marked as that of oratorio was in Ontario. Generally the organizational, financial, and artistic problems involved in producing opera proved too formidable to stage performances without serious compromises. A typical example of such compromise was the production of an Italian opera in Victoria in the 1880's. A leading singer refused to sing her part in anything but Italian, while the rest of the cast sang in English, the language in which the conductor had studied the work as a young man.

A quick summary of operatic progress is given in the following list of performances which were the first of each respective opera, according to the documents inspected.

> Bellini, *Norma*, Toronto, 1853
> Verdi, *Il Trovatore*, Toronto, 1859
> Weber, *Der Freischütz*, Toronto, 1860
> Rossini, *Barber of Seville*, Quebec, 1864
> David, *Le Désert* (Symphonic Ode), Montreal, 1866 (local production)
> Boieldieu, *La Dame Blanche*, Quebec, 1860's (local production)
> Wagner, *The Flying Dutchman*, Montreal, 1871 (local production)
> David, *La Perle du Brésil*, Quebec, 1878 (local production)
> Wagner, *Lohengrin*, Montreal, 1888
> Wagner, *Tannhäuser*, Toronto, 1891–2 season
> Mascagni, *Cavalleria Rusticana*, Toronto, 1891–2 season
> Verdi, *Otello*, Montreal, 1904
> Puccini, *La Bohème*, Montreal, 1904
> Wagner, *Parsifal*, Montreal, 1905
> Wagner, *Die Walküre*, Montreal, 1905

MUSIC FESTIVALS: The most typical signs of musical growth were the festivals held in many cities across the country. These were characteristic of the period generally, as well as of Canada, for an admiration of musical mass effort was widespread in Europe and the United States. Only a few festivals were competitive. An important example of such a competition was the band festival held in Montreal in June 1878. It attracted 19 military and civilian bands from 10 cities as far apart as Quebec in the east and Waterloo and Stratford in the west. Calixa Lavallée was among the judges. Two of the top prizes went to Montreal bands, and from this resulted the charge of prejudice and some serious disagreement among the judges. Nevertheless the event was a significant one, for never before had so many Canadian musicians from so many cities gathered together in one place.

Most festivals were concentrated efforts of music-making in which co-operation rather than competition was the ruling principle. The entire musical resources of a city would be called into action and reinforcements imported from neighbouring towns. Giant choruses and orchestras with over one hundred players would thus be assembled.[1] In Montreal such music festivals were held in 1877 and 1895, in Toronto in 1886 and 1894, in Quebec in 1883, and in Hamilton in 1887. We have already described the song festivals of the German communities in Ontario. One may be inclined to condemn all these affairs as having been spectacles rather than concerts, but it would be a serious error to underestimate their importance as stimuli to musical enterprise. One should keep in mind, for instance, that the Montreal Philharmonic Society was born out of the festival of 1877. Through the combined attractions of music and spectacle many people were for the first time exposed to art, and many others, with some previous training, were persuaded to join choirs or orchestras.

FIRST VISITS AND FIRST CONCERT PERFORMANCES: During the late nineteenth century nearly all the world-famous artists who visited the United States also performed in Canada. Some of these artists with the dates of their first known performance in Canada are recorded in the following list (see pp. 102–3 for guest artists before Confederation):

Christine Nilsson, between 1870 and 1872
Henri Wieniawski, 1872
Anton Rubinstein, 1872

[1]These efforts had a model in the Boston Peace Jubilees of 1869 and 1872 in which some Canadians had participated.

Hans von Bülow, 1876
Eduard Remenyi, 1880
August Wilhelmj, 1880
Rafael Joseffy, 1880

Leopold Godowsky, 1886
Lilli Lehmann, 1886
Ignaz Paderewski, 1892
Eugène Ysaye, 1895

Conductors who visited Canada with their American orchestras included Theodore Thomas, Emil Paur, and Anton Seidl.

An idea of advance in concert repertoire may similarly be gained by tabulating some performances which can reasonably be considered the first in Canada, whether given by Canadian artists or by a visiting organization.

ORATORIO AND MASS

Haydn, *The Creation*, Hamilton, 1858 (excerpts in Saint John, 1842, rehearsed in Halifax 1842)
Handel, *The Messiah*, Toronto, 1857
Handel, *Judas Maccabeus*, Toronto, 1858
Haydn, *The Seasons*, Hamilton, 1860
Mendelssohn, *Elijah*, Toronto, 1874
Mendelssohn, *St. Paul*, Toronto, 1876
Mozart, *Requiem*, Montreal, 1888
Elgar, *The Dream of Gerontius*, Montreal, 1906

SYMPHONIES

Haydn, "Surprise" Symphony, Hamilton, 1855 (unabridged?)
Mozart, Symphony no. 40, Quebec, 1857
Beethoven, Symphony no. 6, Montreal, 1871
Beethoven, Symphony no. 7, Toronto, 1893
Schubert, "Unfinished" Symphony, Montreal, 1894
Dvorak, "New World" Symphony, Toronto, 1895
Beethoven, Symphony no. 9, Montreal, 1897
Beethoven, Symphony no. 3, Montreal, 1902

A SHORT HISTORY OF FOLK-SONG COLLECTING: After the middle of the nineteenth century, folk song in Canada reached a critical stage. Folk singing was still widespread and immigrants from many countries added their songs to the rich treasure. Indeed new songs were still being constantly created, finding inspiration in such new types of work as railroad-building and mining. But while the railroad crews made up their songs,[2] they paved the way

[2]Mrs. Edith F. Fowke of Toronto cited the following examples to me: "The Jolly Railroad Boy" from Ontario and "Drill Ye Heroes, Drill" from Newfoundland.

for trains that were to carry concert artists, orchestras, and opera troupes to Canadian cities, announcing the triumph of the European concert repertoire. The impact of modern technology affected people's mode of living and thus their modes of enjoying music. The steamboat and railroad spelled a slow death to the song of the *voyageurs*. Louis Harap has summed it up neatly:

As the nineteenth century wore on, industrialism uprooted the common people, pulled them out of occupations which had called forth folk song, made city amusements more accessible, spread education and newspaper reading, and finally brought them the phonograph, the radio, and the movies. As a consequence of these conditions, folk song decayed rapidly; to an ever-increasing extent it was supplanted by "popular" song.[3]

Two musical cultures began to exist side by side: the declining culture of folk music and the rising culture of concert and "popular" music. They were almost mutually exclusive. Folk music was relegated to isolated regions, while musicians and amateurs in the cities tended to ignore it as something trivial and primitive. They were far too busy absorbing the printed literature of imported music—in light or serious vein—to study and foster the oral traditions handed down through generations of early Canadian settlers.

One force at work in French Canada prevented the split between folk and sophisticated music from becoming complete: the force of nationalism. French Canadians always nurtured an ardent patriotism, and many folk songs had become identified with the display of patriotism (see page 138). With the prospect of the submergence of their culture under that of English-speaking North America, the pride in local traditions was even further strengthened.

While it was the social and political climate that kept folk song alive in town and country, the credit for first having applied the tools of scholarship to the songs belongs to two individuals, a professor of medicine and man of letters, François Alexandre Hubert LaRue (1833–81), and a public servant and musician, Ernest Gagnon (1834–1915). Both men had studied in France and there had become infected with the new literary and musical movement which we call nationalism.

Before describing the achievement of these scholars, let us trace the story of folk-song collecting in Canada from its very beginnings.

[3]Louis Harap, *Social Roots of the Arts* (New York, 1949), p. 125.

The first person to take notice of aboriginal music in Canada was Marc Lescarbot, the Parisian lawyer who wrote down Indian songs in New France in the early seventeenth century (see p. 9). Other Frenchmen, although they had not crossed the Atlantic, began to interest themselves in the customs of the Canadian Indians. In 1633 Jean de Laet in his *Novus Orbis* reprinted the words and pitch names of an Indian song from Lescarbot. Its fascination lay in the fact that it contained the word "Alleluya." Possibly this word proves missionary influence; possibly there was an accidental similarity of sound. In *L'Harmonie universelle* (1637) Father Mersenne quoted the music of a "chanson canadoise" to demonstrate his view that musically illiterate people always sing in the diatonic scale. He had obtained the song from a sea captain and the notation cannot be considered accurate.[4]

Voyageur songs were collected first by Ferdinand Wentzel, a Norwegian who served with the North West Company in the early years of the nineteenth century, spending most of his time in the Athabasca and Mackenzie regions. In Masson's *Les Bourgeois de la Compagnie du Nord-Ouest* we read:

Mr. Wentzel was a musician; [Sir John] Franklin even says, "an excellent musician!" This talent of his brightened the long and dreary hours of his life and contributed to keep all cheerful around him. A collection of the voyageurs songs made by him is in our possession, but they are mostly obscene and unfit for publication.[5]

In 1823 Lieutenant George Back, who accompanied one of Sir John Franklin's Arctic expeditions, published a collection of *Canadian Airs* in London. It included 73 pages of music with accompaniments and English translations. A few years later Edward Ermatinger, a fur-trader of Swiss descent, whose education in England had included music, noted down eleven *voyageur* songs in the far west of Canada, where he travelled in the service of the Hudson's Bay Company. They have been preserved in manuscript and were published for the first time by Marius Barbeau in the *Journal of American Folklore* in 1955. As Barbeau points out,

[4]See Julien Tiersot, *La Musique chez les peuples indigènes de l'Amérique du Nord* (Paris, 1910). Rousseau and others "arranged" Mersenne's example, adding to the distortion.

[5]L. F. R. Masson, *Les Bourgeois de la Compagnie du Nord-Ouest*, vol. I (1890), part 2, p. 71.

their special interest is twofold: they are the first collection of *voyageur* songs to be preserved and they reveal that there is no basic difference in the versions of the same tunes sung in the West and in the St. Lawrence valley.

A number of *chansonniers* appeared in French Canada about the middle of the nineteenth century, usually without printed music. Johann Georg Kohl, a German geographer and writer who visited Canada in the 1850's, was told that the French Canadians were still singing their old songs and bought all available collections. To his disappointment he noted that the books contained very few real folk songs and instead a great number of songs recently imported from France. Even those called *chansons canadiennes* usually proved to have been written by priests and other educated people.[6] Kohl himself made a valuable contribution with his observations on Ojibwa Indian and *voyageur* music of the Lake Superior region in his book *Kitchi-Gami* (1860).

It remained to Hubert LaRue to discover the value of folk songs as historical and national documents. His studies, which were published in *Le Foyer canadien* in 1863 and 1865 under the title "Les Chansons populaires et historiques du Canada," are of literary and political rather than musical interest and are focused on the comparison between French and Canadian versions of the same songs. As a matter of fact, many of the poems which LaRue exhibits are not genuine folklore and have borrowed their melodies from older songs.

A companion pioneer work in music appeared in 1865. The name of its author, Ernest Gagnon, is still a household word in Canadian music, for the *Chansons populaires du Canada* has become a classic in its field. The collection has maintained its popularity until this day, and in 1956 went into its tenth edition (conforming to the second edition of 1880). It gives the words and music of over a hundred songs which Gagnon noted down during excursions to the countryside of Quebec. He did not attempt to arrange or harmonize the melodies. This fact and the inclusion of a commentary for each song and an essay on the musical structure of the songs add to the value of the book.

[6]Johann Georg Kohl, *Reisen in Canada* . . . (Stuttgart, 1856), pp. 178–9. English translation: *Travels in Canada* . . . (London, 1861), I, 202–4. This book contains many interesting references to music.

What was Gagnon's background? What musical equipment did he have for collecting folk songs? He began his musical education in Canada and finished it in Paris under Auguste Durand (composition) and Henri Herz (piano).[7] From 1864 to 1876 he was organist at the Quebec Basilica. In 1866 he was chosen director of the Union Musicale in that city. At the same time he taught music at Laval Normal School and Quebec Seminary and acted as the first president of the Quebec Académie de Musique. The interests of this many-sided personality extended to literary and historical studies. Gagnon's writings include a biography of Louis Jolliet and two volumes of historical essays, published posthumously. In addition to all these activities, Gagnon for thirty years went about his daily work as secretary of the Quebec Department of Agriculture and Public Works. Recognition came through his election to the Royal Society of Canada and as *officier de l'instruction publique* in France and by a doctorate from Laval University.

Gagnon's output as a composer was small; but his interest in folklore prompted him to harmonize a number of Canadian songs and Christmas carols. As an organist his strength lay in improvisation. Arthur Letondal has contrasted Gagnon's musical outlook with that of Antoine Dessane, saying that Dessane favoured the classics, Gagnon the French and Italian music of his day. Dessane's interest lay in counterpoint and fugue, whereas Gagnon's first love was melody.

The repercussions of LaRue's and Gagnon's publications were widespread. In France their work kindled surprise and delight in the unsuspected knowledge that French traditions had been preserved so well and so richly in Canada. In Canada Gagnon's book demonstrated the dignity and beauty of folk music at a time when it was too often considered barbaric and primitive. Both men helped to widen the French Canadians' consciousness of their cultural heritage. Thus a French scholar, Julien Tiersot, who made a study of French songs in Canada at the beginning of the twentieth century, was able to conclude that "French popular song

[7]An interesting episode during his Parisian years was Gagnon's visit to François Auber and to Rossini (1858). Rossini inquired about the character and customs of the French Canadians and listened to Gagnon with serious attention. See Arthur Letondal, "Ernest Gagnon, Ecrivain et folkloriste," *Qui ?* (March 1951).

in Canada, far from being despised by the educated classes, has remained in favor with them as much and even more than among the lower classes, to whom it has long been relegated in France." The interesting point is that folk songs remained popular among the urban middle classes, though more recent research has shown that Tiersot underestimated the wealth of folk song among the "lower classes." This error was due to that fact that Gagnon's collection was accepted in the musical world as an exhaustive work, comprising all that was worth while recording.

Only a few other studies of folk music appeared in the late nineteenth century, notable among them being Ernest Myrand's *Noëls anciens de la Nouvelle-France* (Quebec, 1899) and Alexander T. Cringan's publication of over ninety Iroquois songs with commentary in the annual *Archaeological Reports* of the Ontario Provincial Museum of 1898, 1899, and 1902. Not until the early twentieth century did Marius Barbeau, Edward Sapir, E.-Z. Massicotte and others begin the serious and systematic investigation of folk music in Canada. Where Gagnon had given us a small glimpse, his successors opened up a wide vista of folk art; and whereas the older collectors appraised aboriginal and folk music with the narrow criteria of contemporary art music, the next generation learned to approach this music on its own terms. It must be admitted that Gagnon attributed value to folk songs only to the degree that they conformed to the grammar of modern art music. In a survey of North American Indian music he estimated that aboriginal chants assumed a rhythmic and modal shape bordering on art only under the impact of European influence.[9] Few composers or scholars of a later generation would share the appraisal of the Gagnon collection given in 1914 by J. E. Middleton, which expresses much the same bias:

From the academic musical standpoint the melodies have little interest. They are unconventional to excess. Many of them are not to be classified either in the major or the minor mode. There is more than a trace of Gregorian in them. What would a modern composer do with a theme like "Ah, qui me passery le bois," which ends on the second

[8]Julien Tiersot, *Forty-Four French Folk-Songs and Variants from Canada, Normandy, and Brittany* (New York, 1910), Preface.
[9]Ernest Gagnon, "Les Sauvages de l'Amérique et l'art musical," *Congrès international des américanistes, Québec 1906* (Quebec, 1907), pp. 179 ff.

of the major diatonic scale? As Gagnon very properly says, harmonization of these folk airs is too great a task.[10]

In an age where such an outlook appears outmoded and where the study of Canadian folklore is recognized and supported by universities and governments alike it should not be forgotten that to Ernest Gagnon belongs the merit of first having demonstrated the value of folk music in the fabric of Canadian culture.

CHURCH MUSIC: Our description of musical life again and again stresses the role played by the churches as focal points of musical practice, experience and employment. It is precisely because church music was so closely interwoven with other musical activities that it cannot be easily isolated from the historical fabric. For this reason and because it would involve the description of the liturgy and history of a dozen or more sects and denominations which flourished in nineteenth-century Canada, a systematic treatment of the subject must remain outside the scope of this book. What might hold true of the musical service in the Baptist or Methodist Church would hardly be valid for the Anglican or Roman Catholic Church. At one extreme there were sects which frowned upon "ungodly" singing; at the other, there were such high dignitaries as Bishops Jacob Mountain and A. W. Sillitoe who personally fostered both sacred and secular music-making. Many churches provided the musical nucleus from which sprang choral societies, and many organists made fine contributions to the improvement of musical knowledge and taste in their capacity as performers and teachers. For many communities the church acted as the local concert hall. Here many people received their earliest musical impressions in childhood, here they first became acquainted with the great oratorios and organ compositions.

There is no lack of source material in church records, hymn books and contemporary periodicals for a study of the literature for choir and organ and the technical and aesthetic level of performance. Church music was the subject of lively discussion and polemics: the design of organs, the place of music in worship, the training and duties of church musicians, the quality of the music

10J. E. Middleton, "Music in Canada," *Canada and Its Provinces* (Toronto, 1914), XII, 648.

performed—these were the foremost topics. In so far as generalization about church music in nineteenth-century Canada is possible, one might say that it was comparable to that of provincial England and France. As Charles Peaker has observed, ". . . the early settlers . . . thankfully received the forms of worship and the music of the church that came to them from older lands."[11] Thankfully they may have received, but not always with proper discrimination. J. E. P. Aldous, the Hamilton organist, knew why he attacked the widely used American hymn collection of Moody and Sankey with its "jingling tunes and puerile harmonies" in his speech at the Ontario Music Teachers' Association convention in 1886. Sometimes such low standards of taste were the fault of a church committee or minister ignorant of music who overruled the better judgment of the choirmaster, but only too often the musician himself was to blame.

While the prevailing taste left much to be desired, however, the technical quality was adequate: fine church choirs existed in every city, organs of varying sizes were numerous, and there were many fine organists. The following quotation from the Toronto *Musical Journal* of January 15, 1888, confirms the superiority of technique over taste and demonstrates the spirited tone of controversy:

THE MUSICAL JOURNAL desires to give forth no uncertain sound with regard to its views on Church Music. We are looking hopefully for the day when we shall have in our midst some reliable institution for the training of choirmasters and organists for the service of the church. Technique, without a trained taste and sound theoretic tuition, is a growing danger against which sacred music needs prompt protection. How lamentably ill-judged are the majority of the "voluntaries" we hear in our churches!

Just what the writer had in mind comes to light in the issue of February 15:

Mr. Torrington, we are glad to learn, is rapidly completing his arrangements for the establishment of the College of Organists, which was projected some months ago.

The promoters included prominent organists from various cities, but the plan did not come to fruition until 21 years later. In this

[11]Charles Peaker, "Church Music, Other than Roman Catholic," *Encyclopedia Canadiana* (Ottawa, 1957), II, 381.

interval many new churches had been built and there had been a large influx of organists from Great Britain, many of whom possessed excellent training. On October 27, 1909, a number of church musicians met at the Brantford Conservatory of Music to establish a College of Organists in Canada, similar to that existing in England. The first general council of the Canadian Guild of Organists (now the Royal Canadian College of Organists) met in Toronto in 1910, and the first convention took place in that city in 1911 with delegates representing five provinces. Dr. Albert Ham, organist and choirmaster at St. James Cathedral in Toronto was the first president. Although the College was never intended to become a teaching institution, its first aim was to set up examinations in organ playing. Through granting the diplomas of Associateship and Fellowship, as well as through the lectures, discussions and recitals at its annual conventions, the R.C.C.O. has raised the standards of church music in Canada immeasurably above those prevailing in the nineteenth century.

In the field of Roman Catholic church music the need for improvement was recognized by Ernest Gagnon whose *Accompagnement d'orgue des chants liturgiques* (1903) helped to eliminate the use of tasteless chromatic harmonizations. In the same year Pope Pius X issued the famous *Motu proprio* which laid down the functions and qualities desirable in sacred music. The reforms based on this document have had far-reaching effects.

MUSIC EDUCATION: Music education was at once an agent and a product of the increased musical activity which we have observed in all parts of Canada: choral and orchestral societies cannot flourish without a system of elementary instruction and music education receives an important stimulus when choirs and orchestras are waiting to engage talent.

In the early days many leaders of choirs and bands had, as well as rehearsing the pieces to be performed, given as much instruction in the rudiments of musical theory and performance as was needed at the moment. In the late nineteenth century such instruction was taken over by agencies who were concerned with teaching all that was necessary to become a skilled practitioner of a particular branch of music, leaving it to the individual pupils to apply their skill in any way and place they might. There were four such agencies, the public school, the private music teacher, the conservatory and the university, each with its particular function.

Until the middle of the nineteenth century music was at best an incidental activity in public schools, depending largely on the talent and inclination of individual teachers. In order to give music a regular place on the curriculum it was necessary to train qualified teachers. In Ontario, a pioneer in the field, the foundations for the training of music teachers were laid in 1847 when James P. Clarke was appointed music teacher at the Toronto Normal School.[12] In the following decades music teaching made a gradual appearance in some Ontario schools. Toronto and Hamilton have had a continuous history of music instruction since the 1870's. Hamilton is reported to have had a school orchestra as early as 1887.

Few men have played as important a role in the growth of Ontario school music as did Alexander T. Cringan (1860–1931). Trained in Britain, Cringan arrived in Canada in 1884. At this time there was much experimentation in Toronto with the different sol-fa systems. Cringan's able demonstration of the tonic sol-fa method resulted in its adoption. A few years after his arrival he was appointed Superintendent for the Toronto Public Schools and published a *Canadian Music Course* in three volumes together with a *Teacher's Handbook*, expounding the tonic sol-fa system. These were long recognized as standard textbooks. Cringan was also made director of a teachers' course in practical music, theory, and methods, established by the University of Toronto for the Ontario Department of Education.

In Halifax, to give an example from another province, music has been a subject of public-school instruction since 1867. The first School Music Festival was held there in 1870. In Quebec, singing was part of the school curriculum as early as the seventeenth century. Two centuries later we find the names of many prominent musicians associated with the teaching of music in schools. R. O. Pelletier and the brothers Gagnon were normal-school instructors. Many convent schools emphasized music teaching; and, indeed, opportunities for musical education were richer for girls than for boys.

By the end of the nineteenth century, school music had much advanced in Canada, but was still not a universal feature. The

[12]G. Roy Fenwick, *The Function of Music in Education* (Toronto, 1951).

plan of studies usually concentrated on rote- or sight-singing and on the elements of notation, but rarely on instrumental music.

In the decades after Confederation a crisis arose in the field of private music instruction, available as yet from independent teachers only and not from conservatories. As prosperity increased and time for pursuits of leisure grew more abundant, music lessons became a fasionable part of education; indeed they were almost an inevitable part of a young lady's training. This demand swelled the ranks of music teachers. Along with the genuine teachers, however, there undoubtedly came into existence an army of charlatans, frequently adopting foreign-sounding names to impress their pupils' parents, and interested in amassing fees rather than in advancing musical art. In addition there was a variety of well-intentioned but poorly qualified instructors: impoverished widows teaching piano to neighbourhood children, young students eager to finance their own lessons, and so forth. Many parents and pupils lacked discrimination in selecting a teacher, and the results were often disastrous.

All over the country sincere musicians began to protest. Gustave Smith, a distinguished French musician in Ottawa, in a survey made in 1882 of 25 years of musical development, deplored the passing of the days when music teachers regarded their work as a profession rather than a *métier* and when the chase for dollars and luxuries had not yet corrupted the custom of spontaneous music-making among friends.[13] The Toronto *Musical Journal* castigated in no uncertain terms the situation existing in 1887:

Now . . . there are but few Canadian towns of any importance which do not overflow with teachers, and surely there must be thousands of intelligent young people, willing and able to take full advantage of musical instruction. Yet, what awful trash do we constantly hear! What wild scamperings across the long-suffering piano! What silly, sentimental stuff is wailed forth by some of our "very musical" young ladies! I cannot blame them, for how can you expect people who have never, perhaps, heard one note of good music in all their lives, to perform and appreciate what they cannot understand!"[14]

The negative criticism expressed by these writers was intended

[13]Gustave Smith, "Du mouvement musical en Canada," *L'Album Musical* (1882).

[14]"Musical Culture in Canada: A Few Words about Amateurs," *Musical Journal*, Toronto, June 15, 1887.

to draw attention to the need for improvement. Several means were suggested by which the level of musical instruction might be raised: the establishment of conservatories, certification of teachers, and emphasis on the study of classical music.

The history of campaigns and plans for music schools had begun much earlier, however. Quesnel, Sauvageau, and Brauneis, Jr., all designed plans for music schools.[15] Dessane envisaged a national conservatory with a particularly ambitious feature—an orchestra giving six concerts each year. Gustav Schilling, a musicologist from Germany, advertised plans for a Conservatoire de Musique in Montreal in 1863. The studio maintained in common by three of Canada's finest musicians—Lavallée, Frantz, and Mme Jehin-Prume—in the 1870's was a close approach to a conservatory in that it provided instruction in most of the basic subjects: piano, violin, voice and theory. It is unnecessary to continue the list: all our great musical pioneers held a firm belief in the potential talent of Canadians and recognized in the establishment of conservatories and musical societies the best guarantee for raising standards and defeating charlatanism.

The first actual establishment was the Académie de Musique founded in Quebec in 1868. Its founders included the Abbé Lagacé, the principal of the Quebec normal school, and the musicians Ernest and Gustave Gagnon, Frederick W. Mills, Arthur Lavigne and Antoine Dessane. The Académie was incorporated in 1870 by the Quebec government, which also helped to sustain it. This institution did not impart instruction; rather its purpose was to raise the level of music education throughout the province by a system of examinations and by recommending a list of carefully selected pieces for study. The Académie de Musique is still active as a supervisory body which examines students and awards scholarships.

A Canadian Conservatory was established in Toronto about 1876. A small school, it functioned for a decade. The first of the still existing schools to open their doors were the Mount Allison Conservatory, Sackville, N.B., and the Toronto Conservatory of Music, now, under the name of Royal Conservatory of Music of Toronto, the largest of its kind in Canada. Founded and incorporated in 1886 by Edward Fisher (its principal until 1913), it was

[15]The "singing schools" of the eighteenth and early nineteenth centuries cannot properly be considered as forerunners of the modern conservatory.

a large-scale enterprise from the beginning. In September 1887, when the first students were admitted, the faculty numbered about fifty teachers, and the programme of studies included, besides the more common subjects, orchestral and ensemble playing, composition, dramatics, and music history. Faculty and student recitals were a quarterly event. Student enrolment increased from 600 in the first year to 2,000 in 1912. Having quickly outgrown its original quarters, the Conservatory moved to its present building in 1897.[16]

The Toronto Conservatory was followed in 1888 by Torrington's Toronto College of Music, which flourished until its amalgamation in 1918 with the Canadian Academy of Music (founded in 1911). The Academy was a successor of W. O. Forsyth's Metropolitan School of Music and was in its turn absorbed by the Toronto Conservatory in 1924.

A group of music teachers founded the Halifax Conservatory in 1887. Charles Porter was appointed the first principal. In 1954 the conservatory joined with the Maritime Academy of Music and assumed the name Maritime Conservatory of Music.

In Hamilton a Musical Institute (later College of Music) was founded in 1888 by D. J. O'Brien. It was short-lived, as was the Hamilton School of Music founded the following year by John Edmund Paul Aldous. The still flourishing Hamilton Conservatory of Music was opened in 1897, succeeding a music school founded in 1890 by C. M. L. Harris. Harris remained the principal of the Conservatory for 15 years. Later Bruce Carey and William H. Hewlett directed the school.

The first Conservatory of Music in Montreal is said to have been established in 1876.[17] Records fail to indicate its length of existence. In 1895 Edmond Hardy founded the Conservatoire de Musique de Montréal, an institution which was subsidized by lottery and offered free tuition. Its staff included many well-known Montreal musicians, such as Oscar Martel, Charles Labelle, Achille Fortier, and Arthur Letondal. After five years it had to close its doors, as the lottery was stopped by the Dominion government. The next French music school of importance, the Conservatoire National de Musi-

[16]Plans for the construction of a new building were announced in 1960.
[17]E. Lapierre, *Calixa Lavallée* (rev. and enlarged ed.; Montreal, 1950), p. 109. Mrs. J. W. F. Harrison, "Canada," *The Imperial History and Encyclopedia of Music*, volume Foreign Music (New York, etc., *ca.* 1909), p. 236 quotes 1868 as the opening date.

que, was founded in 1905 by Alphonse Lavallée-Smith. By 1912 the school had issued 250 graduation diplomas.

The most influential of the English-language conservatories in Montreal were the Dominion College of Music, established in 1894 with the chief aim of holding examinations and issuing diplomas, and the McGill Conservatorium, which opened in 1904 under the directorship of Charles A. E. Harriss. In 1908, when McGill University created a professorship in music, Harriss was succeeded by Dr. Harry Crane Perrin, former organist of Canterbury Cathedral.

Conservatories in other cities would make a long list. In 1913 about fifty were in existence, but an even larger number had already closed for reasons of financial or organizational failure. As time went on, the number of conservatories decreased, and only a few progressive and well-organized ones survived the early decades of the new century.

It is a fair guess that the amazing number of music schools in the early period included a good many of the two-or-three-teacher variety, inflated by a grandiose name, "the small private dwelling on a back street, boasting a large gold sign, and evidently the pet hobby of some enthusiastic but untrained amateur."[18] It is difficult for a historian to single out the genuine music schools from among the many names.

A prominent feature of many conservatories was a system of examinations which enabled the pupil to have his skill tested at various stages of development. These examinations could be taken not only at the conservatory but in so-called "local centres." This system, borrowed from England, was particularly helpful in a country of vast distances. The conservatory would conduct examinations in the practical subjects in various cities by appointing resident music teachers as examiners or by sending out members of its own staff. Examinations in theoretical subjects were supervised by a local examiner and marked at the conservatory. This system enabled a pupil to obtain a certificate from a recognized institution without making a time-consuming and costly trip.

Local-centre examinations were conducted in Canada from *ca.*

[18]See S. Frances Harrison, "Historical Sketch of Music in Canada," *Canada: An Encyclopedia of the Country* (Toronto, 1898–1900), IV, 389; quotation from p. 390.

1899 by a British organization, the Associated Board of the Royal Schools, representing the Royal Academy and the Royal College of Music. The Toronto Conservatory had already established local examinations in 1898, opening centres from Halifax to Victoria. McGill Conservatorium followed suit in 1910. The local-centre examination system has become a major factor in musical education and has extended the influence of the conservatories far beyond their home cities.

We have already traced the beginnings of music teaching in the "higher ladies' academies" and boys' colleges (see p. 112). The first musician with the academic title Professor of Music was George W. Strathy. He held this position at the University of Trinity College, Toronto (founded 1852), in the early years of the university. Apparently Strathy's position did not carry much responsibility with it, for in 1881 Trinity's student paper pointed out that the university "had a Professor, but we have seen nothing of him—no graduates—no lecture—no examinations—it is time for a change."[19] The students here made reference to a privilege granted Trinity College in its charter, namely to give degrees in the various arts and faculties, including music. This criticism must have moved the authorities to action, for in 1883 a music syllabus was drawn up and three succeeding annual examinations towards the Bachelor of Music degree were instituted. In 1886 four degrees were conferred. A special feature of the course was the appointment of a registrar in England and the simultaneous holding of examinations in Toronto and London. This arrangement attracted many candidates in England, far more indeed than in Canada. Between 1886 and 1891, 193 students applied and 89 degrees were granted, both baccalaurcates and doctorates.

Trouble was brewing, however. Examiners and musical representatives of Oxford, Cambridge, and other British universities objected strongly to this invasion of their traditional rights and in particular to the fact that a Canadian institution granted degrees to students who had never set foot in Canada. They were afraid that such "in absentia degrees" would open the way to all kinds of bogus

[19]*Rouge et noir*, vol. II, no. 2. Much of the information about music at Trinity College is taken from *A History of the University of Trinity College, Toronto,* ed. T. A. Reed (Toronto, 1952), pp. 98–100, and from the University of Trinity College, Toronto, Faculty of Music, *Memorials Presented to Lord Knutsford . . .* (London, 1890).

degrees, and felt that the Trinity degrees were undoing the laborious efforts among English universities to impose really trustworthy tests of literary and musical attainment.[20] Without the official authorization of their universities they presented a memorandum to the Colonial Secretary in 1890, asking him to take action to stop this practice. Greatly aroused, the authorities of Trinity refuted the charges by pointing out that the requirements for the degrees were as strict as those upheld by British universities and claiming that Trinity's London examiners were men of high musical qualifications. However, in order to avoid friction and because the University of Durham had instituted a similar system of examinations in England, Trinity ceased to accept candidates in England after February 1891.[21]

Faculties of music as such did not exist in Canadian universities until after World War I, but the University of Toronto, Trinity College, and McGill, and Dalhousie, and Bishop's Universities offered examinations for degrees in music before that time. These examinations followed the time-honoured British type, dividing musical studies into harmony, counterpoint, fugue, history, analysis, and orchestration. Most degrees were of the bachelor level, but about fifty doctorates (a large number honorary) were conferred before 1914.

Instruction towards these degrees was given by conservatories, while the examiners were appointed by the universities. In order to tighten their relationship, and for economic reasons, many conservatories became affiliated with universities. University supervision meant the raising of teaching standards and the strengthening of financial security. The Toronto Conservatory was affiliated with Trinity College from the beginning but later became linked, like the Toronto College of Music and the Hamilton Conservatory, with the University of Toronto. This relationship continued until 1918, when the university created its own faculty of music. Similar affiliations took place between the Halifax Conservatory and Dalhousie University (1898); the music department of Albert College in Belleville, Ontario, and Victoria (Toronto) University; the

---

[20]For the English point of view in this affair, see F. W. Joyce, *The Life of the Rev. Sir F. A. G. Ouseley, Bart.* (London, 1896).

[21]This is the date given by Reed, *Trinity College*, p. 100. Elsewhere, however, I find a note dating the "scandal" 1895.

London and Brantford Conservatories and the University of Western Ontario; Le Conservatoire National de Musique and the Université de Montréal. McGill Conservatorium, founded in 1904, was fully incorporated into the university in 1908, and the first Bachelor and Doctor of Music degrees were conferred in 1911.

All these educational agencies combined—schools, conservatories, and universities—represent an impressive achievement for a young country. But no matter how excellent the opportunities for study, what was still lacking was the atmosphere of the European cities with their famous composers and virtuosi, rich libraries, and abundance of musical performances. It is not surprising that most Canadian students planning to take up music as a career sought advanced instruction outside Canada. There were exceptions, such as Arthur Lavigne and Joseph Vézina, fine musicians who received all their training in Canada, but these were few. The closest goal for students was Boston (Contant, Vogt), the most frequent ones Paris (Couture, Fortier, E. Gagnon, G. Gagnon, Lavallée, Lucas, etc.) and Leipzig (Blachford, Clench, Field, Forsyth, G. Gagnon, Lauder, A. Read, Vogt, Welsman, etc.), and a few Canadians studied in Berlin (Fairclough, Laliberté, Tripp, S. P. Warren).[22] It is a matter of record that while abroad, many of these students distinguished themselves brilliantly and won great honours.

MUSIC JOURNALS AND CRITICISM: An important aid to musical education was the music journal. Following the 1840's and 1850's, during which several literary journals issued sheet-music supplements and printed concert reviews, periodicals devoted entirely chiefly to music made their appearance in the 1860's. The dozen and a half musical periodicals that were founded between then and World War I varied in size, purpose, and quality. The majority were addressed to laymen and students rather than to professionals and were concerned with the spreading of basic knowledge about the "art of music." These journals represent valiant attempts to uphold refinement and culture amid a world of pioneering and commercialism. Many an inaugural editorial statement reflects a conscious desire to contribute to the improvement of

[22]W. Waugh Lauder was a pupil of Liszt. This claim has also been made for two immigrants to Canada, George W. Strathy and Clara Lichtenstein, but their names do not appear in several lists of the composer's pupils inspected by the author.

musical conditions in Canada. This aim was not always achieved in practice—for instance, much of the sheet music found in music journals catered to the popular demand for *salon* music instead of fostering the appreciation of good music—but many individual pages were devoted to campaigns for reforms in church or school music and other fields.

The bulk of the periodicals consisted of short articles, paragraphs of comment and advice to students, concert reviews, anecdotes, advertisements, professional cards, lists of new publications and miscellaneous news items. Articles, which appeared rarely, favoured subjects of a general nature, such as "Music and Beauty" or "Descriptive Music," and were belletristic rather than scholarly in approach. True to the avowed aim of instructing and entertaining at the same time, the journals abounded in success stories of famous virtuosi and anecdotes from the lives of the great composers. One can also find a few biographical sketches of Canadian musicians, but all in all more articles are reprints from foreign journals than original contributions. The most valuable Canadian contribution in the early music journals is Gustave Smith's series "Du mouvement musical en Canada" in *L'Album Musical* (1882). Though it is concerned with trends rather than documentation of facts, this somewhat gloomy appraisal of musical conditions represents one of the first serious attempts to assess musical achievement in Canada.

The first music journal, *L'Artiste* (1860), was obviously a premature effort, for only two issues appeared. The life-span of *Les Beaux Arts* was a little longer; a project of Gustave Smith and Adélard J. Boucher, it was published monthly from April 1863 to May 1864, when the publishers announced that too many readers had failed to pay their subscription fee. *Le Canada Musical,* (1866–7, 1875–81), published by Boucher, may be considered a continuation of the previous magazine. The first periodical in English was the *Musical Journal* of Toronto (1887–8), a witness to the foundation of the Toronto Conservatory of Music and the Toronto College of Music.

Most of the music journals founded in the following decades were short-lived—*Arcadia, Le Canada artistique,* and *L'Art musical* were promising publications—but at least three flourished for a long period of time: *Le Passe-Temps* (1895–1948), the *Canadian Music Trades Journal* (1900–32), and *Musical Canada* (1906–33). The

Toronto Conservatory has issued periodicals or bulletins (interrupted during the years 1913–18, and with frequent changes in title and format) from 1902 on.

The growing complexity of musical life is reflected in the specialization of music journals after the turn of the century: the *Conservatory Bi-Monthly* (Toronto) represented educational interests; *Musical Canada* was a mirror of concert life; and the *Canadian Music Trades Journal* served a business group that had grown to large dimensions. In addition, music was also served by the regular music columns or sheet-music supplements of various newspapers and magazines.

Early Canadian music journals are invaluable (though far from complete) documentary sources for historians: they furnish the thousands of little facts from which can be pieced together the story of Canadian musicians and musical societies. At the same time, the journals disappoint by their regionalism (Montreal and Toronto are two different worlds of music), their very limited historical perspective, and the rareness of systematic surveys of the Canadian scene. They do reflect, however, both in form and contents the growth of concert life from the crude amateurism of the 1850's to the accomplished professionalism of the early twentieth century.

PROFESSIONAL SOCIETIES: Another by-product of the increased activities of musicians was the formation of professional organizations which established ties between musicians within a certain locality or branch of activity. A Montreal Musicians' Guild, founded in the 1870's by Charles Lavallée (Calixa's brother) and others, was the fore-runner of the present-day union.[23] The next decade saw the formation of the Association des Corps de Musique (1887) and the Ontario Music Teachers' Association (1885). The last changed its name to Canadian Society of Musicians in 1887. It aimed to draw music teachers together to share the results of study and professional experience and to join forces in the struggle to make music more respected and appreciated. The lectures, discussions and resolutions at the annual conventions were concerned with promoting public-school music instruction, improving taste in church music and licensing music teachers. Leading figures in this

[23]The first Toronto meeting of a musicians' union took place in 1887.

organization were Dr. Charles A. Sippi of London and Edward Fisher and Arthur E. Fisher of Toronto. The Canadian Society of Musicians was intended to be a Dominion-wide organization of music teachers, but after the sixth annual meeting (in Hamilton, 1890) there is no further record of its activities.[24]

INSTRUMENT MANUFACTURING: If the rapid expansion of musical activity needed further demonstration, ample proof could be found in the instrument-building industry. In the advertisement section of almost any contemporary magazine or trade directory one stumbles across pictures of pianos, parlour organs, melodeons, and a variety of other popular keyboard instruments—monstrosities of furniture design most of them. These instruments were considered a social amenity in much the same way as television sets are today. Nor were they mere ornamental pieces of furniture: in the days before the phonograph and radio, the piano was the focus of family entertainment.

Statistics speak convincingly on this subject. In 1869 musical instruments to the value of $220,000 were imported into Canada. This figure had risen to $389,000 in 1885 and (to take the same interval of time) to $416,000 in 1901. The export figure was only $7,600 in 1869 but rose to $144,000 in 1885, and surpassed the import figure in 1901, when it amounted to $545,000. Practically the entire export consisted of keyboard instruments. Great Britain, South Africa, Australia, New Zealand, and the United States absorbed most of them. There was one important difference between pianos and organs, however. Pianos and piano parts accounted for much of the import (mostly from the United States) but very little of the exports; organs, on the other hand, made up 90 per cent of the export. In 1901, for instance, 12,000 pianos were built, but the export figures include only 500 pianos as compared with 8,000 organs (mostly reed organs). In other words, the home market was able to absorb most of 12,000 pianos in 1901 and most of 30,000 in 1912. In that year there were 30 piano factories in Canada, employing about 5,000 people.

Not all factories turned out complete instruments. Some specialized in the production of piano actions, strings, keys, or organ pipes.

[24]The present Ontario Registered Music Teachers' Association was founded in 1936.

Many piano and organ parts were also imported from other countries. In fact, some of the smaller factories were only assembly plants and cabinet workshops. String and wind instruments of the orchestral type were not produced on a mass scale. A few craftsmen skilled in this field have already been mentioned on page 117.

Only a few of the better-known firms can be named here. Instrument-building was concentrated in the provinces of Ontario and Quebec. Many of the makers there maintained agencies or retail stores in the other provinces. After Confederation, Toronto became the largest single production centre for instruments, producing more than a third of all the pianos made in Canada. Two of the largest firms were A. & S. Nordheimer (later called Nordheimer Piano and Music Co.), music dealers and importers who branched out into building pianos about 1890, and Theodore Heintzman, who established himself as a maker of pianos in 1860. When Nordheimer went out of business in 1928, Heintzman & Co. absorbed the firm. Two other piano factories established in Toronto during the 1880's were Newcombe & Co. and the surviving Mason & Risch.

Apart from those in Toronto, a surprisingly large number of manufacturers was located in smaller towns. The piano firm of Weber and Co. (begun in 1871, as successor to John Fox) flourished in Kingston, Ontario, while the factories of the still existing firms of Willis & Co. Ltd. (1870), Lesage Pianos Ltée (1891), and Quidoz Pianos Ltée (1891), were all established in Ste-Thérèse, near Montreal. The Montreal firm of Pratte et Cie began making pianos in 1889 and claimed to have produced the first Canadian player-piano in 1900, the year when one of its instruments won a *grand prix* at the Paris World Exposition.

Several manufacturers in Ontario produced both pianos and organs: the defunct Dominion Organ and Piano Co. (1871?) of Bowmanville, the Sherlock-Manning Piano Co. (1875) of London (later moved to Clinton), and the defunct W. Bell & Co. of Guelph. The last was the most important Canadian manufacturer about the turn of the century and even opened a branch factory in London, England.

Among the firms specializing in building organs were the D. W. Karn & Co. of Woodstock, Ontario, and Casavant Frères Limitée of St. Hyacinthe, Quebec. Pipe organs, like string instruments, were not usually mass-produced in factories but were constructed in workshops. Information about many of the master organ-builders in French Canada can be found in Gérard Morisset's *Coup d'œil sur les arts en Nouvelle-France* (Quebec, 1941). One of the late nineteenth-century pipe-organ firms deserves closer description within the framework of this book, because it has developed into Canada's most famous organ company. The beginnings of the Casavant organs date from before the middle of the nineteenth century, when Joseph Casavant (1807–74), a descendant of a seventeenth-century Canadian soldier-trumpeter, built his first organs in his own workshop.[25] When he retired from business in 1866 he had 16 instruments to his credit, among them the organs for the Roman Catholic cathedrals of Ottawa and Kingston. His work was then taken over by his former apprentice and assistant Eusèbe Brodeur, who continued the firm under his own name until the 1890's. The present-day firm was established in 1879 by Casavant's sons and apprentices Joseph-Claver (1855–1933) and Samuel (1859–1929), after they had perfected their skill in Europe.[26] Their craftsmanship first gained reputation in their native province (Notre Dame Church in Montreal, 1886–91) but soon orders were received from Ontario and the United States. An organ built in 1892 for the Ottawa Basilica (and apparently replacing the one their father had built) was their first electrical instrument. Up to 1903 the brothers Casavant had directed the construction of 335 organs. In that year they employed 70 workers. By 1914 they had produced about 600 organs and had 200 employees, as well as 20 at a branch workshop in South Haven, Michigan. By 1959 the number of Casavant organs was 2,550. These instruments can be heard in churches and concert halls not only in Canada but in many other parts of the world, giving eloquent proof of the excellence of Canadian craftsmanship.

[25]See F. Elie, *La Famille Casavant* (Montreal, 1914).
[26]The date is sometimes given as 1880. The firm was founded in December 1879 and began work in the following year.

10 / The Early Twentieth Century: Performance

CULMINATION AND NEW BEGINNINGS: The work of the pioneers bore fruit in the musical period which coincided, roughly speaking, with the beginning of the new century and lasted until World War I put a stop to many peacetime activities. The colonial phase of music in Canada reached its climax in an era of general prosperity and rapid population growth. A large influx of British capital helped to open up the West and to industrialize the East. Population increased by 34 per cent during the first decade of the century alone.

The Canadian writer John Castell Hopkins pointed out in 1900 that art and music "are cultivated tastes, and for their full fruition require the leisure which only comes to matured communities and the wealth which only results from a fairly developed country. Toward the end of the century both these conditions are becoming apparent."[1] The following years lived up to this promise by providing more leisure and wealth. On the other hand, musical taste did not come to "full fruition": there was too much in musical literature to assimilate in such a short time. But what mattered was that people had better opportunities than ever before to become familiar with the standard concert repertoire.

Canada had definitely become music-conscious, as she had been in the pre-industrial age. Considering these years in relation to nineteenth-century pioneer work one can point out many fine

[1]John Castell Hopkins, *Progress of Canada in the Nineteenth Century* (Toronto, Brantford, and Guelph, 1900), p. 520.

achievements. The variety and quantity of musical events completely disprove the currently held assumption that until the 1930's or 1940's Canada was a musical desert. On the contrary, in the early twentieth century a far greater percentage of the population took an active part in music than do now. Mechanically reproduced music was in its infancy: if one wanted to enjoy music between public concerts, one still depended mostly on one's family and friends. There was more time for study and rehearsal. It was a rare day when the living-room piano stood silent, a rare week when a band or choir could not be heard in public. The cultivation of oratorio, the performances by visiting or local opera troupes and outstanding American orchestras (in concert halls generally more adequate than those of fifty years later), the boom in instrument-building, and the publication of sheet music—these were unique highlights in Canada's musical history, not outshone by later developments.

Along with the increase in performance came an increase in composition. One is tempted to consider the lively activity in composition around the turn of the century as a phenomenon pointing to the future rather than the culmination of earlier developments. Closer examination shows that stylistically the compositions are firmly linked to the nineteenth century, just as is the organist-choirmaster and bandmaster type of composer. Notwithstanding their importance as teachers, the influence of these men on composers of younger generations was negligible. One cannot find in the works of Couture, Forsyth, or Harriss the roots of the music of Champagne, MacMillan, or Weinzweig. If we describe turn-of-the-century composition as the "fruition" of a period, we find our justification in the impressive number of respectable oratorios, light operas, and small-scale works of various types that were produced.

The opening years of the twentieth century saw more than the harvest of half a century of intensive pioneering; they also saw the planting of new seeds. New characteristics could be observed first in the musical life of Montreal and Toronto, but were also felt to a lesser degree elsewhere. Bernard K. Sandwell was conscious of this change when he declared in 1907 that the previous twelve seasons had

. . . seen the culmination of the musical life of the old provincial-town society—a culmination which lasted considerably after the ways of that society had begun to disappear from our midst—and the complete collapse of that musical life before the invasion of new and more metropolitan characteristics, habits and modes of thought.[2]

Many of the great musical pioneer associations went into eclipse and made room for organizations of a different kind. The Toronto Philharmonic Society ceased to function in 1894, the Montreal Philharmonic Society in 1899, and the Septuor Haydn of Quebec in 1903. In the musical organizations of the "old provincial-town society" Sandwell observed a strongly developed community spirit, for the musical character and reputation of a city was a direct reflection of the personality and ability of its musical leaders.

Let us now examine some of the "new and more metropolitan characteristics, habits and modes of thought," making use of Sandwell's and our own observations. The basic change was that the increase in wealth and population and the improvement of transportation facilities made artistic interchange possible on a far wider scale. This interchange had three facets: visits, immigration, and emigration.

Visits by international celebrities were no longer exceptional events. Backhaus, Carreno, Elman, Flesch, Hofmann, Kreisler, Kubelik, Melba, Nordica, Rachmaninoff, Artur Rubinstein, Schumann-Heink, Slezak, Ysaye, and Zimbalist—all these were heard in the five years before 1914. Although most of their visits were limited to Ontario and Quebec, a number of artists ventured as far west as Winnipeg or Vancouver; for example, Clara Butt, Johanna Gadski, Carl Goldmark and Paderewski. The contact with artists of such calibre had a profound influence on Canadian audiences. It resulted in a new sophistication mixed with an insecurity of judgment. Local artists, once heartily applauded, were now regarded with suspicion unless they had conquered the approval of New York or Paris critics. As Sandwell observed, a Montreal address in itself would have made even an Ysaye appear a third-rate artist to Montrealers. It is taking Canadian audiences a long time to develop independent judgment and to overcome the worship of the "name" artist.

A new type of musical organization was necessary to arrange the celebrity visits. It arose in the women's musical club. Organizations

[2]Bernard K. Sandwell, *The Musical Red Book of Montreal, 1896–1906* (Montreal, 1907).

of this type existed in Quebec, Ottawa, Montreal, London, Winnipeg, Vancouver, Victoria and other cities. Usually their functions encompassed the arrangement of concert series by visiting and, less often, local artists. Some clubs also arranged lecture series and established scholarships. A few of the original groups still function at the middle of twentieth century and are as vital a factor as ever in enriching the country's musical life.

As the opportunities of employment for professional musicians increased, great numbers of Europeans were attracted to the New World to work as teachers, organists, or performers in theatre orchestras and bands. Britain supplied the largest number of these immigrants (to be discussed as a group on pp. 220–3) and Germany maintained the steady flow begun in the days of Glackemeyer and Brauneis, Sr.; but for the first time musicians came from a great variety of European countries. In the 1890's a group of Belgian orchestral musicians settled in Montreal, including Jean-Baptiste Dubois (cellist), and the brothers Joseph and Jean Goulet (violinists). Luigi von Kunits (violinist and conductor) was an Austrian, Henri Miro (conductor and composer) a Spaniard, and Viggo Kihl (pianist) a Dane. The famous Hambourg family was of Russian-Jewish background. It is unnecessary to stress what a benefit Canada derived from this diversity of background and experience among the musicians in her midst.[3]

At the same time as European musicians crossed the Atlantic, more and more Canadian-born musicians sought their fortunes abroad. This is not as strange as it sounds. Canada needed the teaching skill and cultural maturity of European musicians; but she was too little developed to provide permanent employment for certain types of musicians, such as opera singers and concert virtuosi. And Canada was producing by this time a quite remarkable number of good singers. Canadian voices resounded in leading roles in the great European opera houses, and were largely responsible for the growing recognition of Canada as a musical country.

The results of this lively interchange of artists manifested themselves most clearly in the growth of professionalism and the sharpening distinction between amateur and professional performances.

[3]The same variety of cultural traditions was embodied among all ranks of music-loving immigrants. However, the full contribution of these immigrants to the musical profession was realized only among their children. From the 1920's on Canadian orchestras in particular would be unthinkable without players of Ukrainian, Jewish and Italian origin.

Visiting celebrities no longer had to share an evening with local brass quartets and choruses or the side attractions of a touring company; instead they were responsible for the entire programme, unless they took part in an oratorio or played a concerto. Orchestras underwent a similar process of emancipation from the role of a group of instrumentalists newly assembled from time to time to support an oratorio or opera. The growing supply of trained musicians made possible the formation of permanent orchestras in the larger cities. No longer was it necessary to restrict orchestral programmes to works of overture length, even though to introduce "heavy" symphonies and concertos to a public reared largely on popular and religious music proved a slow process.

Thus choral and orchestral groups became separate organizations and a separate survey of them is justified in the following pages, which will draw a more detailed picture of musical life at the beginning of the twentieth century.

CHOIRS OUTSIDE TORONTO: Fine choirs existed in all parts of Canada, though it must be admitted that in French Canada interest in vocal music was confined chiefly to operatic and solo singing. Among the English-speaking population, choral music represented a more deeply rooted tradition connected with religious worship and strengthened by the influence of British immigrant musicians who brought their love of oratorio from their mother country. Its sociable nature also focused interest on choral singing. Furthermore, much less time is required to train a good choir from scratch than to drill a mediocre orchestra.

It is impossible to register here the hundreds of church and secular choral groups active in the decade before World War I, probably the richest choral decade in Canadian history. Towns as small as Lethbridge in Alberta, Indian Head in Saskatchewan, Nanaimo in British Columbia, and Truro in Nova Scotia all had choral societies. Only a few typical or outstanding groups can be listed here, proceeding geographically from east to west.

The Orpheus Club of Halifax was organized in 1882 as a male choir with about 75 singers. Its principal leaders were Charles Porter and Harry Dean. Because of the shortage of men after 1914 it admitted women to its ranks and became known as the Philharmonic Society. The Orpheus Club did some of its work in oratorio and opera.

The Festival Chorus of New Brunswick (about 1900) represented a typically Canadian experiment. Choral groups in various regions rehearsed the same music in preparation for final rehearsals and performances in a central locality.

In Quebec City choral work was carried on in the early years of the century by the Union Musicale, the Union Chorale Palestrina, and the Union Lambillotte.

The Montreal choir of St.-Louis de France was founded in 1891 by Charles Labelle. Under a later director, Alexander Clarke, this French-Canadian group gave a memorable rendition of Pierné's *Children's Crusade*. Horace W. Reyner led a short-lived Handel and Haydn Society, founded in 1895, and his Oratorio Society of later years introduced many new works to Montreal, among them Elgar's *Dream of Gerontius* in 1906.

Ottawa had a Choral Society of some 175 singers under Edgar Birch. The Elgar Choir of Hamilton, founded in 1904 (now the Bach-Elgar Choir), enjoyed one of the finest reputations in Canada under its first conductor, Bruce Carey. Brantford, among smaller Ontario cities, established its choral excellence early in the century. Its Schubert Choir (1906–49) under Henry Jordan had a distinguished career which included an appearance at the New York World Fair in 1939.

The young provinces west of Ontario likewise produced fine choirs. Winnipeg had an Oratorio Society, a Cecilian Society, and an Elgar Musical Society. In 1913 the province of Saskatchewan, whose total population amounted to only half a million, was reported to have, apart from numerous small choirs, at least seven choirs each with more than 60 singers. Two outstanding Alberta groups were the Edmonton Male Chorus, under Vernon Barford, and the Apollo Choir of 100 singers, the oldest choir in Calgary. In Vancouver choral societies under George Hicks, Fred Dyke and J. D. A. Tripp laid the foundations for a strong tradition. The Victoria Choral Society under Gideon Hicks gave its first concert in 1910. In this city we also find the oldest existing secular choir in Canada, the Arion Club (now Arion Male Voice Choir), organized in 1892 with 25 singers. It gave its first concert on May 17, 1893, under William Greig.

CHOIRS IN TORONTO: The assertion, frequently made by contemporary Canadian critics, that Toronto was the "choral capital" of North America was not an idle boast. One is amazed at the sheer number of people who appeared in public concerts each year in one of the four or five large choral organizations. The National Chorus (1903–28) under Albert Ham was noted for the sweetness of its sound and its spontaneous musical quality. Oratorio was presented by Edward Broome's Oratorio Society (1910?–14?). An interesting scheme, designed to popularize choral singing, was the one undertaken by Herbert M. Fletcher who directed three large choirs, totalling about a thousand singers. The People's Choral Union comprised an elementary and an advanced choir, and those who had successfully sung in both were admitted at the end of two years to the Schubert Choir. Over 7,000 choristers are reported to have gone through Fletcher's training. World War I put an end to the scheme, but the Schubert Choir was revived in 1917 with 300 women's voices. The old Philharmonic Society had a successor in Torrington's Festival Chorus (1894–1912), called together each year for the presentation of Handel's *The Messiah*.

At last we come to the most famous of all Canadian choirs, a choir whose name turns up sooner or later whenever foreign musicians talk about Canada. This is the Mendelssohn Choir, founded in 1894 by Augustus Stephen Vogt (1861–1926). Because of its age and fame we shall describe the early history of the choir at some length, not intending thereby to belittle the organizations previously listed.

The story of the Mendelssohn Choir must also include the story of its founder. Vogt was born in western Ontario of Swiss and German parentage. His father was a builder of small pipe organs. Thus the boy had an opportunity to develop his musical talent. He displayed such talent, indeed, that he was appointed organist at Elmira at the age of twelve. Once having decided upon a professional career, he studied at the conservatories of Boston and Leipzig. It was in Leipzig that, under the impact of the great St. Thomas Choir, Vogt began to envisage in his mind a choir "whose tonal quality and expression should approach that of a fine orchestra," and which would be developed through unaccompanied singing by a select group of trained musicians. Vogt was back in Toronto in 1888, and in 1894 when the old Philharmonic Society came to an end, he grasped the opportunity to convert his dream into reality. He enlarged his choir of Jarvis Street Baptist Church to a group of 75 singers. The new Mendelssohn Choir gave its first concert on

January 15, 1895. As the name suggests, the cultivation of Mendelssohn's *a cappella* psalms and motets was one of its aims. After three years of *a cappella* singing Vogt suddenly disbanded the choir, in spite of its constantly growing popularity. The conductor was not dissatisfied with the group, but he wanted to gain time in which to reorganize it on a different and larger scale. He worked out a constitution which required each singer to pass a voice test each season. These tests enabled the conductor to eliminate singers whose voices had seriously deteriorated and to find a place for gifted applicants. The reorganized choir began to rehearse in 1900, and the first concert took place on February 16, 1901. From 1902 on the choir engaged American orchestras (in Vogt's time the Pittsburgh and Chicago Symphonies) to present accompanied works. This scheme at the same time provided an opportunity for the performance of well-played orchestral music. A highlight of this type of co-operation was the performance of Beethoven's Ninth Symphony with the Pittsburgh Symphony Orchestra under Emil Paur in 1907. The conductor exclaimed after the performance that no European choir could have done it better. The choir's repertoire ranged from *a cappella* Renaissance music to the Requiems of Verdi and Brahms.

In 1905 the Mendelssohn Choir began to give concerts in American cities, first in Buffalo, later in New York (first in 1907), Chicago (first in 1909), Cleveland (first in 1910), and Boston (first in 1912). After Vogt returned from another trip to Europe to observe choirs and orchestras at first hand, arrangements were made in 1914 with the help of Canadian financiers for an extensive tour through western Europe and Germany. The trip, scheduled for 1915, was cancelled because of the war. The choir, which now numbered over 200 voices, continued under the leadership of Vogt until his retirement in 1917 for reasons of overwork and health. His successor was Herbert Austin Fricker.

According to a review of Vogt's achievement by the Toronto critic Augustus Bridle, the training of the choir in its earlier years concentrated on technical perfection. The result was a "regimental precision" and discipline unheard of before. Once the problems of technique and tone had been successfully solved, Vogt broadened the powers of expression and developed a group of "tremendous beauty, virility, and power." Twenty years' work by a "quiet, persistent, inexorable chorusmaster" had developed a "remarkable instrument of dramatic and emotional expression out of a church choir."[4]

OPERA: The most ambitious operatic enterprise ever undertaken in Canada was the Montreal Opera Company (1910–13).[5] Its leading figures were Albert Clerk-Jeannotte, director (a voice teacher at McGill Conservatorium), Agide Jacchia (later of the Boston Pops) and Louis Hasselmans, conductors, and Charles-Onésime Lamontagne as business administrator. The chief benefactor was Lieutenant-Colonel Frank Stephen Meighen. While the organization was Canadian, most of the principal singers were not. They included such celebrities as the now forgotten Mme Ferrabini and Signor Colombini and the unforgotten Leo Slezak, besides the Canadians La Palme Issaurel and Mme Edvina.

In the first season the company was successful at home, but attendance was poorer on its tour because people expected a mere amateur company. This season consisted of eight weeks of performances in Montreal, one each in Toronto, Rochester, and Quebec, and four nights in Ottawa. Among the 13 operas given, *La Bohème*, *Madame Butterfly* and *Tosca* were played most frequently. The first season involved an expenditure of $80,000 but thanks to the wealthy patron ended without material loss. At this time the company had about 100 members, among them 23 principal singers.

The second season was a bigger artistic success and featured *Aïda*, *La Bohème* and *Carmen* as the chief attractions. No less than 72 performances were given in Montreal and three weeks in Toronto. Unfortunately the artistic success was not matched by financial support. Theatres were not large enough to hold an audience that would make the performance pay; and even the small theatres were not always filled. Perhaps the moral suspicion with which theatre and opera were still regarded in many circles contributed to the lack of support. In any case the company had to disband after a few years, like so many other worthy artistic enterprises in Canada, because it was unable to continue operating at a deficit.

[4]Augustus Bridle, "Dr. A. S. Vogt," *Sons of Canada* (Toronto, 1916), p. 139.
[5]It was known at first as the Montreal Musical Society and at the end as the National Grand Opera Company.

Elsewhere in Canada grand opera was the domain of visiting companies, but light opera, especially that of Gilbert and Sullivan, was well established in the repertoire of amateur and semi-professional groups across the country. Halifax was probably the oldest centre of light opera. *The Mikado* was produced there in 1887, only two years after it had been written. In the same year the D'Oyly Carte company toured the continent, introducing the latest Gilbert and Sullivan operetta, *Ruddigore*. Halifax also established what were probably the first opera classes in Canada. Under the leadership of Max Weil (see p. 213) the Orpheus Club, supplemented by local singers, staged a performance of *Martha* in 1896. Other operas produced with local principals, chorus, and orchestra included *Faust* and *The Bohemian Girl*.

In Montreal, works by Gilbert and Sullivan were produced under the direction of Guillaume Couture, and in the West, light-opera performances are recorded in the earliest history of some communities. *The Pirates of Penzance* was produced in Lethbridge, Alberta, in the 1880's, and fine standards were achieved in Edmonton under Vernon Barford. An opera company was formed in Winnipeg by Dr. Ralph Joseph Horner, who had gained distinction as a choral and operatic conductor in England before going to Canada in 1909. Among other works, Horner produced his own comic opera *The Belles of Barcelona* in 1911.

Some indication has been given as to the kind of grand and light operas selected for performance. Only one striking contrast remains to be observed: the absence of the Mozart operas and the relative frequency of those by Wagner. *Lohengrin* and *Tannhäuser* were performed repeatedly, and *Parsifal* was performed at least once (in 1905 by the Savage Opera Company in Montreal). The *Ring* cycle was scheduled in Montreal in 1914, but later cancelled.

ORCHESTRAS: Beginning with the Germanians at the middle of the nineteenth century, United States orchestras paid occasional visits to Canada. From the early 1870's the Boston Symphony gave performances in Montreal, and later also in Toronto. The Theodore Thomas Orchestra, the New York Philharmonic, the New York Symphony, and the orchestras of Pittsburgh and Chicago were among those touring Canada, often, as we have seen, joining a Canadian chorus in the performance of choral-orchestral works.

Providing the real highlights of the musical season, these orchestras stimulated the desire for good music and provided local musicians with standards to strive for.

A young music student went to hear the Theodore Thomas Orchestra on its visit to Toronto in the early 1890's. She had graduated from the Toronto Conservatory of Music and studied piano concertos by Mendelssohn and Chopin; yet this was the first time she heard a symphony orchestra. Prior to that time, her only introduction to massed musical instruments came from hearing Sousa's Band.[6] This experience was typical. By far the majority of instrumental group performances were provided by resident or visiting bands. On summer days band music could be heard in the parks of every town. Some of these groups were amateur; others achieved high professional standards and undertook concert tours to Canadian and American cities.

Until late in the nineteenth century nearly all Canadian orchestras were mere adjuncts to theatres, dance halls, choral societies and churches. Only theatre orchestras and dance or military bands provided regular employment. Concert orchestras had to be assembled for each particular performance or series of performances. They consisted of a core of theatre and band musicians and were augmented by local amateur players and professional performers from neighbouring Canadian and American cities. Such pooling of resources sometimes resulted in orchestras of gigantic proportions (for instance, Joseph Vézina brought together 125 instrumentalists to perform with a choir of 300 at the Quebec Winter Carnival of 1894), but it could not offer a substitute for permanent, well-disciplined ensembles.

In the 1880's "orchestral clubs" were formed in some cities (examples are the Victoria Amateur Orchestral Society and Torrington's Orchestra in Toronto, both previously mentioned) with the purpose of training amateurs and providing an outlet for professional players. The success of such groups depended on a dozen factors: the proportion of players available in each section of the orchestra, the personal relationship between conductor and players, the width of the gap between the best and the poorest musicians, and so on. How typical was the "amateur clarinet player . . . who could not

<hr>

[6]Louise McDowell, *Past and Present: A Canadian Musician's Reminiscences* (Kirkland Lake, Ontario, 1957), p. 31.

or would not keep time" and who would indulge in long verbal duels when called down by the irate conductor for coming in wrong.[7] What usually happened in the end is told by a Victoria musician:

In later years, some of the older members resigned, and because the newer ones failed to take the same musical interest, the rehearsals were quite frequently poorly attended, and . . . on many occasions . . . the following instruments would line up in front of the conductor: 'cello, drums, flute, cornet, bass viol. It will readily be seen that very indifferent headway could be made with such a combination of instruments. . . . On other occasions, a violin, drum and flute . . . would be ready for work, but the conductor would look sadly at the members, regret his inability to take any of Haydn's Symphonies, or standard overtures with such a peculiar combination, and a decision to retire homewards was inevitably the order. Finally the Orchestra went the way of many other musical societies, and the assets, which were not very great, were divided among the few remaining and loyal members.[8]

Only in the last decade of the century was the formation of independent concert orchestras tackled in a serious way. The most impressive efforts in that direction were made in Montreal, where a considerable amount of orchestral music had already been heard in the concerts of the Philharmonic Society. The pioneer of orchestral music was Ernest Lavigne (1851–1909), brother of the Quebec musician, Arthur Lavigne. After spending several years of study in Europe, Ernest returned as an excellent cornet virtuoso and became involved in the organization of bands, first in Quebec and later in Montreal. In the latter city, he founded the Fanfare de la Cité, a fine body of players, which compared well in competitions with American bands. The Fanfare began to provide free concerts in 1885 and four years later became a principal attraction of the Parc Sohmer, a newly opened amusement garden named after a piano firm. Lavigne then proceeded to establish a symphony orchestra with the purpose of providing music at the park on summer days. He recruited most of the musicians in Belgium in 1890 and began with a season of light concert and operatic music. However, many of the musicians had come in the hope of becoming

[7]J. S. Loudon, "Reminiscences of Chamber Music in Toronto during the Past Forty Years," Canadian Journal of Music (July–Aug. 1914), p. 52.

[8]Herbert Kent, "Musical Chronicles of Early Times," Victoria Daily Times, Dec. 21, 1918.

teachers at a projected conservatory. When this project failed many returned to Belgium. The Parc Sohmer concerts were interrupted for some time but were continued later under different conductors, the last of whom was Jean Josaphat Gagnier, until 1919.

Fortunately a few of the Belgian musicians decided to stay in Montreal, conservatory or no conservatory. Among these were two violinists from Liège, Jean Goulet (1877–) and his brother Joseph (1870–1951). Joseph Goulet, violin soloist with Lavigne's orchestra, was to become the next important organizer of orchestras. Orchestral history in Montreal was very complicated during the following few years, and sources give contradictory information. Couture's Symphony Orchestra of Montreal may be mentioned as one of several short-lived organizations. It was formed about 1894 on a co-operative basis and its repertoire included the first two Beethoven symphonies, Schumann's "Spring" Symphony, and Mendelssohn's "Italian" Symphony. Out of the remnants of this orchestra, Goulet, who had meanwhile conducted theatre orchestras, organized a new orchestra. It appeared in the season of 1897–8, bearing the conductor's name, but was later renamed Montreal Symphony Orchestra. It gave four or five concerts each season and flourished for over a decade. Its repertoire included symphonies by Haydn, Mozart, Beethoven, Mendelssohn, and Schumann but not those by Brahms and Sibelius. Eventually the cultivation of orchestral music passed into the hands of the Montreal Opera Company Orchestra, which presented a number of symphony concerts in addition to its operatic work.

Formation of a symphony orchestra was proposed in Toronto in 1895 but five years passed before the Toronto Permanent Orchestra started rehearsals. It did not live up to its name. The decisive year was 1906 when Frank S. Welsman (1873–1952) organized an orchestra at the Toronto Conservatory of Music with about 60 players. Two concerts were given during the first season and in 1908 the orchestra assumed semi-professional status and changed its name to Toronto Symphony Orchestra. It testifies to the growing maturity of musical conditions in Toronto that both the conductor and the concertmaster, Frank Blachford (1879–1957), were natives of the city. (There are further parallels in the careers of the two musicians: both were Leipzig-trained, and both were staff members of the Toronto Conservatory of Music for many decades, the one teaching piano, the other violin.)

In the years before the war the orchestra gave an average of 18 performances each season, including popular concerts, concerts with choirs, and out-of-town engagements. The maintenance of the young orchestra was guaranteed by a group of business men headed by Herbert C. Cox. Nearly 20 different symphonies were played in the first six years, no longer, as before, in single movements, but in their entirety.[9] Analysis of the programmes reveals a good share of Tschaikowsky, Wagner (to whom an entire evening was devoted in 1911), and Beethoven, whose Third and Seventh Symphonies were among the more ambitious works to be studied by the orchestra. On the other hand, symphonies by Schumann, Brahms, and Franck, and the works of Bach, were missing. Music of recent date was heard very rarely, but Strauss's *Death and Transfiguration* and parts of Debussy's *Petite Suite* should be mentioned as exceptions. Typical "warhorses" were *Finlandia* and the *Meistersinger* Prelude.

The war years presented the orchestra with increasing problems of personnel shortage and financial difficulties. It ceased to function in 1918. The present Toronto Symphony Orchestra is the successor of the New Symphony Orchestra founded in 1923 with Luigi von Kunits as conductor.

For a number of years Earl Grey, the Governor-General, awarded a trophy for amateur orchestra playing. It was won in 1907 by the Société Symphonique de Québec and in the two succeeding years by the orchestra of the Canadian Conservatory, the Ottawa Symphony Orchestra. The Société Symphonique was founded in February 1903.[10] Its core was the famous Septuor Haydn, whose former leader, Arthur Lavigne, became the orchestra's first president. Joseph Vézina (p. 126) was the conductor from the beginning until his death in 1924. The Société (now Orchestre) Symphonique de Québec boasts of being the oldest existing Canadian orchestra with a continuous history.

An Amateur Orchestral Society was established in Ottawa in

[9]Although it seems contradicted by these figures, we should record Leo Smith's view: "In Canada . . . orchestral music is popular generally when it presents simple and tuneful operatic examples only; and the symphony is a tedious something which has to be put up with." *Canadian Journal of Music* (March–April 1915), p. 157.

[10]The date of foundation is sometimes given as 1902. For an explanation see A.-P. Tanguay, "L'Orchestre symphonique de Québec," *Musique et musiciens* (April 1954).

1894 with some 60 players. Until 1900 it was directed by F. M. S. Jenkins. In concerts it often joined forces with the Ottawa Choral Society. In 1903 the Canadian Conservatory established a String Orchestra under Donald Heins (1878–1949), a violist and music teacher newly arrived from England. A few years later Heins expanded the group into the Ottawa Symphony Orchestra which remained under his baton for about twenty years. Curiously enough in the early years of the century there was another Ottawa Symphony Orchestra, conducted by J. Albert Tassé (1879–1951), a violinist, which later changed its title to Ottawa String Orchestra. It had begun in 1908 with a successful season, but during the following year the musician's union withdrew permission to allow the professionals to play without remuneration. As the orchestra had no subsidy and was quite unable to undertake to pay union fees to any of its members, it resolved to carry on without the professional players. This decision eliminated the wind section.[11]

In Halifax, musical activities were enlivened when in 1893 Max Weil, a German-American educated in Leipzig, took up a position at the Halifax Conservatory of Music. We have already spoken of Weil's opera productions. He also led the Halifax Symphony Orchestra in what appears to have been its first concert, in April 1897. The programme included Schubert's "Unfinished" Symphony and some of the conductor's own works. There were 38 players, including 11 women string-players and a number of band musicians. Serious and popular concerts were given for several seasons, and a high reputation was established. Special events were a Wagner concert in 1901 and performances of the incidental music to *Egmont* and *A Midsummer Night's Dream*.

In Hamilton orchestral music was confined to sporadic efforts made from the 1880's on by J. E. P. Aldous, C. L. M. Harris and Fred J. Domville. A chamber orchestra, the Ladies' String Orchestra, proved more durable. Founded in 1908 by Miss Jean Hunter it was led by her for 17 years.

Winnipeg depended for many years on visits of the Minneapolis Symphony Orchestra. Its own orchestral attempts were less successful than those in the choral field. In the 1880's an Apollo Club was organized with some 35 amateur players, and in the early years

[11]This interesting detail about the problem of a Canadian orchestra was supplied to the author by the late Mr. Tassé in 1951.

of the twentieth century Alexander Scott conducted performances of the Winnipeg Orchestral Society. Attempts were made shortly before World War I to establish a permanent orchestra with Gustav Stephan as conductor.

Orchestral history in the prairie and Pacific cities followed the same pattern. In Regina, Frank L. Laubach founded an orchestra in 1908, and in Edmonton, Vernon Barford led an orchestral society. A Vancouver Symphony Orchestra gave a concert in 1899 and later J. D. A. Tripp became an orchestral leader in this city. Saskatoon and Moose Jaw were also among the young settlements that had established amateur orchestras.

One western city, however, rose above the others in its orchestral efforts. The Calgary Symphony Orchestra gave its first concert on November 10, 1913. The city had had a good amateur orchestra some years earlier, but as a local writer proudly observed "The [new] orchestra is in no sense amateur." Indeed Calgary was said to be "now the only city in Canada outside Toronto which supports a professional symphony orchestra."[12] The conductor was the same Max Weil who had been active in Halifax. The 55 players were all professional musicians but some of them had been imported from the United States. For financial reasons this orchestra too did not survive World War I.

CHAMBER MUSIC: The concept of chamber music has assumed two different, though not mutually exclusive, meanings: ensemble playing in the home of any type of music within reach of the particular combination of instruments; and a branch of musical literature, culminating in the string quartet, the performance of which has become more and more a prerogative of professional ensembles appearing in concert halls.

Private ensemble playing was encouraged whenever musicians and amateurs joined for an evening of relaxation.[13] But such meetings were rather rare in pioneer society, for it was hard to find and keep together four or five players of matching technical skill, sight-reading ability, and musical taste and with equal amounts of time, enthusiasm, and patience. More often than not, such

[12]Carlton McNaught, "The Calgary Symphony Orchestra," *Canadian Courier,* Dec. 13, 1913.
[13]See the examples cited in Marcus Adeney, "Chamber Music," *Music in Canada* (Toronto, 1955), pp. 114–15.

music-making thrived on albums of music arranged for trios or "cued" orchestrations rather than on the original literature for the medium.

The enjoyment of chamber music presents more difficulties to the novice than that of most other types of music. Its popularization through public concerts found even more obstacles in a country where instrumental ensemble playing in the home had not become an established part of the social pattern.

Professional chamber ensembles were drawn from among the ranks of conservatory teachers and orchestral players. What were the groups that followed the nineteenth-century pioneer ensembles —the Septuor Haydn in Quebec, the Artistic Association in Montreal, the Toronto Quartette Club, and the Leipzig Trio in Halifax? The most prominent chamber-music ensembles were the Dubois Quartet of Montreal and the Toronto String Quartet. Jean-Baptiste Dubois (1870–1938), a Belgian cellist, was the leading figure in Montreal chamber-music circles after the death of Frantz Jehin-Prume. He participated in several professional trios and organized his own quartet in 1910. Its players were Albert Chamberland, first violin; Alphonse Dansereau (later Eugène Chartier), second violin; Eugene Schneider, viola; and J.-B. Dubois, cello. Its repertoire ranged from Haydn to Franck and Debussy.

The Toronto String Quartet gave its first concert on January 23, 1907. Its original members were Frank Blachford, Roland Roberts, Frank Converse Smith, and Dr. Fred Nicolai. Shortly before World War I, Luigi von Kunits founded the Academy String Quartet in Toronto. Its programmes contained works of great difficulty, such as Schoenberg's Quartet op. 7 (performed 1915) and three of the late Beethoven quartets. Also established in Toronto was the Hambourg Concert Society, a trio consisting of Jan Hambourg, violin; Boris Hambourg, cello; and various pianists in succession.

FESTIVALS: A BOND WITH GREAT BRITAIN: An important factor in this dawning Edwardian period was the strengthening of musical ties with Great Britain, the ancestral home of so many Canadians. These musical exchanges of goodwill were largely owing to the organizing talent of an English-born musician who had settled in Canada as a young man. Charles

Albert Edwin Harriss (1862–1929), the son of an organist, was educated at St. Michael's College, Tenbury, under Sir Frederick Ouseley, where he acquired a thorough background in the English cathedral tradition. He went to Ottawa in 1882 and settled in Montreal in the following year. Active as an organist, choirmaster and leader of musical societies, he was appointed the first director of the McGill Conservatorium in 1904. Besides being a composer in his own right, Harriss was also a tireless propagandist for British music and an organizer of music festivals in several parts of the Empire. He was one of the few Canadians to hold the Lambeth doctoral degree in music, bestowed by the Archbishop of Canterbury.

In 1903 Harriss invited the Scottish musician Sir Alexander Mackenzie to conduct a series of music festivals throughout Canada. Mackenzie gladly accepted, but only on condition that the entire cycle should be devoted exclusively to British music. Modern audiences might not be enticed by so heavy a dose of Parry, Stanford, Mackenzie, Elgar, and Sullivan, but in the spring of 1903 Canadians responded with great enthusiasm to this display of imperial goodwill. The festivals were held in 18 cities from coast to coast. For five weeks Sir Alexander worked with superhuman energy, often conducting three times a day and leading rehearsals on Sundays as well. Four and a half thousand people actively participated in the concerts. Even though some choirs were very new, the conductor was amazed at the singers' enthusiasm and ability. As a matter of fact, some of the choirs had been formed specially for the occasion, and, what is more important, many kept together for years after. In some towns, such as Brandon (Manitoba) and Moncton (N.B.), Mackenzie's festivals were the first occasions on which an orchestra was heard.[14]

Another musical demonstration of British-Canadian friendship took place in the fall of the same year. This time the Dominion government extended the invitation, and the visitors were the 45 musicians of the Coldstream Band under J. Mackenzie-Rogan, joined in Canada by the singer Kathleen Howard. The band toured all of eastern Canada but did not venture west of Toronto, where it performed at the Canadian National Exhibition. On a single day

[14]Sir Alexander C. Mackenzie, *A Musician's Narrative* (London, 1927). The book includes a chapter on the Canadian trip.

at the "Ex" 70,000 people listened to two concerts given by the band. The most outstanding aspect of the tour was the British patriotism displayed by Canadians, said to have been more British than the British themselves. In the course of some 70 concerts, "God Save the King" was requested to be played 150 times, "Rule Britannia" 126 times, and "The Maple Leaf" 120 times. All patriotic songs received wild applause. "I have never known more attentive listeners, particularly during any melody of a patriotic character. . . . and when we played patriotic airs they nearly yelled themselves hoarse in the intensity of their feeling," wrote the conductor in his memoirs.[15]

Another visitor was Sir Frederick Bridge, organist of Westminster Abbey, who in 1908 gave a series of lectures on English cathedral music. His tour was organized by Dr. Harriss and stretched as far as Vancouver. Sir Edward Elgar, too, visited Canada on his North American tour with the Sheffield Choir in 1911.

These British visitors were very much impressed by the hospitality and musical enthusiasm they met in Canada. As Mackenzie-Rogan said: "I had no idea until then of the fine taste for music prevailing in the Dominion. I remember it all even now with glowing pride and pleasure." . . . "I came to the conclusion that throughout Canada there is an instinctive fondness for the best class of music."[16]

To reciprocate, the indefatigable Dr. Harriss organized a British-Canadian Music Festival in London. It took place on June 27, 1906, and included a number of Canadian features: the Canadian singer Pauline Donalda was the leading soloist; Harriss' choric idyl *Pan* and Mackenzie's *Canadian Rhapsody* were among the works performed. Visits to England by the Calgary Light Horse Band and the Victoria College Glee Club (Toronto) further strengthened musical ties.

These festivals and visits had important effects on both sides of the Atlantic. In Canada choirs and festivals were called into life, and in England the reports of the visitors returning from Canada must have enticed many a young musician to consider a career in the Dominion.

[15]J. Mackenzie-Rogan, *Fifty Years of Army Music* (London, 1926). p. 154.
[16]*Ibid.*, pp. 152, 154.

COMPETITIVE MUSIC FESTIVALS: One British musical institution which was adapted to the new environment with great success was the competitive music festival which had developed rapidly throughout Britain after its inception in 1885.

A brief outline will explain the festival routine in its developed Canadian form to those not familiar with it. Months before the festival, a committee of music teachers and organizers draws up a syllabus of pieces, arranged in various "classes" as to medium of performance and number and age of performers. Each class consists of one or more contest pieces. The syllabus is then published and contestants begin to study the music in the class they have chosen.

Each day of the festival features a number of contests to which audiences are admitted for a modest fee. Each contestant or group of contestants in a class performs the same piece or pieces. When all the contestants in a class have been heard, the adjudicators, usually Canadian or British musicians of distinction, hand down their judgments together with critical advice. At the end of the festivals the winners often appear in special concerts. Sometimes, in addition, there are non-competitive concerts. Although the winners of these receive trophies and medals rather than cash awards, they will be at an advantage in obtaining scholarships for musical studies from some other source.

May 5, 1908, marked the beginning of competitive music festivals in Canada. The first was organized in Edmonton upon the initiative of the Lieutenant-Governor of Alberta, George Bulyea, who in turn acted on a suggestion of Governor-General Earl Grey, a man anxious to foster the arts in Canada. The chief organizers of the Alberta Musical Competition Festival were two English-born musicians in Edmonton, Vernon Barford (1876–   ), organist, choirmaster and conductor who is still active in 1960, sixty years after settling in the city, and Howard Stutchbury, baritone and choirmaster. Two adjudicators came from Winnipeg. Thirty contestants (individuals or groups) competed. This was not, perhaps, a large number, even considering that Edmonton had only about 15,000 inhabitants, but the idea caught fire and at the fourth festival there were already 28 classes of contest. The main emphasis was on choral singing. A performance of the combined choruses (about 200 singers) and 50 instrumentalists before some 2,000 listeners became a highlight at each year's festival.

Saskatchewan was the next province to have a festival. Here the event was organized on a province-wide basis from the start. The number of entries grew from 25 in 1909 to 265 in 1914. In British Columbia and Manitoba festivals took place in 1909 but became annual events only after World War I. A Western Ontario Musical Festival Association was organized in 1914 and intended to hold its first annual competitions in London in 1915. The War put a stop to the plan.

In spite of this rapid progress of the competitive festival from one part of Canada to another, "the evidence does not suggest that the movement owes its growth entirely to the idea's having been caught up from province to province. Rather does it appear that in many cases the seeds from which blossomed the movement in the western provinces were brought from the Mother Country by people born and bred in the atmosphere of the British festivals."[17] Wherever the seeds were brought from, it is no accident that they found such fertile ground in the western provinces. In the competitive festival, for which individuals and groups study in separation but join in community, the thinly populated western provinces found their musical institution par excellence. These festivals provide more than an opportunity to measure one's own musical progress and to listen to performances that are often of surprisingly high quality. They provide occasions for social gatherings of friends and relatives from different parts of a region and they cultivate, in the contestants, the spirit of sportsmanship. It is doubtful whether anywhere in the world people travel greater distances for the sake of music.

[17]Richard W. Cooke, "Competition Festivals," *Music in Canada* (Toronto, 1955), p. 200.

11 / The Early Twentieth Century: Artists

BRITISH IMMIGRANTS: In the introduction to chapter x we have spoken of the benefits Canada reaped from the increased number of immigrant musicians arriving after the turn of the century. We listed the names of a few non-British immigrants, merely stating that the British formed the largest section. In the light of our remarks about the strengthening of musical bonds between England and Canada and about the resulting encouragement of immigration to Canada, we should consider the role of the British immigrants more closely.

The Massey Report stresses the contribution made by this large group in the following words:

We might suggest that the work of English organists in Canada from about 1880 to 1920 would form the subject of a valuable social and historical study. The names of a few of these in Toronto and Montreal and in some other cities came to be nationally known and are still remembered; but the work of the scholarly musicians who brought to so many of our smaller towns an important part of the world's great music should not pass unrecorded.[1]

A study such as is suggested here would probably reveal that Canadians owe to this group of musicians an intensification of musical life, a reinforcement of hitherto weak institutions rather than the beginnings or the very existence of musical culture in Canada.

[1]Royal Commission on National Development in the Arts, Letters and Sciences, Vincent Massey, Chairman, *Report* (Ottawa, 1951), p. 19.

Our survey of the nineteenth century has shown that the pioneers were natives of Canada and immigrants from Great Britain, the United States, Germany, France, Belgium, and other countries, and that a great mass of their common European heritage was assimilated under their leadership. While British-born musicians had always formed a large section of the profession outside French Canada, they began to dominate the musical scene only near the turn of the century. This is revealed by the following list which names some of the more important British immigrants (until 1914) with the date of their arrival and the city of their chief activity.

1816	Stephen Codman	Quebec
1835	James Paton Clarke	Toronto
1857	Frederick H. Torrington	Montreal, Toronto
1874	John W. F. Harrison	Ottawa, Toronto
1877	John Edmund Paul Aldous	Hamilton
1882	Charles Albert Edwin Harriss	Montreal
1884	Alexander T. Cringan	Toronto
ca. 1885	William Henry Hewlett	Hamilton
1893	Joseph Humfrey Anger	Toronto
1890	Percival Illsley	Montreal
1894	Edward Broome	Montreal, Toronto
1895	Vernon Barford	Edmonton
1897	Albert Ham	Toronto
1902	Donald Heins	Ottawa, Toronto
1903	William Dichmont	Winnipeg, Vancouver
1906	Charles O'Neill	Quebec, U.S., Toronto
1907	John William Bearder	Ottawa
1907	Herbert Sanders	Ottawa
1908	Harry Crane Perrin	Montreal
1909	Ralph Horner	Winnipeg
1910	William Henry Anderson	Winnipeg
1910	George Ross	Moncton
1910	Leo Smith	Toronto
1911	George Coutts	Vancouver, Toronto
1912	Alfred Whitehead	Montreal, Sackville
1913	William A. Montgomery	Halifax
1913	Healey Willan	Toronto
1914	Dalton Baker	Toronto, Vancouver

To this list could be added the names of scores of other musicians of equal or lesser stature who made a strong impact on musical conditions in cities and towns in every region of the country. Many of them, though by no means all, were trained as church organists and choirmasters in cathedral schools or conservatories and consequently their most immediate influence was the improvement of the musical part of the church service, which hitherto had all too often been ruled on by church committees or ministers ignorant of music. The musicians established new standards for performance and replaced many of the sentimental and musically worthless anthems and hymns with more suitable and dignified music. Not in vain had they grown up in the era of the renaissance of English church music.

The British influence on music education was perhaps even more far-reaching. It is reflected not only in such institutions as the competitive festival and the graded examination system but above all in the higher branch of music education. British-born musicians held a virtual monopoly in the faculties or departments of music in Anglo-Canadian universities from the beginnings of these faculties until about 1950.[2] Since then, in direct contrast to their former abundance, there has been a dearth of British musicians in university positions. The concentration of the syllabus on academic harmony and counterpoint and its relative neglect of musical history (not to mention musicology) were the hallmarks of this period in university development.

A study such as the Massey Report has suggested would have to take into account some controversial opinions. It cannot be denied that about 1940 a reaction began to develop among younger Canadian musicians against "the long dependence on a 'mother' country [which] has let our resources of native talent be stifled or exported."[3] They felt that many of the older British-born musicians ignored the fact that British methods and values in music education were not necessarily suitable for Canadian conditions, and kept the doors of music schools closed to influences from other countries. The charge of sterility was levelled against the composers among the immigrants. "Before our time," stated one of the younger composers, "music development was largely in the hands of

[2]The most notable exceptions were the first dean of the faculty of music at the University of Toronto, Augustus Stephen Vogt, and his successor, Sir Ernest MacMillan. The latter received much of his training in Great Britain.
[3]Barbara Pentland, "Canadian Music, 1950," *Northern Review* (Feb.–March 1950), pp. 43–6.

imported English organists, who however sound academically, had no creative contribution to make of any general value."[4] There is both truth and exaggeration in these charges. Undoubtedly the majority of the "imported English organists" were musicians of great culture and thorough training. While rooted in the musical climate of the late Victorian period in Britain, their experience also encompassed the music of Wagner and Strauss, Debussy and Ravel. They clung to tradition, but they also possessed strong convictions. And it was men with a fixed scale of values who were needed in Canadian conservatories and faculties of music in their formative period.

EMIGRANTS BY NECESSITY: The movement of musicians across the borders of Canada proceeded in both directions. The Canadian-born musicians who went to live in other countries usually belonged to one of two groups: those teachers and performers who left mainly because the field for employment was too narrow or because they had established valuable contacts in the more developed countries where they studied; and the virtuosi and opera stars who would have left Canada even under more mature conditions. Great artists from any country belong to the world at large and rarely confine their activities to one country.

The first group comprised organists, pianists and violinists, most of whom settled in American cities (rarely far from the Canadian border), and who generally taught music as well as performing it. If inclusion in standard musical dictionaries is any measure of merit, many of these Canadian-born musicians must have been persons of distinction. We shall give brief sketches here of those only who won recognition before World War I, but the flow of Canadian musicians across the border to the south and to Europe did not stop at that time. On the other hand, Canadian writers pleading for better opportunities of employment have often exaggerated the number of musicians who have left the country. One must not forget the great number of performers, teachers and composers who remained at home. Nevertheless the list that follows is a pathetic commentary on the failure of Canadian society to give employment for much of the talent it had produced.

JOHN B. SHARLAND (1837–1909) was born in Halifax. He achieved
[4]*Ibid.*

prominence in Boston as conductor of choral societies and school music supervisor. He also compiled songbooks.

HUGH ARCHIBALD CLARKE (1839–1927), son of the Toronto musician James P. Clarke left Canada as a young man and became an outstanding organist and professor at the University of Pennsylvania in Philadelphia. He wrote textbooks and composed.

SAMUEL PROWSE WARREN (1841–1915) was born in Montreal as the son of an organ-builder of American birth. He studied in Berlin from 1861 to 1864 and settled in New York City as an organist. He became one of the foremost concert organists in the United States.

ARTHUR DUMOUCHEL (1841–1919), a native of Rigaud, P.Q., studied in Leipzig and Vienna. He appears to have been the first Canadian to receive a doctoral degree in music (1872). He became an organist in Albany, N.Y. Dumouchel and Lavallée are the first Canadian composers credited with symphonies.

CALIXA LAVALLÉE (1842–1891), while spending some adult years in Montreal and Quebec, achieved his greatest success in Boston. (See also pp. 132–43, 239–41.)

SALOMON MAZURETTE (1848–1910) of Montreal completed his studies in piano and organ in Paris and settled in Detroit in 1873. He undertook many tours as a concert pianist.

OSCAR MARTEL (1848–1924), a French-Canadian violinist, was a child prodigy who completed his musical education in Belgium. He appeared in concerts with Mazurette and settled as a teacher at a Chicago music school.

PHILIP CADY HAYDEN (1854–1925) of Brantford, Ontario, received his advanced musical training in the United States. He became a school music supervisor and editor of the *School Music Magazine*.

KATE SARA CHITTENDEN (1856–1949), a native of Hamilton, was head of the piano department at Vassar College from 1899 until 1930 and became known as a composer of *études* and other pieces for students.

PHILÉAS ROY (1857–1939) studied with Calixa Lavallée and was organist and bandmaster in his native Quebec until 1899, when he moved to New York. There he was active as organist and taught piano at the New York College of Music.

WILLIAM WAUGH LAUDER (b. *ca.* 1858), the son of a Toronto barrister and an authoress, was Canada's outstanding pianist of the nineteenth century. He spent several years studying in Leipzig where he went in 1878 and has been called the "only Canadian who can justly claim the honour of being a pupil of Liszt."[5] The contact with Liszt took place

[5]"Music in Canada," *Musical Times*, April 1, 1885.

in Weimar and Rome, where he went with von Bülow and other Liszt disciples in the winter of 1880. He gave performances before royalty and the Pope, and in Venice he played to Wagner arrangements of his operas arranged by various musicians. His teachers gave him very high recommendations.

One of the reasons that he did not gain wider reputation as a performer may have been his predilection for the "lecture recital," a form of entertainment in which he was a pioneer. In 1889 it was reported that he had given no less than 350 recitals in Ontario alone. To trace his career after his return from Europe is difficult. He occupied positions of musical director at a School of Music, Art, and Languages in Toronto, at Hellmuth Ladies College in London, Ontario, and in the late 1880's he moved to the United States. There we can trace him as a teacher in Kansas and Illinois, at the New England Conservatory, as director of the College of Music of Cincinnati Wesleyan College (1889–93). The record of his career ends in Chicago early in the twentieth century. Posterity has not remembered this great talent: no reference book records the date of his death.

FRANCOIS BOUCHER (1860–ca. 1936) studied the violin in his native Montreal and at the Liége Conservatory. In the 1880's he was much in the limelight as a violin virtuoso in Montreal and Ottawa, where he opened a music store and led a string quartet. He was one of the first violin teachers at the Toronto Conservatory of Music but later settled in the United States, where he taught at the Kansas City Conservatory of Music from its founding 1906.

ALFRED DE SÈVE (1860–1928) was born in Montreal, but spent many years of his career as a violinist in Boston, where he was concertmaster with the Boston Philharmonic Orchestra and a teacher at the New England Conservatory. He died in Montreal.

HARRY MARSHALL FIELD (b. 1860 or 1861), a native of Aurora, Ontario, studied the piano with von Bülow and Martin Krause in Germany. After his *début* in Leipzig in 1887 he returned to Canada and was appointed teacher at the Toronto Conservatory of Music. Nine years later he accepted an invitation to become assistant to his former teacher Krause in Leipzig. He appeared as soloist with European orchestras and eventually settled in London where he was still living in 1936.

KATHARINE BURROWES (ca. 1865–1939) was born in Kingston, Ontario. She became an expert in methods of teaching piano to children and published many articles on this subject. She maintained her own piano school in Detroit.

LAURA (LEMON) HEATH (1866–1924) was born in Guelph. She

went to London in 1890 to study music and did not return.. She wrote some piano and violin music and published many songs, including the widely-known "My Ain Folk" and a *Canadian Song Cycle*.

PAUL AMBROSE (1869–1941), born in Hamilton, was organist in New York City and Trenton, N.J. In Trenton he was also director of music at the State Normal School. He spent the last years of his life in Hamilton and in 1939 was elected president of the Canadian College of Organists.

GEORGE HERBERT FAIRCLOUGH (1869–1954) was also born in Hamilton. He obtained his training in organ and piano and in composition in Toronto and Berlin. He became head of the organ department of the University of Minnesota school of music and for several terms was president of the Minnesota Music Teachers' Association.

GEORGE ALFRED GRANT-SCHAEFER (1872–1939), a native of Williamstown, Ontario, was an organist and music teacher in Chicago from 1896 on. He was a prolific composer known especially by his songs and operettas.

EDWARD BETTS MANNING (1874–1948) from Saint John, N.B., studied composition with MacDowell, Humperdinck and Vidal. From 1908 to 1911 he was supervisor of music for New York public schools and later taught at Columbia University. He composed works for orchestra, chamber ensemble, and voice. His opera *Rip van Winkle* was performed in New York City in 1932.

JEANETTE DURNO (b. 1876), a pianist from Walkerton, Ontario, studied in Chicago and then in Vienna with Leschetitzky. She gave concerts in Europe and North America. Later she taught piano in Chicago, after which she moved to California.

BRUCE CAREY (1877–   ), born in Hamilton where he founded and brought to fame the Elgar Choir, became a staff member of Pennsylvania and Cornell Universities and gained renown as choral conductor in Philadelphia and Bethlehem.

L. J. OSCAR FONTAINE (b. 1878), born in St.-Hyacinthe, P.Q., was a pupil of Leon Ringuet and R. O. Pelletier. He played organ in Fall River and New Bedford, Massachusetts, but after 1918 he taught only. Many of his pieces for the piano were published.

CEDRIC WILMOT LEMONT (1879–1954) was born in Fredericton, N.B. He studied in Boston and settled in Chicago in 1907. He was an organist and piano teacher whose many anthems and piano pieces achieved wide circulation in print. He specialized in student pieces and *études*. The figure of some 600 published compositions probably exceeds that of any other composer of Canadian birth.

OPERA STARS: Certain decades have been extraordinarily fertile in the production of Canadian artists. The years from 1841 to 1851 brought forth a wave of French-Canadian organists and composers, and the 1890's, to take another example, saw the birth of many of the leading musical personalities of the twentieth century, including Sir Ernest MacMillan, Wilfrid Pelletier, and Claude Champagne. With very few exceptions, all Canadian singers who achieved fame before World War I were born in the years 1875–85: Marie Edvina (1875), Edmund Burke (1876), Rodolphe Plamondon (1876), Beatrice LaPalme-Issaurel (1878), Edward Johnson (1881), Forrest Lamont (1881), Pauline Donalda (1882), and Eva Gauthier (1885). To this group may be added Florence Easton (1884), a native of England who spent her childhood in Toronto, and Kathleen Howard (ca. 1880), a native of Niagara Falls, Ont. who moved to Buffalo as a child and whose career led to the stages of Covent Garden and the Met. It would be of great interest to investigate the interaction of musical, social, and educational forces which produced such a great number of singers in one particular decade. Surely the phenomenon was the result of more than sheer coincidence.

It can be stated without exaggeration that this group of Canadian artists—not poets, novelists or painters, but singers—was the first to win a reputation abroad. It is also noteworthy that the majority of these singers were women. All of them would have made splendid ambassadors for Canadian culture, had it not been for the unfortunate fact that few of them were known abroad as Canadians. Edward Johnson launched his operatic career in Italy as Edoardo di Giovanni because his manager expected the public to accept the singer more readily if they took him for one of their countrymen. Similarly, many of the other singers were labelled by critics and managers with the nationality of the country where they made their headquarters or where they had received their advanced training. It is doubtful whether many of them objected to this transformation, because in those times European audiences would not put much trust in an artist identified as a Canadian. Indeed, these artists usually did not even consider Canada as the base of their operations, and made only a few isolated visits there.

The careers of these artists were abnormal in another respect. Normally an artist strives for national recognition before he ventures to perform in foreign countries. In Canada the process was almost the reverse. After giving a few student recitals a young artist heading for a concert or operatic career had to turn to the stages of other countries. Hence the Canadian public learned about the achievements of Canadian artists only through the critics of New York, London and Paris. This state of affairs had a stifling effect upon the formation of artistic judgment among Canadian audiences—and critics. It became a habit to bestow praise upon celebrities from abroad and to withhold it from local artists until the nod of approval had been given by the critics in the world's musical capitals. Only the development of radio and television has provided young artists with the possibility of proceeding from a Canadian to an international reputation.

When a country or a historical era produces a group or school of composers, writers, painters, or other artists there usually appear a number of "forerunners" or "pathfinders" before the great masters step onto the scene. It is a strange fact that the very first in a long line of Canadian singers was also the most famous one the country has produced until the present time and that she preceded the group of singers born between 1875 and 1885 by a full thirty years. It is equally remarkable that her Canadian background was not a handicap but in fact an asset to the musical education of this singer. A noted English critic, Herman Klein, has pointed out that Emma Lajeunesse (1847–1930) became the celebrated singer whom we know under the name of Mme Albani largely because of the thorough musical training she received in her childhood. Her strict though kind teacher was her own father, Joseph Lajeunesse, a musician of seventeenth-century Canadian stock who performed on the piano, organ, harp and violin. Her mother, of French-Canadian and Scottish descent, was an amateur singer. Young Emma was determined on a singer's career from the beginning and under her father's guiding hand rapidly developed a great faculty for sight-reading and quick memorizing. She became a versatile performer and appeared as a singer, harpist, and pianist in her first recitals, which took place in and near Montreal from 1856 on. Her training even included composition, and one work, "O Salutaris" found its way into print.

A public subscription for the financing of her further studies having come to naught, Emma and her family moved *ca.* 1866 to Albany, N.Y., where Emma accepted a position as soprano soloist and, later, substitute organist at the Roman Catholic cathedral. Here she became acquainted with the masses of Mozart, Beethoven, and Cherubini. The bishop and others encouraged her to continue her studies in Europe, and after money was raised through concerts she left for Paris in 1868. She studied there for some time and then proceeded to Milan, where she became a pupil of Lamperti, one of the finest teachers of the Italian style of singing.

Lamperti selected the city of Messina for her operatic debut because audiences there were very critical. If the young singer succeeded in Messina she would succeed wherever she went. Her *début*, as Amina in *La Sonnambula*, took place in 1870 and received an ovation. It was around this time that the stage name Albani was suggested to the singer. It was chosen in honour of an old Italian family, but its coincidental similarity with the name of the city that had encouraged her studies greatly pleased her.[6] After Italy and Malta came England (1872), where Albani was at once appreciated and where she made her first oratorio appearance. The following years were crowded with tours and engagements in Paris, St. Petersburg, Moscow, Berlin, and New York, but England became her permanent headquarters. She appeared at Covent Garden almost every season until 1896, and married Ernest Gye, the son and successor of its manager in 1878.

The Canadian singer was now in the forefront of operatic celebrities, no small achievement in an age which boasted Patti, Tietjens, Nilsson, and Lucca! Her life now became typical of a starring artist, filled with tours from country to country, meetings and friendships with famous composers, command performances before royalty, and rewards and honours from all sides. Gounod's *Mors et Vita*, Dvorak's *The Spectre's Bride*, and Sullivan's *Golden Legend* were written with Albani's voice in mind. These titles suggest that the soprano had become the leading oratorio singer

[6]Emma Albani, *Forty Years of Song* (London, 1911), pp. 34–5. However, the extremely reliable scholar and dictionary-maker Nicolas Slonimsky, in a letter to myself, suggests that the singer invented the story of how she got her stage name. He points out that contemporary sources always asserted the name was chosen in honour of the American city. Some of the early sources even suggested that her birthplace was Plattsburg, New York.

in England. She was engaged to sing at many of the British music festivals where enormous audiences flocked to hear her. From the lighter soprano roles which marked the earlier part of her career she turned to more serious roles. Her mastery of Wagnerian roles distinguished her above her older rivals. She introduced the parts of Senta, Elsa and Elisabeth to England, and celebrated her last and perhaps greatest triumph as Isolde. Desdemona in Verdi's *Otello*, which she introduced at the New York Metropolitan Opera, was another of her great roles.

Her voice was distinguished by technical neatness and flexibility as well as a considerable range and beauty of tone. The smooth and pure quality of her coloratura passages made her exceptional even in an age of florid singing. She could sing well in many languages and was a good actress. Only her power and warmth of interpretation did not quite match the many virtues of her performance.

Although Albani made her American debut in New York in 1874, she did not sing in Canada until 1883. The singer who had once been discouraged from entering an operatic career by her countrymen (see p. 112) was now received like royalty and proudly hailed as "our Canadian" Albani. Thousands of citizens lined the streets of Montreal and delegations came from many cities to welcome her. Extended tours of Canada followed in 1889 and 1896-7, when she toured from Halifax to Vancouver. The Canadian Pacific Railway put a car at her disposal, and when she passed through Ottawa she stayed at the home of the Prime Minister, Sir John A. Macdonald. Her last visit to Canada was in 1903. Again every appearance was a triumph.

Near the end of the century Albani retired from opera but continued to perform in concert. She toured many countries of the British Empire, including Australia, New Zealand and India. There was, however, an undeniable decline in her vocal powers. After a farewell concert at the Albert Hall in London she devoted herself entirely to teaching. Two of her most talented pupils were the Canadians Eva Gauthier and Sarah Fischer. All but forgotten by the public and suffering from financial reverses, the prima donna received her last great honour in 1925 when she was made a Dame of the British Empire. Albani died in 1930, having been a resident of England for over half a century, yet always remaining a French

Canadian at heart. All that now remains of her great art are a handful of wax-cylinder recordings, made about 1904, which have become treasured collector's items.

Short biographical notes will have to suffice for the other Canadian singers who gained fame before World War I. They are listed in chronological order.

MARY HOPE MORGAN (1862–1936) was the first Anglo-Canadian singer to appear in European opera houses and the first to return to Canada to reside. A native of Toronto, she went to Paris in 1892 to perfect her soprano voice. After her *début* in Naples as Marguerite in *Faust* she appeared in several European opera houses. Reasons of health forced her to turn from the stage to the concert platform and to teaching. In 1906 she settled in Toronto, where she had already made a triumphant appearance six years earlier. She was responsible for training a number of outstanding Canadian singers of a younger generation.

Mme EDVINA (1875–1948), soprano, was born in Montreal but her family moved to Vancouver in her childhood. She was of French-Canadian parentage and her real name was MARIE LOUISE LUCIENNE JULIETTE MARTIN. She studied in Paris and made her *début* at Covent Garden in 1908. She sang in London for some years and later was a member of opera companies in Boston and Chicago.

Another native of Toronto, the basso-cantante EDMUND BURKE (1876–   ), turned from the study of law to that of singing. He first appeared in opera in France in 1906 and was engaged at Covent Garden from 1910 to 1918.

RODOLPHE PLAMONDON (1876–1940) of Montreal turned from a career as a cellist to that of a tenor. Guillaume Couture was his first voice teacher. He celebrated his first triumphs in Paris and became a well-known figure at the Opéra, the Opéra Comique, the Colonne Concerts, and the Schola Cantorum. He appeared in opera and oratorio and concert performances of works by Bach, Mozart, Berlioz, Wagner, and many other composers, not only in Paris, but also in London, Vienna and Munich and at the New York Metropolitan Opera. He also taught many Canadian singers after returning to his homeland in 1928.

BEATRICE LA PALME (Mme ISSAUREL) (1878–1921) of Beloeil, P.Q., likewise began her career as an instrumentalist. She won the coveted Lord Strathcona bursary (McGill University) to enable her to study violin at the Royal College of Music in London. The bursary was twice prolonged, but she switched from violin to voice. Her *début* as dramatic soprano took place at Covent Garden and she later sang at the Paris Opéra Comique, the Lyon Opera, and the Century Opera House in New York. She excelled in Wagnerian roles and in the parts of Mimi, Rosina, and Marguerite. Her singing with the Montreal Opera Company won her great applause. When her health began to decline she settled in Montreal, teaching voice until her untimely death.

EDWARD JOHNSON (1878-1959) was born in Guelph, Ontario, and from boyhood on sang in churches and choirs. In 1907 he went to New York to train his tenor voice. There he was a church soloist and also sang in oratorios and concert recitals. Later he was selected for a part in Oscar Straus's *Waltz Dream* at the Broadway Theatre. Having gained experience in these varied types of singing Johnson went to Florence to study with Vincenzo Lombardi. He made his *début* in the title role of Giordano's *Andrea Chenier* in Padua in 1912 and from 1913 to 1919 was engaged at La Scala in Milan, taking leading roles in Wagner and Puccini operas. He toured the Latin American countries and Spain with the La Scala company. In 1919 he returned to the United States to sing, first, with the Chicago Opera Co., and from 1922 to 1935 with the New York Metropolitan Opera, where he sang in the world *premières* of several American operas. From 1935 to 1950 he was general manager of the "Met." After his retirement he returned to Canada, and took an active interest in the development of music there, especially in his capacity of chairman of the Board of the Royal Conservatory of Music in Toronto.

FORREST LAMONT (1881-1937), a tenor, was born in an Ontario village but was brought up in Massachusetts. His operatic career began in Italy in 1914 and was continued in 1916 in the United States. He settled in Chicago and specialized in Wagnerian, French and Italian operas.

PAULINE LIGHTSTONE (1882/3–)[7] of Montreal has become known to the world as PAULINE DONALDA. She studied at Royal Victoria College in Montreal and later in Paris, making her *début* as a dramatic soprano in Nice in 1904 in the role of Manon. In the following years she established a reputation as a prima donna second only to that of Albani among Canadians. She appeared in the opera houses of Paris, Brussels, Moscow, London, and New York, impressing audiences with the richness of her voice and her great talent for acting. She created the leading soprano part in Ravel's *L'Heure espagnole* and excelled in the roles of Marguerite, Mimi, and Gilda. In the early 1920's she turned from singing to teaching and for many years maintained her own

[7]Her parents, of Russian- and Polish-Jewish origin, were originally named Lichtenstein. The name Donalda honours Sir Donald A. Smith (Lord Strathcona), the benefactor of Royal Victoria College, Montreal.

singing-school in Paris. In 1937 she returned to Montreal where she is making a great contribution to musical life as a teacher and as founder-director of the Opera Guild (1941). This organization each season stages one or two operas, including many that have never been heard in Canada before.

EVA GAUTHIER (1885–1958), a protégée of Sir Wilfrid Laurier, pursued her musical studies in Paris and Italy. She aroused the active interest of Albani, whom she accompanied on several tours. In 1909 the young mezzo-soprano made her operatic *début* in Parma, the next year she appeared at Covent Garden in Debussy's *Pelléas et Mélisande*. Later she became a resident of New York City. Throughout her life she was interested in a great variety of music. She spent several years in Java, making a study of Malayan music; she championed the contemporary music of various countries; and she was one of the first concert singers to include songs in the popular idiom on her programme (1923).

INSTRUMENTAL VIRTUOSI: While the gifted singers inevitably turned to other countries, the careers of instrumental virtuosi showed a more varied pattern. Nearly all the earlier virtuosi were unable to make solo appearances the centre of their careers. Instead their livelihood was gained by teaching, playing in churches or orchestras, and other means. The first generation found its way to the United States. Samuel Prowse Warren, Calixa Lavallée and Waugh Lauder may be cited as examples. The members of the next generation usually assumed important positions in Canadian cities. We have previously spoken of the pianist Frank S. Welsman and the violinist Frank Blachford. In Montreal Albert Chamberland (1886–) had a career closely parallel to Blachford's in Toronto, being the leading concertmaster and chamber music performer for many decades.[8]

Instrumental virtuosi who regularly made extensive concert tours appeared later and were fewer in number than Canadian opera singers. Only a few had paved their way to international recognition by the time World War I broke out. Two of these, Lynnwood Farnam and Kathleen Parlow, were to win international fame equal to the great singers we have mentioned. Two others, who were to become famous after the war as organist and pianist respectively, had aroused attention as child prodigies. Their names were

[8]These names may serve as examples. Readers are referred to the many organists, pianists, and violinists mentioned elsewhere in this book.

Ernest MacMillan (1893–) of Toronto and Ellen Ballon (1898–) of Montreal.

It would be exaggerated to claim world fame for ESTHER LEONORA (NORA) CLENCH (1866–1938), a native of St. Mary's, Ontario, but this violinist did win acclaim in several countries. She studied in Leipzig under Adolf Brodsky and obtained a special prize for her excellent progress. After being concertmistress in an orchestra in Buffalo, she studied with Ysaye in Brussels, toured Europe and made London her headquarters. She was honoured by an invitation to play before Queen Victoria. Early in the century she founded a ladies' string quartet which gave prominent hearing to contemporary composers such as Debussy and Hugo Wolf. After her marriage in 1908 she withdrew from the concert stage and eventually retired with her husband to Toorak in Australia.

ALFRED LALIBERTÉ (1882–1952) of St. Jean, P.Q., was a scholarship student at the Stern Conservatorium in Berlin. He perfected his pianistic education with Teresa Carreño and Alexander Scriabine and became an exponent of the latter's music. The young pianist appeared in recital in Berlin, Paris, Brussels and London with great success but returned to Canada in 1911 to reside in Montreal. He devoted his time to playing, teaching and composing.

LYNNWOOD FARNAM (1885–1930) was born in Sutton, P.Q. Like Beatrice La Palme he was a winner of the Lord Strathcona bursary and studied his instrument, the organ, at the Royal College of Music in London. From 1904 to 1913 he successively occupied positions as organist in Montreal, Boston, and New York. At the same time he made extensive concert tours, achieving fame in North America and Europe. His repertoire included the complete organ works of Bach.

KATHLEEN PARLOW (1890–), a native of the young town (now city) of Calgary, won her first laurels as violinist when she performed before Queen Alexandra in London. In 1906 she went to St. Petersburg to study with Leopold Auer and made her formal début in Berlin at the age of 17. This marked the beginning of a long and distinguished career which includes solo performances with the major European and American symphony orchestras and innumerable recitals in Europe, the Orient and North America. In 1940, after making her home in the United States for several decades, Miss Parlow accepted an invitation to come to Toronto where she now teaches at the Royal Conservatory and appears frequently in recital. She is also a great champion of chamber music and has had a string quartet of her own since 1929.

THE SETTING: The best way to gain a proper perspective on composition in Canada is to compare its development with the other basic musical activities—performance and education. Chronologically, no branch can claim priority in Canada. In seventeenth-century New France music was performed in church services; it was taught in the schools directed by priests and nuns; and several clergymen possessed skill in composition. Towards the end of the eighteenth and during much of the nineteenth century all three activities were united in the figure of the performer-teacher-composer. As cities grew and the consumption of music increased in domestic and public entertainment, in church service and military band, a definite relationship was established between the three branches, much in disfavour of composition.

The new "market" required both performers and music to perform. The former had to be supplied in the flesh, the latter could be imported on printed paper. To obtain performers it was necessary to train local talent for everyday functions and to rely on visiting artists for higher forms of entertainment. The training of local talent involved the development of music education, however modest in scope. To obtain music for performance, on the other hand, there was no need to train composers: a wealth of printed music of any type could be imported for a few dollars. The use of original composition was restricted to such specific needs as patriotic events, dedication of new churches, paying homage to a particular person, and so on.

In consequence the performer and teacher became a person of immediate usefulness, the composer a remote and legendary figure. The first outstanding musicians that Canadians had an opportunity to hear and see in person were vocal and instrumental virtuosi, not composers. We find here one reason why the worship of concert stars could develop to the extreme it did.

It was natural that under the circumstances a young musician planned his career in terms of performing and teaching and not of composing. If ambitious, he was fired by the prospect of travelling and winning the applause and laurels of a virtuoso. It is no wonder that Canada produced great singers and organists before she produced great composers.

For its full fruition, creative talent requires a mature social and intellectual environment. Such an environment was very slow in taking shape during the late nineteenth century. Fortunately, however, the creative urge is not entirely dependent on the external social setting. The setting can restrict or stimulate it, but not entirely thwart its expression. Even though there was little immediate need for composition, many young musicians took up the study of theory and composition in a more than perfunctory manner. When they returned from their studies abroad, they were cut off from the main stream of musical development. Making a living as organists, bandmasters or music teachers left them little time for serious composition. Hope for a performance, let alone material gain, was slight. To mature fully a composer needs a stimulating exchange of opinion with his colleagues, the interest and criticism of a wide circle of intelligent music lovers, and publishers eager to make new music known. Canadian composers lived too far away from the great composers of the time to allow personal contact and discussion, audiences were chiefly interested in performers and limited in their appreciation of serious music, and publishers were rarely willing to venture outside the field of strictly utilitarian music. A composer could at best hope for only local reputation. It is doubtful whether a work by a Toronto composer such as Forsyth or Ham was ever played in Montreal or Halifax, or whether the names of Contant and Couture were known in Toronto and the West.[1] All these circumstances combined to condemn most composers to stagnation in a sterile eclecticism.

[1]Professional jealousy may have had something to do with this if we are to believe the rather strong words of the *Musical Journal* of February 15, 1888. The

This brings us to the question of style, a matter on which it is difficult to speak with authority because we lack printed or manuscript copies of many compositions. The few works available for inspection, however, indicate that there are compositions of genuine beauty and craftsmanship besides countless inferior ones. Nevertheless serious Canadian compositions were essentially exercises in the assimilation of European models. Their beauty is more often borrowed than original, reminding us that Canadian culture was still in its colonial stage. Speaking about literature, Edward McCourt has defined colonialism as

a deferential spirit which acknowledges, as an act of faith, the superiority in all things literary of the Mother Country, and seeks no more than imitation of her models. It is not a spirit of emulation; the writer infected with colonialism does not attempt to write as well as Keats or Shelley or Scott; he attempts only a shadowy imitation. From this colonialism, scarcely one of our 19th century poets is free.[2]

Canada's composers, too, echoed what Mendelssohn, Gounod, Tschaikowsky, and Grieg had already expressed more powerfully, and many of their works were outdated the moment they were written. Almost none survive in performance today.

It must be conceded that there was no alternative to colonialism. Clearly one could not have expected a distinctively Canadian school of composers at the end of the nineteenth century. Had it been possible it would have been foolish to ignore European traditions and instead to try to build up a completely new school of composition based entirely on aboriginal music and local folk songs. Nevertheless it is to be regretted that composers made very few attempts to find inspiration in the folk song of eastern Canada which still existed in abundance. The Canadian environment is reflected at best in the occasional title, the words of a song, or the libretto of an operetta. Trained in European "learned" music, most composers disdained "low" and "simple" folk music. A few French-Canadian composers arranged folk songs into rhapsodies and medleys, and some foreign composers followed suit. Sir Alexander Mackenzie's

Journal stated in an editorial on jealousy among Canadian musicians that "there are a few good composers in this province [Ontario]—conscientious and clever writers—but their productions are invariably denounced by rivals as so much 'rubbish,' and publishers consequently handle them very cautiously."

[2]Edward McCourt, "Canadian Letters," *Royal Commission Studies* ("Massey Report"; Ottawa, 1951), p. 67.

Canadian Rhapsody and the Belgian Paul Gilson's *Fantasie cana-dienne*, both for orchestra, were published in Germany by Breit-kopf & Härtel. The Frenchman Eugène Gigout wrote a *Rhapsodie sur des airs canadiens* for organ. Canadian musicians who harmon-ized or arranged Canadian songs, making them available for choral or instrumental performance, remained an insignificant minority. Use of English-language folk songs in compositions was prevented altogether by the vast geographical distance between the Atlantic provinces, which were rich in folk song, and the cities of Ontario, where most Anglo-Canadian composers resided. In addition immigrant composers and performers were so much prejudiced in favour of their native culture that it rarely occurred to them to study the musical traditions of Canada or to include works by local composers in their recitals. Canadian cities were mere distributing centres for music brought from foreign countries.

By the turn of the century Canada had produced a sizable num-ber of musicians for whom composition was a dominant interest. No apologies need be made for the fact that most of them composed only sporadically and that there were few whose catalogue of works reached large proportions; these included Lavallée, Contant, Cou-ture, Vézina, Forsyth, Lucas and Lemont. It is equally true that many of their larger compositions date from their student days abroad or from the time they had left Canada to settle elsewhere. Lavallée, the best known of them, also provides the best example.

Apart from a number of operas, oratorios and orchestral settings of the mass, most of the works written in Canada were in smaller forms and were meant for practical use in church, military parades, dance halls, or music lessons rather than for concert performance. The amount of music written on commission or called forth by public events was small. A composition contest was announced by the Ontario Music Teachers' Association in 1887, but it brought no results because of a strange qualification which admitted only professional composers, of which there were too few at that time by any mode of definition. Occasions such as the inauguration of a church, a visit of royalty, or the reception of a new governor-general inspired both musicians and amateur composers. Confedera-tion, for instance, was celebrated in a cantata by such a serious musician as Jean-Baptiste Labelle and, on a lower musical level, by Sergeant H. Dixon, in a *Confederation Galop* written in 1865 in anticipation of the event and described by its publisher as "a stirring composition [which] ought of itself to impel every one to vote for Confederation." *Canada's Welcome* was the title of a masque with music by A. A. Clappé. It was performed in Ottawa in 1879 to celebrate the arrival of Governor-General the Marquis of Lorne and his wife the Princess Louise.

FRENCH-CANADIAN COMPOSERS IN MONTREAL: Our survey of composers, which will embrace the period from Confederation to World War I, begins with the musicians of French Canada, where a greater number appeared at an earlier time than in the English-speaking regions. The first place among nineteenth-century Canadian composers is held by Calixa Lavallée. Among Canadian-born composers he stands high in the quantity of his music and ranks first in the variety of media attempted. Furthermore, he was the first whose music was widely performed both in Canada and in the United States, and he was the only one of Canada's early composers whose music has been revived in recent years with some success. The renewed interest in Lavallée was prompted by curiosity about the creator of "O Canada," but it has proven rewarding from a purely musical point of view as well.

The small fraction of Lavallée's works which is preserved in print or manuscript includes the comic opera *The Widow* and the melodramatic musical satire in two acts *Tiq (Settled at Last)*, the offertory *Tu es Petrus*, the *Hymne à la paix dedié a toutes les nations du monde*, the "Bridal Rose" Overture, and a number of piano pieces and songs. The full list of Lavallée's compositions is not yet known. Among the many works that have been lost or not yet located are two more stage works; a three-act comic opera *Lou-Lou* and *Le Jugement de Salomon*; a cantata in honour of the arrival of the Marquis of Lorne and Princess Louise; two symphonies; two orchestral suites; overtures and marches for band; thirty studies for piano; some chamber music; and uncounted piano pieces and songs.

The dominant impression gained from the surviving scores is that Lavallée possessed an inexhaustible gift for melody—facile and trivial at times, but always spontaneous and musical. This music is not overburdened with complexity or originality, but it has great vitality and is popular in appeal without being vulgar. Many numbers in *The Widow* (Fig. 6) bear comparison with Bizet, Offen-

FIGURE 6. An excerpt from Lavallée's *The Widow*.

bach or Sullivan. They have the pulse and sparkle of true theatre music and deserve to be revived in performance. It is a pity that the surviving works represent only the lighter aspect of Lavallée's style, for his skill in combining three songs contrapuntally in the cantata for the Marquis of Lorne (see p. 137), would seem to indicate that the symphonies and chamber works probably contained passages of greater contrapuntal and harmonic interest than *The Widow* or the "Bridal Rose" Overture.

That Lavallée was more than a bread-and-butter composer of workaday music is revealed by his response when a well-known publisher of band music held out to him the prospect of quick fortune if he would write a series of pieces for cornet band. "I am not seeking fame or advancement on that question," Lavallée replied. "I would rather devote my time to compositions which, if less profitable, are more artistic. I would rather be remembered for a few artistic compositions than to [*sic*] grow rich in other lines of musical effort."[3] This idealistic attitude is confirmed in the judgment of a Canadian writer who had met Lavallée: "Lavallée must be regarded as the first native-born Canadian creative composer—first in time, in genius, in versatility of achievement and in meritorious musicianship."[4]

There have been critics who would disagree with the last part of this statement. They have maintained that Guillaume Couture, the Montreal organist and conductor of the Philharmonic Society, surpassed Lavallée as a musical scholar and theorist. This is another way of saying that Couture was the more academic and Lavallée the more imaginative composer. Couture was indeed a more disciplined thinker, one who cherished the orthodox rules of harmony. This preoccupation with the study of harmony was his strength as well as his weakness. "Il voyait, avant tout, dans la musique, des règles harmoniques dont on ne pouvait sans danger se départir. C'est que Couture était doué d'une sensibilité surtout intellectuelle."[5]

Couture's compositions are not as numerous or as varied in form as Lavallée's. Apart from a string quartet written in his student years and a few other pieces, all his music is religious in purpose. Two highlights stand out from his career as a composer: first, when he was a student in Paris, the performance of some of his choral and orchestral works in Paris under Edouard Colonne; and second, the completion of his masterwork, the oratorio (or, to be exact, lyrical religious poem) *Jean le Précurseur* in the year before his

[3]Obituary, New York *Times*, Jan. 31, 1891.

[4]D. J. Logan, "Canadian Creative Composers," *Canadian Magazine* (1913), p. 489.

[5]Léo-Pol Morin, *Papiers de musique* (Montreal, 1930), p. 80.

death. Unfortunately this work, which was published in France, was not performed until February 6, 1923 (at the St.-Denis Theatre, Montreal), eight years after Couture's death. This music exhibits a wealth of colour and contrast. The three parts of *Jean le Pré-curseur*—"La Nativité," "La Prédication," "Le Martyre"—contain a great variety of reflective and dramatic passages. Solos which rarely assume the proportion of arias, recitatives, and accompanied and unaccompanied choral passages are linked by instrumental inter-ludes and bridges. Each part forms a continuous musical whole. The strong musical points of the oratorio are the use of frequent change or contrast of mood to sustain interest, and the feeling for massive climactic effects. What is lacking in melodic inspiration is made up by contrapuntal ingenuity. There are many exciting passages of choral polyphony, culminating in two elaborate fugues: "Que soit béni le Dieu d'Israël" which ends the first part (Fig. 7), and "Elle a fait retentir les échos du désert" near the end of the last part. If Canadian conductors were less preoccupied with the pro-ducts of the last five or ten years and more anxious to explore the whole range of the repertoire they would discover in *Jean le Pré-curseur* one of the monuments of Canadian music.

Romain Octave Pelletier (1843–1927) was a pioneer musician of Montreal with an unusually wide educational background. In addition to becoming a notary public, Pelletier received musical training in England (with the famous organist William Thomas Best), Paris (with Widor and Marmontel), Brussels and Germany. He occupied the organist's bench at St. James Cathedral for two periods totalling over forty years. As an organist he did much to propagate the works of Bach (not without incurring criticism for playing Protestant music in Catholic churches); as a pianist he excelled in Chopin. Canada has produced few music teachers equalling Pelletier in skill and influence. He taught solfeggio at Jacques-Cartier Normal School for several decades, and his private pupils included many outstanding Canadian musicians of a younger generation: Champagne, Laliberté, Lavallée-Smith, Lucas, Reed and Tremblay, to mention but a few. A few textbooks on piano pedagogy illustrate his teaching experience. As a composer his output was, like that of Couture, mostly restricted to church music

FIGURE 7. The beginning of the fugue "Que soit béni le Dieu d'Israël" from Couture's *Jean le Précurseur*. With permission of the copyright owners.

for choir and organ. He was essentially an improviser and committed few of his musical thoughts on paper. The few printed compositions included *Six Organ Pieces*, and his mastery of Gregorian accompaniment on the organ is documented in *L'Accompagnement du nouveau manuel de chants liturgiques* which appeared in 1889. A Montreal musician has characterized the personalities of Pelletier and Couture in these words: "Pelletier sentait la musique; Couture la pensait."[6]

Alexis Contant (1858–1918) was organist at St. Jean-Baptiste Church in Montreal for over thirty years. He was also known as a pianist and accompanist and taught piano in several colleges and convents in the Montreal area. His teachers had been Joseph A. Fowler and Calixa Lavallée. He also studied with Lavallée in Boston, where he replaced the ailing master in some concerts. Contant's pupils include such well-known Canadian musicians as Wilfrid Pelletier, J. J. Gagnier, Rodolphe Mathieu, and Claude Champagne. His compositions include numerous songs, sacred pieces, and *salon* pieces for the piano. The most important works are three masses with soloists, chorus, and orchestra; a march for the consecration of Pope Pius X; a *Marche héroïque*; an oratorio, *Caïn*; and a symphonic poem, *Les Deux Ames*. Of the masses, the third is considered the greatest. It was intended for the inauguration of a new St. Jean-Baptiste Church in 1903, but its performance was turned down because of the prohibitive expense involved. A performance was arranged later in the same year at the Monument National under Edmond Hardy. Other compositions by Contant were included on this programme, which may be considered the first orchestral-choral concert devoted to one Canadian composer.

Caïn is a work in three parts: "La Haine," "Le Sang," and "La Promesse." Jehin-Prume and Lucas had written oratorios before, but the claim appears justified that this was the first Canadian oratorio to be performed. The event took place on November 12, 1905, in the presence of the Prime Minister, Sir Wilfrid Laurier. Joseph-Jean Goulet was the conductor. Two more performances followed. *Les Deux Ames* was finished in 1909 after three years of work and received two performances in Montreal

6Arthur Laurendeau, "Musiciens d'autrefois: Romain-Octave Pelletier," *l'Action Nationale*, XXXV (June 1950), 442.

in 1913. It employs a narrator, chorus, and orchestra. At the time of his death Contant was planning an opera, *Veronica*, to a drama by Louis Fréchette. He completed only the overture.

The opinions of those who know Contant's music differ. Léo-Pol Morin found in *Caïn* and *Les Deux Ames* "une grande insuffisance de métier et une imagination à la fois généreuse et d'un goût discutable."[7] More recently, Romain Gour has stated: "Ces œuvres témoignent d'une constante évolution, depuis le style à la mode du temps à l'emploi heureux de la dissonance jusqu'au chromaticisme."[8] Contant's idol was Gounod; he was also deeply interested in the scores of Wagner and Saint-Saëns. Whatever the weaknesses of his music, he must be respected for his courage to tackle large forms of composition at a time when most composers in Canada restricted themselves to smaller forms. Nor must it be forgotten that Contant never studied with any but Canadian teachers.

Two other composers from Montreal who were held in high esteem by the critics of the early twentieth century were Achille Fortier (1864–*ca.* 1939) and Amédée Tremblay (1876–1949). The grouping is suggested by certain parallels in their careers, both of which started in Montreal and led to Ottawa. Both men were organists and published arrangements of French-Canadian songs. Unlike Tremblay, however, who was mostly self-taught, Fortier had the advantage of studying in Paris. He was the first Canadian student to enrol in the regular composition course of the Conservatoire. After five years he returned to Montreal, taught music, and later became a government translator in Ottawa. His manuscripts, some of which were destroyed by fire, consisted of church music, songs, and piano pieces. The largest work was a mass with orchestral accompaniment which was performed in 1896. His music is said to have been romantic, with traces of Fauré, and more modernistic than the music of his Canadian contemporaries. Tremblay was organist at the Roman Catholic Basilica in Ottawa from 1894 until 1920. Later he was organist in the United States. His published works include songs and an organ suite. He also wrote a Mass in D flat, a Requiem, and an operetta, *L'Intransigeant*, which was performed in Ottawa about 1906. It appears that the most produc-

[7]Morin, *Papiers de musique*, p. 76.
[8]Romain Gour, "Alexis Contant, pianiste-compositeur," *Qui?* (Dec. 1953), p. 40.

tive period of both Fortier and Tremblay was before World War I. Certainly they did not play a great role in Canadian musical life after this time.[9]

A respected organist and music teacher was Alphonse Lavallée-Smith (1873–1912; not a relative of Calixa), the founder in 1905 of the Conservatoire National de Musique in Montreal. He received his first music lessons in Nicolet, P.Q., and later studied in Paris with Widor and Guilmant. He composed numerous vocal and sacred composition. A Prelude and Cantata, with music by Lavallée-Smith and words by Louis Fréchette, was performed in 1903. His largest work is the operetta Gisèle.

The Montreal composers mentioned so far were all organists or pianists, and their works stemmed chiefly from the Roman Catholic church service. There were also a number of violinists (whom we have spoken of previously) who wrote extensively for their own instrument. The most important of them was Frantz Jehin-Prume, the Belgian violin virtuoso who spent nearly half his life in Canada. It is doubtful whether his two violin concertos and other works for violin and orchestra were written specially for a Canadian performance, but many of them were composed after his first visit to Montreal. The list of Jehin-Prume's works, numbering to opus 88, also includes works for violin and piano, cadenzas for several classical violin concertos, and transcriptions. There is no record of a performance of his largest work in a different form, an oratorio written in 1886 and dedicated to Pope Leo XIII.

Jules Hone (1833–1913) belonged, like Jehin-Prume, to the group of Belgian violinists born in or near the city of Liège. He had been a pupil of François Prume and, after conducting in New York for a few years, settled in Montreal. There he was influential as a teacher and conductor. Some of his violin pieces and a violin method were published in Belgium and the United States. His compositions were not confined to his own instrument. He harmonized Canadian and Irish folk songs, dedicated a Marche militaire to Dr. Sun Yat-Sen, the founder of the Chinese republic, and wrote an opera, The Grandee, which was performed in Montreal in 1899. Hone's talented pupil, Oscar Martel (see also p. 224), wrote a number of virtuoso pieces for his own recitals. They include a violin

[9]Tremblay's son George Amédée, born in Ottawa in 1911, is a composer in the United States.

concerto and a set of *Airs canadiens variés* for violin and piano. Alfred de Sève (see also p. 225), in turn a pupil of Martel, wrote many recital pieces for violin, as well as piano and church music, some of which was published in the United States.

The achievements of Ernest Lavigne (see also p. 210) lay chiefly in the fields of cornet-playing and conducting. He also made a name for himself as the writer of some seventy songs. Twenty-five of these were published in an album in 1901. They contain music of typically French sparkle and lightness.

Three other composers began their careers about the turn of the century, although their period of maturity lies beyond the time under discussion. Frédéric Pelletier (1870–1944), the son of R. O. Pelletier, was a church musician and critic who composed church music; Emiliano Renaud (1875–1932), a pianist and church musician active in Canada and the United States, wrote nearly two hundred compositions, many of them published; and Alfred Laliberté (see also p. 234), was a pianist who returned to Montreal in 1911 after his studies in Europe, strongly impressed by the music of Scriabine and Medtner.

FRENCH CANADIANS OUTSIDE MONTREAL: Montreal was the undisputed centre of composition not only of French Canada but of the whole country. (In addition to the French Canadians already listed, a few Anglo-Canadian composers of Montreal are still to be discussed.) Comparatively few French-Canadian composers were active outside Montreal. The most prominent of these was Joseph Vézina, the bandmaster and conductor of Quebec City. His fifty-odd pieces for band are divided about equally between marches and dances, a few of which are still performed. The list of Vézina's band music is rounded off by a few overtures and fantasies, including the *Mosaïque sur des airs populaires canadiens*. The fame of this work is based on the fact that its first performance (1880) marked also the first performance of one of the "airs populaires Canadiens," Lavallée's "O Canada." As a composer of marches and dances Vézina was most fertile between 1875 and 1900. Then he turned to the writing of operettas. Of his three works in this form, *Le Lauréat* (1906) and *Le Fétiche* (1912) are based on plots set in Canada. The title of the third, *Le Rajah* (1910), suggests an exotic setting.

Octave Chatillon (1831–1906) wrote six masses for the Nicolet Seminary where he was a teacher. He also wrote cantatas, band music, and instrumental pieces, and was author of several stage plays. One of these, *La Prise de Québec*, appeared in print.

Napoléon Crépault (1849–1906) was organist at the church of St.-Roche in Quebec in the 1880's. His Mass in G and *La Communion des Saints* were performed at this church. His reputation rested on a collection of vocal works, *La Ruche harmonieuse*, and another of piano pieces, *Les Joies du foyer*.

Louis-Philippe Laurendeau (*ca.* 1860–1916), a native of St.-Hyacinthe, wrote innumerable compositions and arrangements for band as well as a manual, *The Practical Band Arranger*. Working for Carl Fischer, Inc., and other American publishers he had probably more of his music published than any other Canadian composer except Cedric W. Lemont. He died in Montreal.

Léon Ringuet (1858–1932 or 1933) was a bandmaster and organist in St.-Hyacinthe. Many of his band marches and piano pieces have been published.

BRITISH IMMIGRANTS: The composers in the English-speaking cities of Canada, like their French Canadian compatriots, earned their living as organists, music teachers, or choirmasters. They were fewer in number, however, and the immigrants were as numerous as the native Canadians. They too were chiefly attracted by the sacred vocal composition and the *salon* piece, and works of larger dimensions were usually of the vocal type. The lack of symphonies, concertos, quartets, and sonatas appears almost complete, if we disregard a few works written outside Canada.

Once more our survey begins with the city of Montreal, for here the most ambitious and perhaps most gifted of the early immigrant composers spent much of his time. We have already sketched the activities of Charles A. E. Harriss as an organizer of music festivals and music educator (p. 216). These accomplishments tend to overshadow his merit as a composer. Few Canadian composers were as lucky with regard to the publication of their music: the entire known list of Harriss's music consists of published works, and the publishers include the best-known English, American and Canadian names in the field. The majority of the works are songs, choral pieces, and organ music, but Harriss's compositions culminate in seven large vocal-orchestral works. These are the dramatic sacred cantata *Daniel before the King* (1890), the opera *Torquil* (published 1896), a "Festival" Mass (1901) dedicated to the Countess of Minto, the "Coronation" Mass for Edward VII (1902), the choric idyl *Pan* (1904), the ballad "The Sands of Dee" (performed 1907), and the ode *The Crowning of the King* (1911). *Pan*, when performed in England in 1906, was described as imaginative and picturesque music, "an interesting essay in what might be termed the symphonic style of choral composition." One of the perform-ances of *Torquil* took place in Montreal on May 25, 1900, with a cast under the direction of the composer and the Boston Festival Orchestra. Throughout the opera the style is that of a serious musical work (Fig. 8). One can detect in it affinities to various masters of the romantic era, and echoes of the harmonic vocabulary of Wagner's *Tristan* come as a pleasant surprise in a Canadian composer of the turn of the century.

Dr. Percival Illsley (1865–1924) was a fine musician who contributed to musical life in Montreal as an organist and pedagogue at the Dominion College of Music and later the McGill Conservatorium. His most important work is the cantata *Ruth*, which dates from 1894.

The most active and erudite English composers who settled in Toronto before 1910 were Albert Ham (1858–1940) and Edward Broome (1868–1932). Both have been mentioned as prominent choirleaders. Dr. Ham, the organist at St. James Cathedral (1897–1933) and the first president of the Canadian Guild (now Royal College) of Organists, came to Canada in 1897. He lectured at the University of Toronto and was at one time dean of the Faculty of Music at Bishop's University in Lennoxville, P.Q. The bulk of his published compositions consists of church music and marches for piano or band. His largest works are the cantata *The Solitudes of the Passion* (published 1917), an Advent cantata, and a suite for orchestra. Ham also wrote a number of manuals on organ technique, voice training, and theory. According to W. O. Forsyth, Ham's music was "rich and sincere, and strongly impregnated with freedom and optimistic gladness." His orchestral scores stimulated patriotic enthusiasm.[10]

[10]W. O. Forsyth, "Canadian Composers," *Canadian Journal of Music*, II (June 1915), 20.

Like F. H. Torrington, Edward Broome spent over a decade in Montreal and after an interval of some years settled in Toronto. He earned his doctorate in music from Trinity College, Toronto, in 1908 and established a reputation as leader of the Oratorio Society and as a teacher of singing and organ at the Toronto Conservatory. His published compositions, numbering one hundred, include anthems, part-songs, and songs for solo voice. Two compositions are for chorus and orchestra, *A Hymn of Trust* (Psalm 18) and *Sea-Song*. Broome started his career in Wales and kept close musical ties with that country after his immigration to Canada. He won many prizes at the Welsh National Festivals, including one for his largest work, the opera *The Siege of Cardiff Castle*, which he completed in 1908.

Robert S. Ambrose (1824–1908), who came to Canada from England at the age of ten and who settled in Hamilton, deserves mention as the composer of one of the most widely circulated of all Canadian compositions. His sacred song "One Sweetly Solemn Thought," published first in 1876, appeared in the catalogues of about a dozen publishers in the next thirty years (it was even arranged for brass ensemble) and is still found in recent collections of songs.

FIGURE 8. An excerpt from Harriss' *Torquil*. With permission of Whaley, Royce & Co. Ltd.

FIGURE 8 (*continued*)

Among the Anglo-Saxon immigrant musicians there was at least one American-born composer of rank. This was Charles H. Porter, organist, conductor and conservatory principal in Halifax (see p. 153). As well as church music and songs he wrote an overture, a sonata, and a symphony, but some of these works may have been written in Leipzig where he studied with Reinecke and Jadassohn. Porter's piano pieces are reported to suggest Chopin and to be of great difficulty.

ANGLO-CANADIANS: In order of chronology the list of Anglo-Canadian composers begins with Hugh Archibald Clarke of Toronto and Samuel Prowse Warren of Montreal, both of whom went to the United States as young men (see p. 224). Another Montreal musician, Joseph A. Fowler (1845–1917), organist at a Roman Catholic church and author of two masses with orchestral accompaniment, does not rank high as a composer, judging from the score of one of the masses. Thus we are justified in calling Angelo M. Read (1854–1926), William Reed (1859–1945) and Wesley Octavius Forsyth (1859–1937) the first notable Canadian composers of British ancestry. Although Angelo Read was born near St. Catharines, he received his musical training in the United States and at Leipzig and Vienna. He was active in Buffalo and other American cities but remained associated with St. Catharines, where he was musical director of Ridley College. A dramatic cantata, *David's Lament* (1903), heads the list of his compositions, which also include orchestral overtures, piano pieces and church music.

William Reed began his studies with R. O. Pelletier and at the age of nineteen was selected from among thirty applicants to play the organ at Keble College in Oxford and to study organ and composition. His career included positions as organist in Sherbrooke, Montreal, Toronto, and finally Quebec. He became known to a wide public as a concert organist, but unfortunately deafness early threatened his career. Eventually Reed turned entirely to composition. His published sacred choral works and his organ pieces form an impressive list. The *Grand Chœur* in D major for organ is considered by such an authority as Henri Gagnon, the Quebec organist, as one of the finest organ works ever written by a Canadian.

Wesley Octavius Forsyth, a native of Aurora, Ontario, studied piano and composition with Zwintscher, Krause, Ruthardt and Jadassohn in Leipzig and with Epstein in Vienna. After his return to Canada he was active as a critic and piano teacher in Toronto, first at the Metropolitan School of Music which he directed, then at the Canadian Academy of Music and the Toronto Conservatory of Music. Two orchestral suites and a *Romanza* are said to have been performed in Leipzig, and in 1889 he already had enough music to his credit to stage a recital in Toronto entirely devoted to his own compositions. Forsyth's prolific pen never rested till the end. His works bear opus numbers from 1 to 71; they were published by at least 17 different publishers in Canada, Germany, England and the United States. Not only was Forsyth the first widely-known composer born in Ontario but probably no other Canadian composer who remained in his native country throughout his professional career has had as much music published. The early orchestral works, the Prelude and Fugue op. 18 in C minor for organ and the Prelude ("canon in the second") and Fugue ("strict, for three voices") op. 25 in A♭ major for piano document his mastery of the craft of composition. His heart, however, was in song-writing and in short piano pieces with descriptive titles (Fig. 9). A warm lyricism and a genuinely pianistic idiom is revealed both in the virtuoso pieces in the grand romantic tradition and in the simpler works written for his students. Some of his music bears a resemblance to that of his friend Cyril Scott.

The fact that Clarence Lucas (1866–1947) spent only a few years of his professional life in Canada suggests that he should be classified, within the framework of this book, as an emigrant musician, along with such composers as G. H. Fairclough, G. A. Grant-Schaefer, Edward B. Manning, and C. W. Lemont (see p. 226). Unlike these men who became absorbed by the United States, however, Lucas remained well-known to Canadian critics and was hailed as the most outstanding living Canadian composer even two decades after his departure. A native of the Niagara Peninsula, Ontario, he received his early musical training in Montreal and later studied in Paris with Gounod, Massenet, Théodore Dubois, and others (1886–9). He taught in Toronto and Utica, N.Y., for some time and obtained his Bachelor of Music degree from the University of Toronto in 1893. His later career

FIGURE 9. The opening of Forsyth's "Frühlingsabend."

was carried on in London, New York, and Paris. He was also associated in editorial capacity with the *Musical Courier* and the publishing firm of Chappell & Co. He died in Paris.

Lucas approaches Lavallée in productivity and variety of compositions. By 1913 he had over 130 works to his credit. Of his seven operas, at least two were performed: *The Money Spider* (London, 1897) and *Peggy Machree* (England, 1904; United States, 1907). His sacred vocal-orchestral music includes an oratorio, *The Birth of Christ* (Chicago, 1902), and a Requiem Mass written in 1936–7. In the orchestral field Lucas wrote a symphony, two symphonic poems, and overtures to *Othello*, *As You Like It*, and *Macbeth*. His works in smaller forms feature organ and piano music most prominently. Finally, Lucas's compositions include about seventy songs. Some of these were written to his own words, as were also some of the stage works. In the opinion of his colleague W. O. Forsyth, "Lucas' works are all impregnated with seriousness. He writes easily. His melodies flow gracefully, and sometimes they haunt one with their plaintive wistfulness."[11] About the piano music Forsyth declared: "His piano pieces have the real piano idiom. They not only require from the pianist fine technical resources, but they sound well—rich, harmonious blends of tone effectively and beautifully contrasted."[12]

Although his output was extremely small, we must mention Augustus Stephen Vogt as the author of some choral pieces that demonstrate his great understanding of choral effect. The most successful were "An Indian Lullaby," "The Sea," and "Crossing the Bar." Vogt also wrote choral arrangements.

As with the French Canadians, we can only mention composers born in the 1880's who did not gain full recognition until after the period under discussion. These were Gena Branscombe (1881–) and Nathaniel Dett (1882–1943), both of whom settled in the United States.

OPERETTA COMPOSERS: While few instrumental works of great length were produced in Canada, the period 1880–1915 witnessed the writing and performance of a fair number of Cana-

[11]*Ibid.*
[12]W. O. Forsyth, "Clarence Lucas," *Canadian Journal of Music*, I (May 1914), 4.

dian operettas. These were usually written for amateur productions with slight vocal and slighter orchestral resources. We have mentioned some of these works written by Vézina, Hone, Lavigueur, Lavallée-Smith, and Tremblay. However, a number of operettas were composed by musicians not otherwise active as composers. Some of the composers are even nameless. H.M.S. Parliament, or The Lady Who Loved a Government Clerk, the libretto of which was printed in Ottawa in 1880, is obviously an adaptation of H.M.S. Pinafore to a political incident. Both borrowed and original melodies were used in a burlesque on the Riel rebellion written by some of the soldiers who had participated in the campaign. This piece, lengthily and explicitly entitled "Our Boys" in the Riel Rebellion (Halifax to the Saskatchewan), was staged in Halifax in 1886 by soldiers of the 63rd Halifax Rifles. Political and military topics were a favourite subject for operettas. Oscar F. Telgmann (1853–1945), German-born founder of the Kingston Conservatory of Music (1892), wrote the music of Leo, the Royal Cadet, an "entirely new and original Canadian military opera, in four acts." This work holds a record among Canadian operas: it is reputed to have received 150 performances, the first in 1889 under the patronage of the Royal Military College in Kingston, and others in Ottawa, Guelph, Toronto, Woodstock, Stratford and Utica, N.Y.[13] Joseph Nevin Doyle of Belleville, Ontario, turned to the exotic and romantic sphere in his operettas The Golden Age (performed in Belleville and Toronto, 1915) and Cingalee. He died in 1916 while working on another, The Enchanted Garden.

The writing of operettas was not confined to the older regions. In Regina, Frank L. Laubach and Charles Shrimpton wrote and produced a successful three-act musical comedy, The Mystic Light, in 1913. Two English composers who settled in Winnipeg early in the twentieth century (too late to be included in our survey of composers) brought forth operettas in 1911: Dr. Ralph Joseph Horner (1849–1926) staged his romantic opera The Belles of Barcelona with his own light opera company, while the vocal score of William Dichmont's (1882–1943) musical play Miss Pepple (of New York) was published in Winnipeg the same year.

SHEET MUSIC: A comparison between the music just surveyed and the lists of Canadian music publishers reveals two separate

13Arthur S. Bourinot, Five Canadian Poets (Ottawa, 1954), p. 22.

worlds. Both activities, composition and publishing, developed simultaneously, but not together. Commercial considerations forced the publishers to specialize in dances, marches and popular ballads rather than serious music. The principal meeting ground was religious and patriotic music. In spite of this cleavage, both parties fared well: the composers, especially those—immigrant or native— who had established contacts abroad during their student years, found English firms (notably Novello) and American firms (notably O. Ditson and G. Schirmer) generous; the publishers prospered by reprinting foreign or printing Canadian popular music.

Music publishing had taken great strides since its beginnings about the middle of the nineteenth century. The number of musical pieces published annually in Canada in the 1880's was about the same as in the 1950's—about 150. In making this comparison one must remember that although the population was much smaller in the 1880's, the phonograph record had not yet challenged the sale of sheet music. The output in the earlier period included few of the instructive beginner's pieces that account for so much of twentieth-century production, but surpassed the later period in ambition of enterprise. Vocal scores and albums with over one hundred pages of music, such as Telgmann's *Leo, the Royal Cadet* (published 1889, 113 pp.), Harriss's *Torquil* (1896, 146 pp.), Dichmont's *Miss Pepple* (1911, 154 pp.) and Ernest Gagnon's *Accompagnement d'orgue des chants liturgiques* (1903, 303 pp.), even though not in every case financed by a commercial publisher, represent publishing achievements virtually unheard of in Canada since World War I.

The advertisements and copyright registrations of sheet music consisted in the large majority of reprints of foreign music. Some firms, such as the Anglo-Canadian Music Publishers' Association (1885) and Edwin Ashdown (1888–ca. 1920), were established by parent companies in England expressly to prevent United States publishers from importing into Canada reprints of British copyrights. Almost all other publishers engaged in the reprint trade to some extent. The bestsellers of the day were the dances and *salon* pieces of men such as Charles D'Albert, John Hatton, Gustave Lange and Sidney Smith and their equivalents in Canada— W. Braybrooke Bayley, Edwin Gledhill, Henry Prince and Moritz Relle. A share of serious Canadian works is found among the publications of A. & S. Nordheimer (later the Nordheimer Piano

& Music Co.), I. Suckling & Sons (ca. 1875–ca. 1894) and Whaley, Royce & Co. (1888) of Toronto; Arthur Lavigne (1868–ca. 1900) and Lavigueur & Hutchison (fl. 1900) of Quebec; Ed. Archambault (1896) and A. J. Boucher (1861) in Montreal, and J. L. Orme (1866) in Ottawa. The last two are the oldest music dealers in business, although neither firm is still active as a publisher.

The bulk of the published Canadian music consisted of music in the patriotic and so-called light or popular vein—marches, galops, waltzes, quadrilles and songs, which were turned out in great numbers by amateurs as well as musicians specializing in this type of music. They deserve attention because they give, through their titles, texts and cover illustrations, a better reflection of Canadian social history than compositions of more artistic and academic aspiration.[14]

The greatest single category of sheet music was that of the patriotic type, identified by titles such as "For Canada and Right," "Canada, the Gem in Crown," or "The Flag of Canada."[15] We have cited some of the patriotic songs of French Canada, written from about 1830 on. The tide of patriotic songs with English texts began to swell about the time of Confederation. The best-known writer in this field was Alexander Muir (1830–1906), a school teacher and later a principal in Toronto. He was born in Scotland but raised in Canada. The story of how his most famous song was written has been told as follows. One October day in 1867, while walking through a Toronto park, a falling maple leaf stuck persistently to Muir's coat. The thought suddenly struck him that he should write about the Maple Leaf, Canada's emblem. When he showed his poem to his wife she suggested that he set it to music. At first Muir went to a music store in search of a suitable melody, but not finding one to his liking, he invented one himself.[16] A

---

[14]Canadian libraries are not well stocked with these documents of a bygone era of musical taste. The libraries of Laval University in Quebec and St. Sulpice in Montreal have examples from French Canada; the music division of the Toronto Public Libraries and especially the National Library in Ottawa are rapidly building up such sections.

[15]"Several tons of them cumber the shelves of the publishers," as one writer put it disdainfully.

[16]A. E. Belcher, "How Alexander Muir Wrote 'The Maple Leaf,' " *Canadian Music Trades Journal* (Aug. 1923), p. 87; also in Toronto *Globe*, July 20, 1923. Belcher heard the story from Muir himself, but many years after the song was written.

supplement to this story was supplied by Muir's friend George Leslie, who has related how on the morning of that day he drew Muir's attention to a patriotic song contest sponsored by the Caledonian Society of Montreal. By evening, the song was written and mailed to Montreal. It won the second prize of $50.[17] "The Maple Leaf Forever," written in the year of Confederation, has long been a favourite in Ontario and other English-speaking provinces, although by the middle of the twentieth century its popularity was overshadowed by "O Canada." Many have been the controversies about the relative merits of these and other national songs. If any is ever officially recognized as a national hymn, it will, no doubt, be Lavallée's song. Muir also wrote other patriotic songs, such as "The Old Union Jack and Canada" and "Land of the Maple Tree." Another stalwart of musical patriotism was English-born Henry Herbert Godfrey (b. 1858). His "Land of the Maple" sold 77,000 copies in the first ten months after its publication in 1897. An album of twenty of his *Patriotic Canadian Songs and Melodies* appeared in 1902.

Some patriotic music was connected with definite political or historical events. Examples are "Le Jubilé de la Reine" for Queen Victoria's golden jubilee in 1887 (by Vézina) and the "Loyal Opposition Galop," "respectfully dedicated to the Right Hon. Sir John A. Macdonald, K.C.B. and the Liberal Conservatives of Canada." Alexander Mackenzie, Canada's first Liberal prime Minister was honoured in the "New Premier Galop" in 1874. Indeed, the list of dedications reads like a recital of dignitaries and politicians.

Next to patriotic sentiment the mighty St. Lawrence River provided the most powerful inspiration. There were "The Rapid St. Lawrence," "Les Canotiers du St. Laurent," and "Les Bords du St. Laurent," but the greatest popularity was achieved by Sabatier's "Promenade sur le fleuve Saint-Laurent." The bridge spanning the river at Montreal, one of the engineering marvels of the time was also celebrated in music. A lithograph picture of the bridge graces the cover of "The St. Lawrence Tubular Bridge Mazurka-Polka" "composed by the author of *The Grand Trunk Railway Galop*." The railway was another marvel of the day. On Dominion Square

[17]J. Ross Robertson, *Landmarks of Toronto*, ser. 6 (Toronto, 1914), chap. xxxvi, "Alexander Muir's Life," pp. 496–586.

in Montreal the Victoria Rifles played in 1887 "A Trip from Montreal to Lachine on the G.T.R." In answer to "popular demand," the score called for "bells, whistles, steam, etc."[18] A journey up the St. Lawrence River takes us to the Great Lakes, pictured in a set of five quadrilles by R. J. Fowler of Montreal (1848). We stop in Toronto to listen to "The Chimes of St. James" (1884).

Also of historical interest are those songs that were dedicated to societies, charity drives, and the like: the "Montreal Skating Club Galop," the "Ontario Agricultural College Polka," the "La Crosse Galop"—dedicated to the La Crosse Clubs of Canada—and "Charity," composed expressly for the Masonic Concert for the Poor in Charlottetown in March 1861. This last was probably the first piece of music printed on Prince Edward Island.

Still another category of sheet music was music given away by stores with advertising on the cover and anything inside from "The Maple Leaf Forever" to marches bearing the firm's name. A few pieces even had texts advertising the firm's wares or services—singing commercials of an older day. An example is "We Dye to Live!" with the chorus "Come! Come! Come! to Parker's Dye Works."

SUMMARY OF COMPOSITION: The foregoing pages demonstrate that for a young and immature country Canada had produced an impressive number of composers by the time of World War I. The music written by these composers did not compare in quality with the masterworks of European literature or in modernism with European *avant garde* music of the turn of the century. But it did cover a wide range of types, from church anthems, parlour songs, and pieces for piano students to choral-orchestral works of considerable proportions, and it also included a sprinkling of serious instrumental music. Much of it was the workaday product of more or less competent craftsmen; some revealed the imagination of sensitive and erudite artists.

Yet all this activity did not produce a regional or national school of composition—a group of composers united by style and convictions, acquainted with each other's work, and clearly distinguished from other groups of composers. Even in Montreal, where composers were most numerous, such criteria did not apply. Composers

[18]*Musical Journal* (Toronto, July 15, 1887), p. 117.

worked in relative isolation from one another, each being more influenced by European music than by that of his Canadian colleagues. The same held true for the composers' relationship to their environment: the memory of local musical traditions was weaker than the inspiring impact of European currents. Not only did the late nineteenth-century and early twentieth-century composers fail to draw inspiration from Canadian traditions—being colonial rather than national in outlook—they also failed to hand down a body of art on which younger generations could build a tradition. The younger generations owe very little to them from a stylistic point of view, preferring as well to seek their models among European masters. This is best illustrated by the fact that when the younger and middle-aged composers of the 1950's speak of the "oldest" or "first" generation of Canadian composers they are referring to Healey Willan, Leo Smith, Georges-Emile Tanguay, Claude Champagne, and others born in the 1880's or 1890's. This is a pity, for it reveals that they have not even a suspicion that there existed one or two earlier generations of musicians who had a strong claim to be respected as genuine and sincere artists.

13 / Assessing Achievement

CONTEMPORARY STOCK-TAKING OF THE MUSICAL
SCENE: The variety of musical activities and institutions in the
late nineteenth and early twentieth centuries could not help but
create a consciousness of achievement and a sense of satisfaction.
A demand arose for a stock-taking of the musical scene, for the
sake of both clarification and documentation. Fortunately this
period delighted in, and could afford, the production of reference
books in multi-volumed deluxe editions; otherwise it would not
have been possible to publish the extensive surveys of music in
Canada which were undertaken in increasing numbers. The turn
of the century is, indeed, the most copiously documented phase of
Canada's musical history. At first surveys of individual cities were
published. For example, brochures were devoted to *Musical
Toronto* (1897; 2nd ed. 1898–9) and *Musical Halifax* (1903–4).
Montreal, however, was presented with a detailed and comprehen-
sive document unparalleled in Canadian musical writing, *The
Musical Red Book of Montreal* (1907), by B. K. Sandwell. Here
was a full-size book given in its entirety to the record of musical
events and personalities of the period 1895–1907. The volume
begins with an analysis of recent Montreal musical history. It
then discusses the chief events, leaders, and programmes of each
orchestra, choral society and visiting opera company. It also
describes music schools, scholarships and examinations, sketches
the biographies of many local musicians, and gives a list of symphonic programmes. To recommend the book as a model would be

futile: money for a publication of this kind is not likely to be raised in many decades.

When F. H. Torrington and Mrs. J. W. F. Harrison contributed articles on musical history and progress to a Canadian encyclopedia in 1898 they had reason to apologize for the difficulty of gathering information.[1] But the four surveys of the musical scene which appeared between 1909 and 1914 in Canadian and foreign reference books have supplied us with profuse though rarely dependable or precise information.[2] The spelling of musicians' names, the years in which musical organizations were founded or dissolved— hardly two writers present us with the identical information. They were further handicapped by a lack of historical information. One of them stated in all seriousness that music in Nova Scotia was "still in its first chapter"; none recorded the contributions of such early pioneers as Quesnel, Glackemeyer or Molt. Instead they honoured musicians of the late nineteenth century with such titles as "father of good music in Toronto," "founder of choral music in Montreal," and so forth. Still we should respect these surveys for what they give, not criticize them for what they lack.

The foremost writer on music in Canada in this period was Dr. John Daniel Logan (1869–1929), who besides writing music reviews in Toronto papers, published several critical essays on composers and musical currents, and was the first actually to undertake writing a musical history of Canada. Unlike his book on Canadian literature it was never published and perhaps not even finished.

All these surveys were published in English. French-Canadian writers were more interested in specific historical subjects. At least two scholars produced works of musical significance: Ernest Myrand in his *Noëls anciens de la Nouvelle-France* (Quebec, 1899, 1907) and Ernest Gagnon in his biography of *Louis Jolliet* (see p. 23) (Quebec, 1902). One survey, at least, took a more practical form than the printed page. It consisted of a concert of

[1]*Canada: An Encyclopedia of the Country*, ed. J. Castell Hopkins (Toronto, 1898–1900), IV (1898).

[2]Mrs. J. W. F. Harrison, "Canada," *The Imperial History and Encyclopedia of Music*, III: *Foreign Music* (New York, etc., *ca.* 1909), pp. 231–53; Edouard Hesselberg, "A Review of Music in Canada," from *Modern Music and Musicians* (International ed.; New York and Toronto, *ca.* 1913); *The Year Book of Canadian Art* (London and Toronto, 1913) (includes articles on various phases of music in Canada by various authors), J. E. Middleton, "Music in Canada," *Canada and Its Provinces* (Toronto, 1914), XII, 643–51.

Canadian compositions, held in Montreal on October 1, 1903. Even though all the composers represented were residents of Montreal—Contant, Fortier, G. Labelle, Laliberté, Lamoureux, Lavallée-Smith, Letondal, R. O. Pelletier, Renaud, and Tremblay —and although the programme included only short vocal and instrumental pieces, it gave the audience the first panorama of Canadian music, the first opportunity to compare and judge the quality of an entire group of Canadian composers.[3]

A BALANCE-SHEET: A balance-sheet of the period just surveyed should list achievements as well as shortcomings. Let us begin with the former. As we have seen, the general state of prosperity and expansion was clearly reflected in musical life. Musical organizations flourished, a reasonably high standard of training was provided by the conservatories, professional standards were established on the concert stage, and at the same time amateur participation in choirs and domestic musical entertainment were at their peaks. Abroad, the success of Canadian-born performers drew attention to the newcomer on the musical map.

The true extent of this achievement becomes clear only when it is realized that mechanical aids (such as the phonograph and the player-piano) for the widespread diffusion, enjoyment, and experience of music were in their earliest stage of development and that patronage by a wealthy class or by government subsidies was virtually unknown. A few military officers in the early days, a number of governors-general in more recent times and a handful of wealthy citizens—these account for isolated instances of underwriting deficits incurred in performances, of hiring musicians for musicales in private homes, of establishing scholarships and prizes, or of financing the building of a concert hall. But such examples were few and far between; they did not constitute a pattern. The only pattern followed by the well-to-do and officialdom was that of treating the arts as stepchildren. The churches were consumers rather than patrons of music, although many showed generosity in making space available for concert rehearsals and performances.

Thus music was promoted essentially by individual enthusiasts— laymen and professionals from all social classes and various national

[3]There had been a few recitals devoted in their entirety to one Canadian composer. The music of Forsyth and Fortier had thus been presented.

origins. Through volunteer societies and other means these music lovers strove tooth and nail to keep music alive and to bring it to the wider public with whom singing and playing was not an everyday activity of home life. Since we have mentioned many musical leaders by name, we should emphasize that the credit for musical pioneer work is shared equally by countless amateurs. Unfortunately, enthusiasm (and box office receipts) alone can never sustain certain types of musical endeavour such as opera, orchestra, and other performing groups employing professional musicians. Because of the absence of a pattern of patronage, these forms of music-making could rarely be sustained for any length of time. Hence performances of good music were too infrequent to produce a widespread and thorough familiarity with the classics among the musical public. Of course, performances of Wagner's *Parsifal*, Schoenberg's String Quartet op. 7, and Beethoven's Ninth Symphony were entirely exceptional events, but even the standard repertoire from Bach to Tschaikowsky was heard only at rare intervals, except in Montreal and Toronto.

What further contributed to the irregularity of concert performances in the cities and to the disparity of musical opportunties between the large cities and the small towns was the failure to pool, distribute and exchange whatever talent was available. Considerable advantages would have accrued to every city and town had it been possible to arrange more tours of individual artists, choirs and orchestras. The Montreal Opera Company went on tour, and a few other examples could be cited, but altogether artistic interchange within the country was woefully small. Basically each city was an isolated musical unit, in more intimate contact with London, Boston or Paris than with its Canadian neighbours. Montreal and Toronto took notice of each other's music only to register contempt or smug superiority: the "musicians of Montreal are as remote from the musicians of Toronto as the Jews were once isolated from the Samaritans," and consequently "it can never be determined which is the more musical city, Montreal or Toronto, without a Royal Commission."[4]

This isolation of musical effort extended over a far wider field than that of performance, although in music education, at least, the provincial competitive festivals and the annual visits of con-

[4]Hesselberg, *Review,* p. vii.

servatory examiners to the cities and small towns of English-speaking Canada acted as centralizing forces.[5] Indeed it may be said that the whole history of music in Canada up to the introduction of radio networks was simply the sum total of many local and regional histories, histories which unfolded in similar patterns but quite independent from one another. Another way of describing the same phenomenon is to point to the lack of national character in musical life. This was more than a question of interchanging performers or of a distinct Canadian style in composition; it was a question of identifying musical effort as Canadian. There was no national opera house and no national music school that might have served as showcases of Canadian talent; there were no nation-wide musical organizations striving for common goals and speaking for the profession as a whole; there were few composers or performers known well in all parts of the country; there was no common Canadian heritage among the different ethnic sections; and last but not least, there were no songs from or about Canada sung in all regions of the Dominion.

Perhaps then the positive aspects of musical life—the vitality of music-making, the rapidity of progress and the abundance of talent—and the retarding factors—lack of patronage, irregularity of concert performances, geographical obstacles, and isolation of effort—permit one to sum up the essential character of the period by saying that it represented the climax of the period of colonial dependence on other countries and that, conversely, it was still marked by an absence of national cohesion.

DEVELOPMENTS AFTER 1914: In the decades after 1914 Canada has moved far in the development of her musical resources and towards a cohesion of effort which characterizes musical maturity. For a detailed description of the modern period readers are referred to the book *Music in Canada* and other literature listed in the section of the Bibliography dealing with "Development from 1914" (p. 286). Only a brief summary of recent trends is attempted in the following paragraphs.

The second decade of the twentieth century marked the beginning of the systematic collecting of folk songs in Canada.

[5]After John Beckwith, "Music in Canada," *Encyclopedia Americana*, V (Montreal, Toronto, Vancouver, Winnipeg, 1958), 440.

Thousands of these have been recorded since, by means of notation, wax-cylinder, or tape recorder, from the Atlantic Provinces and Quebec in the east to Saskatchewan and the west coast Indian settlements. Many songs can be traced to European origins, but some are of North American invention. The most important collections rest in the National Museum of Human History in Ottawa, the Archives de Folklore at Laval University in Quebec, and the Library of Congress in Washington. A great treasure of folk culture has thus been preserved, the extent of which was not even suspected by earlier collectors. Scholarly attention has so far focused on collecting rather than publication and musical analysis because the tradition of folk singing is rapidly moving towards extinction.

Public interest in Canadian folk song was first aroused by a series of festivals of song, dance and handicraft in the late 1920's. Since then a number of song collections and, after 1950, long-playing records and concerts by professional folk singers have popularized a representative number of Canadian songs among a new, urban audience, scattered over all provinces of Canada. In this way the foundations have been laid for a nationally known song repertoire.

The discovery of folk song also provided an impetus to composers. Sir Ernest MacMillan, Alfred Laliberté, Healey Willan, and Ralph Vaughan Williams (to mention one non-Canadian) are among those who harmonized or arranged Canadian songs. Larger works, such as MacMillan's *Two Sketches* and Claude Champagne's *Suite canadienne* (both 1928) characterize a stage at which composers explored folklore in search of a typically Canadian music. Musical nationalism, however, has never developed into a strong stylistic element.

The remarkable growth of Canadian composition towards the end of the 1930's was encouraged by the more mature cultural setting and the advances made in musical education and performance. The main driving force, however, was the dissatisfaction of younger musicians (especially the generation 1908–18) with the conservative outlook of the professors who taught them conventional harmony and counterpoint and with the restrictions placed by box-office considerations on the performance of music later than that of Debussy and Sibelius. They were determined to extend the range of Canadian composition beyond the utilitarian and academic spheres and sought inspiration in the music and teachings of the world's leading contemporary composers from the neo-classicists to the atonalists. Composers such as Louis Applebaum, Violet Archer, Alexander Brott, Jean Coulthard, Jean Papineau-Couture, Barbara Pentland, Godfrey Ridout, Jean Vallerand and John Weinzweig have succeeded in their aims of introducing an idiom that is genuinely contemporary, promoting the performance of new compositions, and providing leadership to younger Canadian composers. The generation born after World War I has reaped the benefit from this leadership and enjoys the added advantage of easy accessibility of contemporary music from other countries in published scores, phonograph records, and live performance.

It was no coincidence that the Canadian League of Composers (1951), the representative organization of Canadian composers, bestowed honorary membership on the two most influential teachers among the older generation, Claude Champagne and Healey Willan. The signal for the new era in musical productivity was given in 1936 when Willan, whose writing so far had been chiefly of church and organ music, turned to orchestral composition with his Symphony No. 1. In 1942 he wrote a radio opera, *Transit through Fire*. Since then new Canadian symphonies, divertimenti, concertos, ballet suites and chamber operas have appeared year after year, and much writing has been done as background music for movies and broadcasts. The stylistic tendencies revealed in this music vary as widely as the temperaments and techniques of the composers. Some critics recognize distinctive Canadian elements in certain compositions; others deny the possibility of such elements in an age where modern means of communication break down national boundaries in art.

This break-down of barriers is due to the advances in the technology of communication and can be observed in every field of musical activity. In Canada the introduction of phonograph records and radio were of even greater importance than in most countries. They have not only increased immensely the opportunities for listening to music but have resulted in a more equal distribution of music throughout the country. This is a great advantage especially to the many outlying and isolated areas which are at a great cultural disadvantage in comparison with the large cities. An audience has thus been reached which never had, or still rarely has an opportunity for hearing good music in live performance.

While the privately owned broadcasting stations concentrate on light recorded music, the government-controlled Canadian Broadcasting Corporation (1936) has contributed greatly to musical culture, partly through the variety and quality of the programmes themselves, partly through its unifying influence. Through its nationwide broadcasts it has contributed more than any other agency towards breaking down regional isolation and establishing national identity in musical life. Furthermore the C.B.C. is an important financial support for artists and performing groups, a promoter of Canadian talent and a propagandist for Canadian composers.

Mass distribution of music has not been an unmixed blessing, however. Radio stations and juke-boxes pour out a flood of popular music of the inferior kind; listening habits tend towards superficiality; and active participation in performance has only too often given way to passive listening. The living room piano, once the centre of home entertainment, stands silent while the family watches television or listens to phonograph records. To some extent these tendencies have been counterbalanced by advances in the fields of music appreciation and performance. Musical culture depends as much on the existence of an intelligent audience as it does on professional performers. The formation of both begins with education. In public and high schools the music programme has been expanded vastly (although unevenly from province to province and community to community), and school choirs and orchestras provide pupils with a practical insight into music-making. The institution of competitive festivals has spread from the prairie provinces to the rest of the country (it has found little appeal among the French-speaking population, however) and involves many thousands of youngsters in performance each year.

Professional students will always widen their horizon by study in other countries, but it is at last possible for them to acquire advanced training from internationally recognized artists at home. The Royal Conservatory of Music in Toronto and the McGill Conservatorium in Montreal are controlled by universities, as are several other conservatories; the Conservatoire de Musique et d'Art Dramatique (1942) in Montreal and Quebec is a scholarship school maintained by the provincial government of Quebec. Many universities have set up music departments or faculties which provide instruction towards academic degrees. The most important are Toronto, Laval, Montreal, McGill and British Columbia. The staff, once composed largely of organist-choirmasters, is recruited in increasing measure from among creative musicians and musicologists.

Great strides have been accomplished in the field of performance, which had been curtailed severely by World War I. The male sections of choirs diminished and orchestras went into eclipse. Recovery was slow. Only about 1930, when the introduction of "sound-track" movies made theatre orchestras superfluous, were concert orchestras revived or established as a device to provide new employment for musicians. Montreal, Toronto, Vancouver and Winnipeg have developed excellent professional orchestras which give subscription series as well as popular and children's concerts and are often heard in broadcasts. Elsewhere semi-professional and amateur orchestras are being trained. Choral singing is less popular than at the beginning of the century, but several choirs continue to maintain high standards and have won international reputation. Performance has also been helped by the establishment of annual festivals in Montreal, Stratford, Vancouver and other places.

Opera has made slow, but steady progress after isolated efforts in the 1920's and 1930's. Landmarks were the formation of the Montreal Opera Guild (1941) and the establishment of an Opera School at the Royal Conservatory of Music in Toronto (1946) and of the Canadian Opera Company (1958). The C.B.C. has also given numerous radio and television broadcasts and transmissions from the Metropolitan Opera House in New York have familiarized Canadians with operatic music.

The increase in professional performance is important not only because concerts are desirable but because it helps to employ Canadian and immigrant talent and reduce emigration, the fate of so many artists in earlier generations. However, the training and encouragement of gifted students and the maintenance of performing organizations are two aspects of musical life that depend strongly on financial patronage. The province of Quebec has provided such assistance for many years and the Canadian government recognized the need for subsidizing artistic effort when it established the Canada Council for the Encouragement of the Arts, Humanities and Social Sciences in 1957. In the few years of its existence the Canada Council has already helped many individual artists through scholarships and other grants and has assured the smooth operation of many worthy musical organizations. Such organized promotion is justified by the existing talent: the 1950's have brought forth a crop of young artists whose international recognition recalls the success of Canadian opera singers about the turn of the century.

Of particular significance is the Canada Council's support of the two most important projects of the Canadian Music Council to date: the *Canadian Music Journal* (1956) and the Canadian Music Centre (1958), an office for the promotion and distribution of Canadian compositions. The Canadian Music Council (1944) is a volunteer organization under the chairmanship of Canada's leading musical personality, Sir Ernest MacMillan, which co-ordinates the activities of many national musical organizations and acts as spokesman for the whole profession. That national organizations represent nearly every branch of music, from education and composition to band music and publishing, is yet another significant example of the growing cohesion in musical life.

In spite of the strengthening of musical institutions through inner growth, the contact with the outside world is as strong as ever. The interplay of local resources and outside influences still furnishes a major theme in Canadian musical history; but the relationship has changed. In the colonial phase of development local institutions were weak and European superiority was acknowledged as a matter of fact. Outside contacts consisted mainly in reliance on British and French traditions, absorption of German training and musical literature, and dependence on United States orchestral, publishing and other facilities. Today contacts show a much wider range. Canadian composers are familiar with the works of their contemporaries in many countries; concert programmes are truly catholic, reflecting few national prejudices or preferences; artists, choirs and orchestras from abroad can be heard frequently in guest performances; books, scores, and recordings from the four corners of the earth are represented in Canadian libraries; teachers and composers from countries as far apart as Denmark, Chile and Austria have settled in Canada.

It could not be any other way in an age where broadcasting and travel by jet plane reduce physical and cultural distances year by year. The relative musical autonomy of nineteenth-century Germany, Italy or France—each with a self-sufficient national repertoire and set of musical institutions—would be anachronistic in the twentieth century. A nationalist phase in Canadian music, in the sense of a withdrawal from world currents for the sake of cultivating regional peculiarities, is an unlikely prospect. On the contrary, strength and achievement will come through cultural exchange between the nations and, indeed, history points towards Canada's joining the family of musical nations as an equal partner, sharing the wealth of a common heritage and contributing an art that is rooted in the Canadian environment and yet valid beyond Canadian borders.

Appendix

BOOKS WITH MUSIC PUBLISHED IN CANADA BEFORE 1850

Le Graduel romain. Quebec, 1800, 1827.
Le Processional romain. Quebec, 1801. 3rd ed.; 1842.
Union Harmony. Saint John, N.B., 1801, 1816, 1831, 1840.
  [At least the first two editions were printed in the United States.]
Le Vespéral romain. Quebec, 1802. 3rd ed.; 1842.
The Vocal Preceptor, by A. Stevenson. Montreal, 1811.
Nouveau Recueil de cantiques. Quebec, 1819.
A Selection from the Psalms of David, arranged by G. Jenkins [from the
  British work *The Psalms of David* by Edward Miller]. Montreal,
  1821.
Elementary Treaty on Music: Traité élémentaire de musique, by T. F.
  Molt. Quebec, 1828.
Colonial Harmonist, by M. Burnham. Port Hope, Ont., 1832.
A Selection of Psalms and Hymns, by W. Warren. Toronto, 1835.
  [Printed in New York. There was also an edition of 1834 which
  did not contain music.]
The Nova-Scotia Songster. Pictou, 1836.
The Harmonicon: A Collection of Sacred Music. Pictou, 1836 or 1837.
  3rd ed.; 1849.
Sacred Harmony, by A. Davidson. Toronto, 1838, 1845, 1856.
Manual of Parochial Psalmody, by H. Horne. Quebec, 1840. [Reprint
  of the fifth edition of the London publication with the same title.]
Messe musicale du sixième tone d'après de la Feillée. Revised and
  augmented. Quebec, 1842.

Recueil de messes, d'hymnes, de prose, de motets, &c. Quebec, 1843.
Lyre Sainte, compiled and arranged by T. F. Molt. Quebec; first instalment 1844, second instalment 1845.
Notions élémentaires, by C. Sauvageau. Quebec, 1844.
Traité élémentaire de musique vocale, by T. F. Molt. Quebec, 1845.
Canadian Church Psalmody, ed. by J. P. Clarke. Toronto, 1845.
A Collection of Original Sacred Music, by F. H. Andrews. Montreal, 1848.
A Selection from the Psalms of David, by G. Talbot; music arranged by W. H. Warren. Montreal, 1848.

It has not been possible to confirm whether the following books include music:
Chansonnier canadien. Montreal, 1825.
Le Chansonnier canadien. Quebec, 1830. [Printed at Trois Rivières.]
Canadian Songster. [Advertised by the Office of the Colonial Advocate, York (Toronto), 1830.]

Selected Bibliography

Excepting those sections devoted to "Developments from 1914" and "Periodicals," which include some material dealing exclusively with the period after 1914, all sections of the Bibliography include only material which deals partly or exclusively with music in Canada before 1914. The sections are as follows: "General Surveys and Reference Material," "Regional and Local History," "Biography," "Composition," "Performance," "Education," "Church and Organ Music," "Instrument Building and Music Trade," "Folk Music," "Developments from 1914" and "Periodicals."

GENERAL SURVEYS AND REFERENCE MATERIAL

Canadian Courier, Oct. 12, 1912. [Issue devoted to music in Canada.]

DALTON, SYDNEY C. "Musical Conditions in Canada," *New Music Review*, VII (1908), 457.

Encyclopedia Canadiana. 10 vols. Ottawa: The Canadiana Company Limited, 1957–8. [See entries beginning with "Musical," and "Music," also "Church Music," "Folk Music," "National Songs," and "Opera."]

[HARRISON, SUSIE FRANCES.] "Canada," by Mrs. J. W. F. Harrison, "Seranus," in *The Imperial History and Encyclopedia of Music*, III; *History of Foreign Music*, ed. by W. L. HUBBARD, pp. 231–53. New York: Irving Squire, *ca.* 1909.

——— "Historical Sketch of Music in Canada," by Seranus [pseudonym], in *Canada: An Encyclopedia of the Country*, ed. by JOHN CASTELL HOPKINS, IV, 389–94. Toronto: Linscott Publishing Co., 1898.

HESSELBERG, EDOUARD. "A Review of Music in Canada," *Modern*

Music and Musicians. International ed.; New York and Toronto: The University Society, *ca.* 1913.

KALLMANN, HELMUT. "A Century of Musical Periodicals in Canada," *The Canadian Music Journal,* vol. I, no. 1 (Fall 1956), and no. 2 (Winter 1957).

——— "Historical Background," in *Music in Canada,* ed. by Sir ERNEST MACMILLAN. Toronto: University of Toronto Press, 1955.

——— "Kanada," in *Die Musik in Geschichte und Gegenwart,* VII. Kassel: Bärenreiter, 1958.

LAPIERRE, EUGÈNE. "Canada, musique," in *Encyclopédie Grolier.* Montreal: La Société Grolier, 1947.

LOGAN, JOHN DANIEL. "Musical Currents in Canada," *Canadian Magazine . . . ,* XLIII (July 1914), 270.

——— "Musical Tendencies in Canada: A Review and a Forecast," *Canadian Magazine . . . ,* XLI (June 1913), 142.

MACMILLAN, JEAN ROSS, compiler. "Music in Canada: A Short Bibliography," *Ontario Library Review,* XXIV (Nov. 1940), 386–96.

MAY, LUCILLE, compiler. "Music and Composers of Canada," *Ontario Library Review,* XXXIII (Aug. 1949), 264–70. [Supplements Jean Ross MacMillan's bibliography.]

MIDDLETON, J. E. "Music in Canada," in *Canada and Its Provinces,* XII, 643. Toronto: Glasgow, Brook & Co., 1914.

MORIN, LÉO-POL. *Papiers de musique.* Montreal: Librairie d'action Canadienne-Française, 1930.

"Music in Canada," *The Nation,* I (Toronto, 1874), 71–2.

"Music in Canada," *The Musical Times,* XXVI (April 1, 1885), 209.

PERRIN, HARRY C. "Music in Canada," *University Magazine,* X (1911), 254.

ROUSSEAU, MARCELLE. "The Rise of Music in Canada," M.A. thesis. Columbia University, 1951.

SMITH, GUSTAVE. "Du mouvement musical en Canada," *L'Album musical,* 1882. [Series of 12 articles.]

THOMPSON, OSCAR, ed. *The International Cyclopedia of Music and Musicians.* 7th ed., ed. by NICOLAS SLONIMSKY. New York: Dodd, Mead, and Co., 1956. [Entries under performing and educational organizations and biography.]

TORRINGTON, FREDERICK HERBERT. "Musical Progress in Canada," in *Canada: An Encyclopedia of the Country,* ed. by JOHN CASTELL HOPKINS, IV, 383–6. Toronto: Linscott Publishing Co., 1898.

WILLIAMSON, NANCY J. "Canadian Music and Composers since 1949," *Ontario Library Review,* XXXVIII (May 1954), 118–22. [Supplements bibliographies by Jean Ross MacMillan and Lucille May.]

The Year Book of Canadian Art, compiled by The Arts & Letters Club of Toronto. London and Toronto: Dent, 1913.

REGIONAL AND LOCAL HISTORY

AMTMANN, WILLIAM. "La Vie musicale dans la Nouvelle France." Doctoral thesis. Strasbourg University, 1956.

BEGG, ALEXANDER, and WALTER R. NURSEY. *Ten Years in Winnipeg.* Winnipeg, 1879.

BLAKELEY, PHYLLIS R. "Music in Nova Scotia (1605–1867)," *Dalhousie Review,* XXXI (Summer 1951) 94, and XXXI (Autumn 1951), 223.

——— "Theatre and Music in Halifax, 1787–1901," *Dalhousie Review,* XXIX (April 1949), 8.

BRIDLE, AUGUSTUS. "Forty Years Ago and Now: Canadian Music from 1876 to 1916, from St. Paul to the Boston Opera Company, A Sketch Outline from Some of Torrington's Interesting Archives," *Canadian Courier,* XXI (December 9, 1916), 12.

CHOUINARD, H. J. J. B. *Annales de la Société St. Jean-Baptiste de Québec,* IV: *1902.* Quebec: Impr. du "Soleil," 1903. [See chap. VII, p. 504.]

———*Fête nationale des Canadiens-français célébrée à Québec en 1880.* Quebec: A. Coté, 1881.

DIXON, F. E. "Music in Toronto, as It was in the Days That are Gone Forever," *Daily Mail and Empire,* November 7, 1896.

FAIRLEY, MARGARET. "Westward with Music," *New Frontiers* (Summer 1956).

FOX, D. ARNOLD. "Music in the Maritime Provinces," in *The Year Book of Canadian Art,* compiled by The Arts & Letters Club of Toronto. London and Toronto: Dent, 1913.

GAGNON, ERNEST. "La Musique à Québec au temps de Mgr de Laval," *La Nouvelle-France* (May 1908). Also in his *Pages choisies.* Quebec, 1917.

———*Louis Jolliet,* 3rd ed.; Montreal: Librairie Beauchemin, 1926.

[GARVIN, A. B.] "Musical Development in Ontario," by KATHERINE HALE [pseud.], *Canadian Magazine* . . . , XXXV (May 1910), 59.

GODFREY, H. H., compiler. *Musical Toronto.* 1st ed.; Toronto: 1897. 2nd ed.; 1898–9.

GOGGIO, EMILIO. "The Italian Contribution to the Development of Music in Ontario," *Canadian Review of Music and Art,* IV (Oct.–Nov. and Dec.–Jan. 1945–6).

Hamilton Musical Festival, 1887. Programme brochure. [Includes "Music in Hamilton."]

HARPER, J. RUSSELL. "Spring Tide: An Enquiry into the Lives, Labours, Loves, and Manners of Early New Brunswickers." Unpublished manuscript. J. R. Harper, c/o National Gallery of Canada, Ottawa.

KALLMANN, HELMUT. "From the Archives," Canadian Music Journal, II (Summer 1958). [Musical documents from British Columbia.]

KENNEDY, NORMAN JOHN. "The Growth and Development of Music in Calgary, 1875–1920." M.A. thesis. University of Alberta, 1952.

KENT, HERBERT. "Musical Chronicles of Early Times," Victoria Daily Times, Dec. 7, 14, 21, and 28, 1918.

LAMBERT, NORMAN. "Music in Alberta and Saskatchewan," in The Year Book of Canadian Art, compiled by The Arts & Letters Club of Toronto. London and Toronto: Dent, 1913.

LAMONTAGNE, CHARLES-ONÉSIME. "Notre Passé musical (fragments)," Amérique Française, XII (Sept. 1954), 221–5.

LEVASSEUR, NAZAIRE. "Musique et musiciens à Québec," La Musique (1919–22).

MASSICOTTE, EDOUARD-ZOTIQUE. "La Musique militaire sous le régime français," Le Bulletin des recherches historiques, XXXIX (juillet 1933), 387–9.

McCOOK, JAMES. "Pioneers Preferred Pianos," The Beaver (Winter 1954–5).

MOREY, HENRY. "Musical Pioneers of the Far West Did Much to Promote Growth of Art," Vancouver Daily Province, Oct. 26, 1927.

"Music in Toronto: Reminiscences of the Last Half Century," Toronto Mail, Dec. 21, 1878.

NESBITT, J. K. "Old Homes and Families," Victoria Daily Colonist, Sept. 25, 1949.

REYNOLDS, ELLA JULIA. "One Hundred Years of Hamilton Music," Hamilton Spectator, June 11 and 18, 1946.

SANDWELL, BERNARD K. The Musical Red Book of Montreal. Montreal: F. A. Veitch, 1907.

SMITH, DOROTHY BLAKEY. "Music in the Furthest West a Hundred Years Ago," Canadian Music Journal, II (Summer 1958).

SPELL, L. "Music in New France in the Seventeenth Century," Canadian Historical Review, VIII (June 1927), 119.

STAEBLER, H. L. "Random Notes on Music of Nineteenth-Century Berlin, Ontario," in Thirty-seventh Annual Report of the Waterloo Historical Society (1949).

TALBOT, HUGO, ed. Musical Halifax: An Annual Devoted to the Interests of the Musicians of Halifax, N. S. Halifax, 1903–4.

TREWHELLA, ETHEL WILLSON. "The Story of Sharon," Newmarket Era and Express. 42 instalments from June 14, 1951 to March 27, 1952.

TRIPP, J. D. A. "Music in British Columbia," in *The Year Book of Canadian Art*, compiled by The Arts & Letters Club of Toronto. London and Toronto: Dent, 1913.

WADE, M. S. *The Overlanders of '62*, edited by John Hosie. (Archives of British Columbia, Memoir no. IX.) Victoria, 1931.

WHEELER, CHARLES H. "Music in Manitoba," in *The Year Book of Canadian Art*, compiled by The Arts & Letters Club of Toronto. London and Toronto: Dent, 1913.

BIOGRAPHY

ALBANI, EMMA. *Forty Years of Song*. London: Mills & Boon, 1911.

Baker's Biographical Dictionary. 5th ed., completely revised by Nicolas Slonimsky; New York: G. Schirmer, 1958. [Includes biographical entries for about 70 Canadians, of whom 25 were active before 1914.]

BENSON, NATHANIEL A. "Edward Johnson," *Canadian Music Journal*, II (Spring 1958).

BRIDLE, AUGUSTUS. "Dr. A. S. Vogt," in his *Sons of Canada*. Toronto: Dent, 1916.

––– "Two Pères de musique," in his *Sons of Canada*. Toronto: Dent, 1916. [On Torrington and Couture.]

CAMPBELL, MARJORIE WILKINS. "When Albani was Queen of Song," *Maclean's Magazine*, June 15, 1953.

CHARBONNEAU, HÉLÈNE. *L'Albani: Sa Carrière artistique et triomphale*. Montreal: Impr. Jacques Cartier, 1938.

CLARKE, HERBERT LINCOLN. *How I Became a Cornetist: The Autobiography of a Cornet-playing Pilgrim's Progress*. St. Louis: J. L. Huber, 1934.

DAVID, L.-O. "Calixa Lavallée," *L'Opinion publique*, IV (March 13, 1873), 121.

DONALDA, PAULINE. "A Jewish Singer's Career," in *Canadian Jewish Year Book*, II (1940–41), 105.

ELIE, F. *La Famille Casavant*. Montreal: La "Croix," 1914.

Encyclopedia Canadiana. 10 vols. Ottawa: The Canadiana Company Limited, 1957–8. [Includes biographical entries for 48 Canadians active in the field of music; 36 of these were active before 1914.]

FORSYTH, WESLEY OCTAVIUS. "Clarence Lucas," *Canadian Journal of Music*, I (May 1914), 4.

GOUR, ROMAIN. "Albani (Emma Lajeunesse), reine du chant," *Qui ?*, I [mars 1949]. English translation by Hugh Poynter Bell. "Albani (Emma Lajeunesse), Queen of Song," *Who ?*, I [mars 1949].

––– "Alexis Contant, pianiste-compositeur," *Qui?*, V (décembre 1953).

——— "Guillaume Couture, compositeur," *Qui ?*, III (septembre 1951).
——— *La Palme-Issaurel: biographie critique.* Montreal: Éditions Eoliennes, 1948.
——— "Rodolphe Plamondon, ténor classique," *Qui ?*, V (juin 1954).
HAMILTON, HENRY COOKE. "Dr. Albert Ham," *Musical Canada*, X (April 1929).
——— "Augustus Stephen Vogt, 1861–1926," *Musical Canada*, IX (June 1928).
——— "Dr. Frederick Herbert Torrington," *Musical Canada*, X (Sept. 1929).
——— "Wesley Octavius Forsyth," *Musical Canada*, X (June 1929).
HARRISON, SUSIE FRANCES. "An Educationist in Music: Dr. Edward Fisher," *Canadian magazine* . . . , XXXIII (1909), 119.
JEHIN-PRUME, fils. *Une Vie d'artiste.* Montreal: Constantineau, n.d. [Biography of Frantz Jehin-Prume.]
LAPIERRE, EUGÈNE. *Calixa Lavallée, musicien national du Canada.* Edition revue et augmentée; Montreal: Granger, 1950.
LAURENDEAU, ARTHUR. "Musiciens d'autrefois: Alfred Desève," *L'Action Nationale*, XXXV (mars 1950), 186.
——— "Musiciens d'autrefois: Guillaume Couture," *L'Action Nationale*, XXXVI (septembre 1950) 19, and XXXVI (octobre 1950), 110.
——— "Musiciens d'autrefois: Paul Letondal," *L'Action Nationale*, XXXVI (décembre 1950), 270.
——— "Musiciens d'autrefois: Romain-Octave Pelletier," *L'Action Nationale*, XXXV (juin 1950), 437.
LETONDAL, ARTHUR. "Ernest Gagnon, écrivain et folkloriste," *Qui ?*, II (juin 1951).
——— "Un musicien oublié (Charles Waugh Sabatier)," *L'Action Nationale* II (octobre 1933), 126.
LOGAN, JOHN DANIEL. "Canada's First Creative Composer," *Canadian Courier*, XI (Jan. 27, 1912), 9. [Calixa Lavallée.]
MARMETTE, JOSEPH. "Prume et Lavallée," *L'Opinion publique*, VI (18 novembre 1875), 541.
MASSICOTTE, EDOUARD-ZOTIQUE. "Les Deux Musiciens Braunies" [*sic*], *Le Bulletin des recherches historiques*, XLI (novembre 1935), 641–3.
MAURAULT, OLIVIER. "Adélard J. Boucher," *La Musique* (janvier 1920).
McDOWELL, LOUISE. *Past and Present: A Canadian Musician's Reminiscences.* Kirkland Lake, Ontario, 1957.
MICHAUD, IRMA. "Antonin Dessane, 1826–1873," *Le Bulletin des recherches historiques*, XXXIX (février 1933), 73–6.

Le Passe-Temps, Numéro-Souvenir: Calixa Lavallée, vol. XXXIX, no. 864 (août 1933).

PELLETIER, ROMAIN. "Octave Pelletier, organiste et pédagogue," *Qui ?,* IV (septembre 1952).

ROBERTSON, J. ROSS. "Alexander Muir's Life," in *Landmarks of Toronto,* chap. XXXVI, pp. 496–586. Ser. 6. Toronto: J. Ross Robertson, 1914.

ROY, PIERRE-GEORGES. "A propos de musique," *Le Bulletin des recherches historiques,* XLIII (février 1933), 353–6. [Brauneis, sr., and Charles Sauvageau.]

Sœurs de Sainte-Anne. *Dictionnaire biographique des musiciens canadiens.* Lachine: Sœurs de Sainte-Anne, 1934.

TRÉPANIER, LÉON. "Oscar Martel, violiniste et professeur," *Qui ?,* IV (mars 1953).

UTTLEY, W. V. "Dr. Augustus Stephen Vogt," *Fourteenth Annual Report of the Waterloo Historical Society* (1926).

VÉZINA. "Joseph Vézina, 1849–1949," *L'Action Catholique,* 17 juillet 1949, magazine section.

WALTER, ARNOLD. "In Memoriam [Edward Johnson]," *Canadian Music Journal,* III (Summer 1959).

COMPOSITION

BRIDLE, AUGUSTUS. "Composers among Us," in *The Year Book of Canadian Art,* compiled by The Arts & Letters Club of Toronto. London and Toronto: Dent, 1913.

Complete List of Canadian Copyright Musical Compositions (Entered from 1868 to January 19th, 1889). Compiled from the official register at Ottawa. [1889.]

FORSYTH, WESLEY OCTAVIUS. "Canadian Composers," *Canadian Journal of Music,* II (June 1915), 20.

KALLMANN, HELMUT, ed. *Catalogue of Canadian Composers.* Toronto: Canadian Broadcasting Corporation, 1952.

——— "Music Composition," in *Encyclopedia Canadiana,* VII. Ottawa: The Canadiana Company Limited, 1958.

LOGAN, JOHN DANIEL. "Canadian Creative Composers," *Canadian Magazine . . .,* XLI (September 1913), 486.

——— "Musical Composition in Canada," in *The Year Book of Canadian Art,* compiled by The Arts & Letters Club of Toronto. London and Toronto: Dent, 1913.

SMITHERMAN, MARY. "Canadian Composers," *Ontario Library Review,* XV (Aug. 1930), 3–6. [Bibliography.]

PERFORMANCE

ADENEY, MARCUS. "Chamber Music," in *Music in Canada*, ed. by Sir Ernest MacMillan. Toronto: University of Toronto Press, 1955.

BREITHAUPT, W. H. "The Saengerfest of 1875," in *Twenty-second Annual Report of the Waterloo Historical Society (1934)*. Kitchener, 1935.

BRIDLE, AUGUSTUS. "Chamber Music in Toronto," in *The Year Book of Canadian Art*, compiled by The Arts & Letters Club of Toronto. London and Toronto: Dent, 1913.

——— "Orchestral Music in Ontario," in *The Year Book of Canadian Art*, compiled by The Arts & Letters Club of Toronto. London and Toronto: Dent, 1913.

CHARLESWORTH, HECTOR. "The Present Status of Grand Opera in Canada," in *The Year Book of Canadian Art*, compiled by The Arts & Letters Club of Toronto. London and Toronto: Dent, 1913.

COOKE, RICHARD W. "Music Competition Festivals," in *Encyclopedia Canadiana*, VII. Ottawa: The Canadiana Company Limited, 1958.

"The Grand Opera House [London, Ont.], 1894–95," *Western Ontario Historical Notes*, IX (Sept. 1951), 120–8. Mimeographed.

Historique de la Société musicale Sainte-Cécile de Québec. Quebec, 1881.

IRWIN, Mrs. D. D. "Behind the Footlights," *Saskatchewan History* (Winter 1956). [On Indian Head Opera House.]

LAMONTAGNE, CHARLES-ONÉSIME, and ROMAIN GOUR. "Frank Stephen Meighen, dilettante et mécène," *Qui ?*, V (mars 1954). ["A complete history of The Montreal Opera Co."]

LAURENDEAU, ARTHUR. "Musique de chambre et musique d'église en Montréal," in *The Year Book of Canadian Art*, compiled by The Arts & Letters Club of Toronto. London and Toronto: Dent, 1913. [Text French and English.]

LOUDON, J. S. "Reminiscences of Chamber Music in Toronto during the Past Forty Years," *Canadian Journal of Music*, I (July–Aug. 1914), 47.

MACKENZIE, Sir ALEXANDER CAMPBELL. *A Musician's Narrative*. London: Cassell, 1927. [Includes chapter on Canadian tour of 1903.]

MACKENZIE-ROGAN, J. *Fifty Years of Army Music*. London: Methuen, 1926. [Includes chapter on Canadian tour of 1903.]

MIDDLETON, J. E. "Choral Music in Ontario," in *The Year Book of Canadian Art*, compiled by The Arts & Letters Club of Toronto. London and Toronto: Dent, 1913.

MOORE, LOUISE A. DEW. "Progressive Alberta," *Canadian Journal of Music*, I (July–Aug. 1914), 58.

SANGWINE, JEAN. "Squire Sowden's Opera House [Souris, Man.]," *The Beaver* (Spring 1960), pp. 50–3.

SMITH, OCEAN G., compiler. *The Toronto Mendelssohn Choir: A History, 1894–1948.* [Toronto,] 1948. [Chap. I written by Hector Charlesworth.]

TANGUAY, A.-P. "L'Orchestre symphonique de Québec," *Musique et musiciens,* II (avril 1954).

WODELL, F. W. "The Alberta Musical Competition Festival at Edmonton," *Musician,* no. 16 (1911), pp. 649–50.

WOOD, CHRISTOPHER. "History and Career of the Toronto Symphony Orchestra," *Curtain Call,* XI (Nov. 1939), 9.

EDUCATION

BECKWITH, JOHN. "Music Education," in *Encyclopedia Canadiana,* VII. Ottawa: The Canadiana Company Limited, 1958.

The Canadian Protesting Committee (edited, compiled, and published by order of). *An Account of the Canadian Protest against the Introduction into Canada of Musical Examinations by Outside Musical Examining Bodies.* Toronto, 1899.

FENWICK, G. ROY. *The Function of Music in Education: Incorporating a History of School Music in Ontario.* Toronto: Gage, 1951.

HAIG, ALASTAIR P. "Henry Frost, Pioneer (1816–1851)," *Canadian Music Journal,* II (Winter 1958).

LEGENDRE, NAPOLÉON. "Le Chant dans les écoles," *Echos de Québec,* II. Quebec, 1877.

McGill University. *Festival of the Conservatorium of Music, to Mark Its Fiftieth Year, 1904–1954.* Souvenir programme.

ROY, PIERRE-GEORGES. "Les Premiers Manuels scolaires canadiens," *Le Bulletin des recherches historiques,* LII (octobre, 1946), 291.

University of Toronto. *The Toronto Conservatory of Music: A Retrospect (1886–1936).* Compiled from material collected by Dr. F. J. Horwood.

University of Trinity College, Toronto, Faculty of Music. *Memorials presented to Lord Knutsford, H. M. Secretary of State for the Colonies, with Appendices, &c.* London: Wm. Brown [1890].

WALTER, ARNOLD. "Education in Music," in *Music in Canada,* ed. by Sir Ernest MacMillan. Toronto: University of Toronto Press, 1955.

CHURCH AND ORGAN MUSIC

CHRISTIE, Rev. GEORGE. *The Use of Instrumental Music in the Public Worship of God.* Halifax: J. Barnes, 1867.

HARRIS, REGINALD V. *The Church of St. Paul in Halifax, Nova Scotia, 1749–1949.* Toronto: Ryerson Press, 1949.

The Jesuit Relations and Allied Documents, ed. by Reuben Gold Thwaites. 73 vols. Cleveland: The Burrows Brothers Company, 1896–1901.

KALLMANN, HELMUT. "From the Archives: Organs and Organ Players in Canada," *Canadian Music Journal,* III (Spring 1959).

LAPALICE, O. "Les Organistes et maîtres de musique à Notre-Dame de Montréal," *Le Bulletin des recherches historiques,* XXV (août 1919), 243.

LAURENDEAU, ARTHUR. "Musique de chambre et musique d'église en Montreal," in *The Year Book of Canadian Art,* compiled by The Arts & Letters Club of Toronto. London and Toronto: Dent, 1913. [Text in French and English.]

MACMILLAN, Sir ERNEST. "The Organ was My First Love," *Canadian Music Journal,* III (Spring 1959).

PELLETIER, J. R. "L'Evolution de la musique réligieuse au Canada français," Mus. Doc. thesis. Laval University, Quebec, 1932.

REED, THOMAS ARTHUR. *Church Music in Canada.* Unpublished manuscript in University of Toronto Library.

Royal Canadian College of Organists. *Golden Jubilee Convention, 1909–1959.* Programme brochure. Toronto, 1959. [Includes "A History."]

INSTRUMENT BUILDING AND MUSIC TRADE

Canadian Music Trades Journal. Toronto, 1900–32. [Until *ca.* 1907 named *Canadian Music and Trade Journal.*]

CHAPAIS, CHARLES. "La Construction des orgues par les Canadiens français," *Congrès de la langue française au Canada,* II (1937), 547.

The House of Nordheimer, 1840–1903. Toronto, 1903. [Written by an employee.]

HUBBARD, R. H. "The Royal Instrument," *Canadian Geographical Journal,* LIII (Dec. 1956), 201.

KALLMANN, HELMUT. "The Publication of Music," in 1961.

KALLMANN, HELMUT, and JOHN BECKWITH. "Musical Instruments, Making of," in *Encyclopedia Canadiana,* VII. Ottawa: The Canadiana Company Limited, 1958.

KEMP, HUGH. "Musical Frères," *Maclean's Magazine,* Oct. 15, 1947. [On Casavant Frères organ builders.]

MASSICOTTE, EDOUARD-ZOTIQUE. "Violons et luthiers," *Le Bulletin des recherches historiques,* XLI (avril 1935), 213–17.

MORISSET, GERARD. *Coup d'œil sur les arts en Nouvelle-France.* Quebec, 1941. [Includes chapter IV, B: "Facteurs d'orgues et luthiers."]

NIXON, D. C. "Making Canadian Pianos," *Canadian Courier,* XII (Oct. 12, 1912), 21.

PORTER, McKENZIE. "The Piano with the All-Canadian Tone," *Maclean's Magazine,* May 11, 1957. [On Heintzman pianos.]

FOLK MUSIC

BARBEAU, MARIUS. "Asiatic Survivals in Indian Songs," *Musical Quarterly,* XX (Jan. 1934), 107.

——— "Folk-Songs of French Canada," *Music and Letters,* XIII (1932), 168–82.

——— *Folk-Songs of Old Quebec.* Ottawa: National Museum of Canada [1935].

——— *Romancero du Canada.* Montreal: Beauchemin, 1937.

——— "Songs of the Northwest," *Musical Quarterly,* XIX, (Jan. 1933), 101.

BARBEAU, MARIUS, and EDWARD SAPIR. *Folk Songs of French Canada.* New Haven, Conn.: Yale University Press, 1925.

CARDIN, CLARISSE, "Bio-bibliographie de Marius Barbeau," in *Les Archives de Folklore,* II, 17–96. ("Publications de l'université Laval.") Montreal: Editions Fides, 1947.

CREIGHTON, HELEN. *Songs and Ballads from Nova Scotia.* Toronto and Vancouver: Dent, 1932.

CREIGHTON, HELEN, and DOREEN H. SENIOR. *Traditional Songs from Nova Scotia.* Toronto: Ryerson Press, 1950.

CRINGAN, ALEXANDER THOM. "Iroquois Folk Songs," in Ontario Provincial Museum, *Annual Archaeological Report, 1902,* p. 137.

———"Iroquois Music," in Ontario Provincial Museum, *Annual Archaeological Report, 1898,* p. 143.

——— "Pagan Dance Songs of the Iroquois," in Ontario Provincial Museum, *Annual Archaeological Report, 1899,* p. 168.

DOYLE, GERALD S. *Old-Time Songs of Newfoundland.* 3rd ed.; St. John's, Nfld.: Gerald S. Doyle, 1955.

FOWKE, EDITH FULTON. "A Guide to Canadian Folksong Records," *Canadian Forum,* XXXVII (September 1957).

FOWKE, EDITH FULTON, and RICHARD JOHNSTON. *Folk Songs of Canada.* Waterloo: Waterloo Music Company, 1954.

——— *Folk Songs of Quebec.* Waterloo: Waterloo Music Company, 1957.

FOWKE, EDITH [FULTON], ALAN MILLS and HELMUT BLUME. *Canada's Story in Song.* Toronto: W. J. Gage, 1960.

GAGNON, ERNEST. *Chansons populaires du Canada.* 10th ed.; Montreal: Beauchemin, 1956.

——— "Les Sauvages de l'Amérique et l'art musical," in *Rapport de la 15ième session du Congrès international des Américanistes, Québec 1906. I,* 184. Quebec: Dussault et Proulx, 1907.

GIBBON, JOHN MURRAY. *The Romance of the Canadian Canoe.* Toronto: Ryerson Press, 1951.

GREENLEAF, ELISABETH BRISTOL, and GRACE YARROW MANSFIELD. *Ballads and Sea Songs of Newfoundland.* Cambridge, Mass.: Harvard University Press, 1933.

D'HARCOURT, MARGUERITE and RAOUL. *Chansons folkloriques françaises au Canada.* Quebec: Presse universitaires Laval, 1956.

Journal of American Folklore. Canadian numbers: Vol. 63, no. 248 (April-June 1950) and Vol. 67, no. 264 (April-June 1954).

LARUE, FRANÇOIS ALEXANDRE-HUBERT. "Les Chansons historiques du Canada," *Le Foyer Canadien,* III (1865), 5–72.

——— "Les Chansons populaires et historiques du Canada," *Le Foyer Canadien,* I (1863), 320–84.

LINDSAY, Abbé LIONEL SAINT-GEORGE. *Notre-Dame de la Jeune-Lorette en la Nouvelle-France.* Montreal: Revue Canadienne, 1900. [Includes chap. XII, p. 249: "La Langue et les chants des Hurons."]

MACLEOD, MARGARET ARNETT. *Songs of Old Manitoba.* Toronto: Ryerson Press, 1960.

MACKENZIE, WILLIAM ROY. *Ballads and Sea Songs from Nova Scotia.* Cambridge, Mass.: Harvard University Press, 1928.

MASSICOTTE, ÉDOUARD-ZOTIQUE, and MARIUS BARBEAU. "Chants populaires du Canada (première série)," *Journal of American Folk-lore* [sic], XXXII (Jan.–March 1919), 1–89.

MILNES, HUMPHREY. "German Folklore in Ontario," *Journal of American Folklore* [sic], LXVII (Jan-March 1954), 35–43.

MYRAND, ERNEST. *Noëls anciens de la Nouvelle-France.* 2nd ed.; Quebec: Laflamme & Proulx, 1907.

ROBERTS, HELEN H., and D. JENNESS. "Songs of the Copper Eskimos," in *Report of the Canadian Arctic Expedition, 1913–16. Report,* XIV: *Eskimo Songs.* Ottawa: King's Printer, 1925.

TIERSOT, JULIEN. *La Musique chez les peuples indigènes de l'Amérique du Nord.* ("Notes d'ethnographie musicale," deuxième série.) Paris: Fischbacher [1910].

DEVELOPMENTS FROM 1914

ARCHER, THOMAS. "Claude Champagne," *Canadian Music Journal,* II (Winter 1958).

BECKWITH, JOHN. "Composers in Toronto and Montreal," *University of Toronto Quarterly*, XXVI (Oct. 1956), 47–69.

——— "Music," *The Culture of Contemporary Canada*, ed. by Julian Park. Ithaca: Cornell University Press, 1957.

BRIDLE, AUGUSTUS. "Who Writes Our Music? A Survey of Canadian Composers," *Maclean's Magazine* (Dec. 15, 1929).

BROOKER, BERTRAM, ed. *Yearbook of the Arts in Canada 1928–1929*, I. Toronto: Macmillan, 1929.

Canadian Library Association Bulletin, IX (March 1953) and XII (April 1956). [Music in Libraries numbers.]

GEORGE, GRAHAM. "Canada's Music; 1955," *Culture*, XVI (Spring 1955), 51–65.

GINGRAS, CLAUDE. *Musiciennes de chez nous*. Outremont-Montreal: Editions de l'Ecole Vincent-d'Indy, 1955.

HOPKINS, J. CASTELL, ed. *Canadian Annual Review*. Toronto: The Canadian Review Co. [Reviews of musical developments in volumes for the years 1922–7, 1930–1, and 1934–6.]

HOULÉ, LÉOPOLD. "Nos Compositeurs de musique," *Transactions of the Royal Society of Canada*, Ser. 3, vol. XL, section 1 (1946), pp. 51–9.

LAPIERRE, EUGÈNE. *Pourquoi la musique?* Montreal: Editions Albert Lévesque, 1933.

MACMILLAN, Sir ERNEST. "Music," in *Royal Commission Studies . . .* Ottawa: King's Printer, 1951.

——— "Orchestral and Choral Music in Canada," *Music Teachers National Association, Volume of Proceedings*. Ser. 40. Pittsburgh: M.T.N.A., 1946.

—ed. *Music in Canada*. Toronto: University of Toronto Press, 1955.

MAZZOLENI, ETTORE. "Our Lively Arts," 2: "Music in Canada," *Queen's Quarterly*, LX, 485–95.

"Music and the Canada Council," *Canadian Music Journal*, I (Spring 1957). [Special issue; includes articles by ARNOLD WALTER and GEOFFREY B. PAYZANT.]

PENTLAND, BARBARA. "Canadian Music, 1950," *Northern Review*, III (Feb.–March 1950), 43–6.

RIDOUT, GODFREY. "Healey Willan," *Canadian Music Journal*, III (Spring 1959).

SMITH, LEO. "Music," in *The Encyclopedia of Canada*, ed. by W. Stewart Wallace, IV. Toronto: University Associates of Canada, 1936.

WALTER, ARNOLD. "Canadian Composition," in *Music Teachers National Association, Volume of Proceedings*, Ser. 40. Pittsburgh: M.T.N.A., 1946.

PERIODICALS

L'Album musical: Journal musical et littéraire. Montreal, 1881–4.
Arcadia: A Semi-monthly Journal Devoted Exclusively to Music, Art and Literature. Montreal, 1892–3.
L'Artiste: Journal religieux, critique, littéraire, industriel et musical. Montreal, 1860.
Les Beaux-Arts: Journal littéraire des arts, des sciences, de l'industrie. Montreal, 1863–4.
Le Canada musical: Revue artistique et littéraire. Montreal, 1866–7 and 1875–81.
Le Canada musical: Revue bi-mensuelle. Montreal, 1917–24 and 1930.
The Canadian Journal of Music: A Monthly Magazine of Musical Life in the Dominion and of Musical News the World Over. Toronto, 1914–19.
Canadian Music: A Registered Monthly Canadian Magazine. Toronto, 1940–1.
The Canadian Music Journal. Sackville, 1956–7, and Toronto from 1958.
Canadian Review of Music and Art (title also: *Canadian Review of Music and Other Arts*). Toronto, 1942–8.
The Conservatory Bi-Monthly [from January 1912 *The Conservatory Monthly*]: *A Magazine for the Music Lover, Student and Teacher.* Toronto, 1902–13.
The Conservatory Quarterly Review: The Official Organ of the Toronto Conservatory of Music. Toronto, 1918–35.
Le Journal musical canadien: Journal des jeunesses musicales du Canada. Montreal, 1954– .
La Lyre: Revue musicale et théâtrale. Montreal, 1922–31.
Musical Canada: A Monthly Review and Magazine (until April 1907 was called *The Violin*). Toronto, 1906–28, and Waterloo, 1928–33.
The Musical Journal (published monthly in the interest of the Art Universal in Canada). Toronto, 1887–8.
La Musique: Revue mensuelle. Quebec, 1919–24.
Musique et Musiciens: Revue mensuelle. Saint-Hyacinthe, 1952–54.
Le Passe-Temps: Revue musicale, artistique (sub-title varies). Montreal, 1895–1948.
Qui?: Art, musique, littérature: revue trimestrielle (s.v.). Montreal, 1949–54.

Amendments to 1987 Reprint

Since the publication of this book in 1960, and to some extent perhaps as a result, research into the history of music in Canada has begun to thrive. Many universities now offer 'CanMus' courses, dissertations examine specific musicians and phases of musical activity in great detail, research projects are carried out by groups and individuals, and the printed literature has increased. A number of libraries and archives have become active collectors of printed, recorded, and manuscript materials relating to music in Canada.

Obviously there is much to revise in this book. Not only could other titles of significant compositions and other names of musicians and musical societies or instrument manufacturers be added, but the literature of music performed and the style of the music composed in various periods could be examined in greater detail. The contributions of certain musicians might be reassessed and the artistic climate probed more deeply in its relationship with the sister arts and the social, intellectual, and political movements of the time.

To make this book available once again without undue delay it was not possible to revise extensively. Some forty-five one-line corrections were made in the 1969 reprint. The following amendments provide a further selection of corrections of name spellings or forms of name, of wrong or imprecise dates, of misattributions of events or accomplishments as 'first' or 'earliest known.' A few significant new sources of information have been indicated, and there are also other types of amendment. As a general rule, the reader is advised to consult the *Encyclopedia of Music in Canada* (1981) (*EMC*) for further detail and research up to 1979 relating to individuals, organizations, cities, the playing and teaching of various instruments, and such topical entries as 'Concerts,' 'Opera performance,' or 'Orchestras.'

p. 19, l. 7   The organ referred to was at the Jesuit chapel, not the parish church. The organ imported in 1663 was placed in the parish church. Willy Amtmann in *Music in Canada 1600—1800* (Montreal: Habitex Books, 1975) questions whether Laval was personally involved in acquiring the organ.

p. 20, n. 34   For a different interpretation of the Latin text see Amtmann, *Music in Canada*, pp. 123—5 and footnotes 32 and 33 on pp. 284—6.

p. 24   The Prose for 'La Fête de la Ste. Famille' appeared in print in *Le Graduel romain* (Quebec 1800) and *Le Processional romain* (Quebec 1801), the first two Canadian books with musical notation.

p. 27   Several rays of light have penetrated the 'dark age' of music in eighteenth-century Canada. See the *EMC* entries on 'Concerts,' section 1, 'Girard, Jean,' 'Grand chantre,' and 'Jourdain dit Labrosse, Paul,' for example. Shortly after *EMC* went into print, Elisabeth Gallat-Morin discovered in Montreal Girard's manuscript anthology of French keyboard music, which is now available in facsimile and transcribed editions.

p. 28, ll. 23—5   Nares' composition bears 'Not unto us, Lord' as its main title.

p. 35, l. 4   As Moore himself pointed out, the similarity between his tune and 'Dans mon chemin j'ai rencontré' extends to little more than the first bar.

p. 48, ll. 2—4   Guillet has quoted inaccurately. The newspaper's title is *The York Gazette*, the ball commenced about (not at) 8 o'clock, and the orchestra (meaning a raised platform or stage, not a group of musicians) was for (not of) the band of the 41st Regiment.

p. 50, ll. 20, 24, 31   Glackemeyer's given names were Johann Friedrich Conrad; he was born in 1759 and arrived in Canada in 1777 with a German regiment, although he can hardly have been a bandmaster at that time.

p. 57   For supplementary information see Frederick A. Hall, 'Musical life in eighteenth-century Halifax,' *Canadian University Music Review*, vol. 4 (1983).

p. 59   For supplementary information see Micheline Vézina-Demers, 'Vie musicale québecoise, 1790—1794, Tendances et influences,' *Les Cahiers de l'ARMuQ*, no. 8 (May 1987).

p. 62, l. 36   According to research by John Hare, Quesnel was probably born in 1746.

p. 63, l. 20   Quesnel visited England and France in 1788—9, shortly before the première of *Colas et Colinette*.

p. 65, l. 14   The correct spelling is 'français.'

p. 65, ll. 30—1   *Colas* received two performances in Montreal in 1790 and two in Quebec in both 1805 and 1807. It has been performed many times and recorded once since its modern revival by Ten Centuries Concerts of Toronto in 1963 (restoration by Godfrey Ridout).

p. 69, l. 1   Pending analysis of all contemporary newspapers and surviving correspondence, diaries, and other archival records, it will not be possible to provide definite 'first' dates. However, the date for Toronto may be changed to 1835, and Kingston (1842) may be added.

p. 79, l. 14   Sauvageau lived until 1849, although his son Flavien did die in the 1846 fire. The same error occurs on p. 82 (l. 11) and in footnote 22.

p. 80, l. 10   The quote in German should end 'so mehr da ich so grosses Verlangen getragen habe den würdigen Beethoven zu sehen. Molt.'

p. 89, ll. 6−7   This should read 'After announcing the psalm he would play the tune on his bassoon ... '

p. 93, l. 21   Schott (1794−1864) was indeed a brother of the music publishers, but his given name was Adam.

p. 94, l. 2   The Philharmonic Society first met in 1846.

p. 95, l. 32   Sabatier (1819−62) was born in France as Charles Wugk. His father was a German immigrant.

p. 96, ll. 32, 38   Labelle died in 1898. The ensemble was called Société philharmonique canadienne de Montréal.

p. 99, l. 1   The dates should read 1845−7, 1848−50, 1854−5, 1872−94.

p. 100, l. 7   The name should read Toronto Vocal Music Society (also on p. 104, lines 29−30).

p. 104, l. 19   Many instances of opera performances between the 1790s and 1846 could be added. See Dorith Cooper's PH.D. dissertation 'Opera in Montreal and Toronto: a study of performance traditions and repertoire 1783−1980,' University of Toronto, 1984.

p. 114, l. 7   Music in *The Literary Garland* spans the years 1838 to 1851.

p. 116, n. 23   The page reference should be 202 rather than 336.

p. 137, l. 7   *La Dame blanche* was performed in 1878 rather than 1879.

p. 140, l. 4   *The Widow* was premiered at New Orleans on 23 November 1881, according to *L'Album musical* of 1 December 1881.

p. 142, n. 16   The quotation is not from the New York *Times* but from *Music and Drama* (vol. 15, no. 14, 31 January 1891).

p. 149, l. 14   Zoellner settled in Berlin in 1861. In 1880 he merely returned from studying in Cincinnati.

p. 151, ll. 25−35   Gustave Smith (1826−96) arrived in Canada in 1856. He moved to Ottawa in 1868. He also wrote *Le Guide de l'organiste* (2nd ed. 1874), *Le Gamma musical* (1887), and *Le Claviste* (1890).

p. 157, l. 24   Georgina Stirling (1867−1935) adopted the stage name Marie Toulinguet, derived from her birthplace, Twillingate.

p. 167, l. 32   The organ builders were Bolton and Baldwin.

p. 175, tabulation   One could add Mozart's *The Marriage of Figaro*,

Auber's *Fra Diavolo*, and Bellini's *La Sonnambula* (all in Montreal in 1840) and change the information for *Norma* to Montreal, 1847, and for *The Barber of Seville* to Montreal, 1840.

p. 179, l. 34   The Barbeau article was published in the April/June 1954 (not 1955) issue of *Journal of American Folklore* (vol. 67), and its title is 'The Ermatinger Collection of Voyageur Songs (ca. 1830).'

p. 186, l. 16   It appears that Cringan paid a preliminary visit to Canada in 1885 and settled in Toronto in 1886.

p. 194, l. 24   *L'Artiste* was preceded by the *Canadian Musical Review* of Toronto. Only its first issue, 1 May 1856, has been located.

p. 194, l. 38   *Le Passe-Temps* was suspended between the January 1935 and January 1945 issues.

p. 196, l. 5   The Canadian Society of Musicians existed until at least 1896.

p. 207, n. 5   The last name of the company was National Opera Company of Canada (1913—14).

p. 208, l. 30   The *Ring* cycle was not cancelled but was performed in its entirety by the Quinlan English Opera Company in March 1914.

p. 214, l. 9   Tripp was a distinguished pianist and teacher but not an orchestra leader.

p. 225, l. 26   Alfred de Sève's dates are May or June 1858 to 25 November 1927.

p. 226, ll. 24, 28, 32   Durno died in 1964, Carey in 1960, and Fontaine in 1950.

p. 230, l. 27   Albani's farewell tour of Canada took place in 1906.

p. 230, l. 35   Eva Gauthier and Sarah Fischer were not formal pupils of Albani but benefited from her advice and interest.

p. 232, ll. 30, 38   Pauline Lightstone (Donalda)'s dates are 1882—1970. She sang in *L'Heure espagnole* in the English, not the world, première.

p. 233, l. 10   Debussy recommended Eva Gauthier for a role in *Pelléas et Mélisande* at Covent Garden but circumstances prevented her participation.

p. 241, n. 3   The quotation is not from the New York *Times* but from *Music and Drama* (vol. 15, no. 14, 31 January 1891).

p. 244, l. 17   Champagne did not consider himself a pupil of Contant.

p. 249, l. 21   The preface to the score of *Ruth* is dated 1894; the copyright date is 1895.

p. 255, ll. 8—9   *The Birth of Christ* is a cantata rather than an oratorio.

p. [273]   The 1828 item should be called *Elementary Treatise on Music . . .* The most important additions to the list are *The New Brunswick Church Harmony*, by Z. Estey (Saint John, N.B., 1835); *Laoidhean Spioradail*, by D. McDonald (Charlottetown, 1835); *The Seraph*, by M. Burnham (Port Hope, Ont., 1844); and *Aiamie kushkushkutu mishinaigan*, by F. Durocher (Quebec, 1847).

p. 280 Hamilton's article on Torrington appeared in the July/August 1928 issue of *Musical Canada*, vol. 9.

p. 281 The article by Pierre-Georges Roy is found in the December 1937 issue of *Le Bulletin des recherches historiques*, vol. 43.

p. 284 The first of the two Kallmann items under 'Instrument Building and Music Trade' was published in revised form as 'Canadian Music Publishing' in *Papers of the Bibliographical Society of Canada 1974*, vol. 13 (1975).

Index